Praise for *The .NET Developer's Guide to Windows Security*

"As usual, Keith masterfully explains complex security issues in down-to-earth and easy-to-understand language. I bet you'll reach for this book often when building your next software application."

—Michael Howard, Microsoft Corporation, coauthor, *Writing Secure Code*

"When it comes to teaching Windows security, Keith Brown is 'The Man.' In *The .NET Developer's Guide to Windows Security*, Keith has written a book that explains the key security concepts of Windows NT, Windows 2000, Windows XP, and Windows Server 2003, and teaches you both how to apply them and how to implement them in C# code. By organizing his material into short, clear snippets, Brown has made a complicated subject highly accessible."

—Martin Heller, senior contributing editor at *Byte.com* and owner of Martin Heller & Co.

"Keith's book is a collection of practical, concise, and carefully thought out nuggets of security insight. Every .NET developer would be wise to keep a copy of this book close at hand and to consult it first when questions of security arise during application development."

—Fritz Onion, author of *Essential ASP.NET with Examples in C++*

"Keith Brown has a unique ability to describe complex technical topics, such as security, in a way that can be understood by mere mortals (such as myself). Keith's book is a must read for anyone attempting to keep up with Microsoft's enhancements to its security features and the next major version of .NET."

—Peter Partch, principal software engineer, PM Consulting

The .NET Developer's Guide to Windows Security

Microsoft .NET Development Series

John Montgomery, *Series Advisor*
Don Box, *Series Advisor*
Martin Heller, *Series Editor*

The **Microsoft .NET Development Series** is supported and developed by the leaders and experts of Microsoft development technologies including Microsoft architects and DevelopMentor instructors. The books in this series provide a core resource of information and understanding every developer needs in order to write effective applications and managed code. Learn from the leaders how to maximize your use of the .NET Framework and its programming languages.

Titles in the Series

Brad Abrams, *.NET Framework Standard Library Annotated Reference Volume 1*, 0-321-15489-4

Keith Ballinger, *.NET Web Services: Architecture and Implementation*, 0-321-11359-4

Bob Beauchemin, Niels Berglund, Dan Sullivan, *A First Look at SQL Server 2005 for Developers*, 0-321-18059-3

Don Box with Chris Sells, *Essential .NET, Volume 1: The Common Language Runtime*, 0-201-73411-7

Mahesh Chand, *Graphics Programming with GDI+*, 0-321-16077-0

Anders Hejlsberg, Scott Wiltamuth, Peter Golde, *The C# Programming Language*, 0-321-15491-6

Alex Homer, Dave Sussman, Mark Fussell, *A First Look at ADO.NET and System.Xml v. 2.0*, 0-321-22839-1

Alex Homer, Dave Sussman, Rob Howard, *A First Look at ASP.NET v. 2.0*, 0-321-22896-0

James S. Miller and Susann Ragsdale, *The Common Language Infrastructure Annotated Standard*, 0-321-15493-2

Fritz Onion, *Essential ASP.NET with Examples in C#*, 0-201-76040-1

Fritz Onion, *Essential ASP.NET with Examples in Visual Basic .NET*, 0-201-76039-8

Ted Pattison and Dr. Joe Hummel, *Building Applications and Components with Visual Basic .NET*, 0-201-73495-8

Chris Sells, *Windows Forms Programming in C#*, 0-321-11620-8

Chris Sells and Justin Gehtland, *Windows Forms Programming in Visual Basic .NET*, 0-321-12519-3

Paul Vick, *The Visual Basic .NET Programming Language*, 0-321-16951-4

Damien Watkins, Mark Hammond, Brad Abrams, *Programming in the .NET Environment*, 0-201-77018-0

Shawn Wildermuth, *Pragmatic ADO.NET: Data Access for the Internet World*, 0-201-74568-2

Paul Yao and David Durant, *.NET Compact Framework Programming with C#*, 0-321-17403-8

Paul Yao and David Durant, *.NET Compact Framework Programming with Visual Basic .NET*, 0-321-17404-6

For more information go to www.awprofessional.com/msdotnetseries/

The .NET Developer's Guide to Windows Security

■ **Keith Brown**

✦ Addison-Wesley

Boston • San Francisco • New York • Toronto • Montreal
London • Munich • Paris • Madrid
Capetown • Sydney • Tokyo • Singapore • Mexico City

Library of Congress Cataloging-in-Publication Data

Brown, Keith, 1967
    The .NET developer's guide to Windows security
/ Keith Brown.
       p. cm.
    Includes bibliographical references and index.
    ISBN 0-321-22835-9 (pbk. : alk. paper)
    1. Computer security. 2. Microsoft Windows
(Computer file) 3. Microsoft .NET. I. Title.

    QA76.9.A25B775 2004
    005.8--dc22
                                    2004013971

ISBN 0-321-22835-9
Text printed on recycled paper
1 2 3 4 5 6 7 8 9 10—PH—0807060504
First printing, September 2004

*To the countless number of programmers
struggling daily to write secure code on
the Windows platform*

Contents

Preface

THIS BOOK WAS WRITTEN for the many thousands of people involved in designing and writing software for the Microsoft .NET platform. It is chock-full of tips and insights about user-based security, which I like to term "Windows security" because it's been around in one form or another since Windows NT first shipped. Given the plethora of books that cover the new security features in the .NET Framework, such as code access security and ASP.NET forms authentication, I decided to write a book to help folks with the basics of Windows security, a topic that most other books miss entirely or get subtly or blatantly wrong. This book is in some sense a second edition of my first security book, *Programming Windows Security*, but I hope that you will find it immensely more approachable and practical. I've tried to distill the Zen of these topics into small tidbits of information—items that link to one another—allowing you to read the book in any order that suits you. I hope that you'll find the format of 75 concise tidbits of information helpful as a reference. The "what is" items focus on explaining concepts, while the "how to" items focus on helping you perform a common task.

Within these pages I cover security features in various versions of Windows based on Windows NT. This includes Windows 2000, Windows XP Professional, and Windows Server 2003, but does not include 16-bit Windows or any of the Win9X flavors (Windows 95/98, Windows ME, Windows XP Home Edition). So, when I talk about "Windows" I'm referring to the versions based on Windows NT. Whenever I talk about the file system, I'm assuming that you're using NTFS, not FAT partitions. Whenever I talk about domains, I'm assuming Windows 2000 or greater. If you're still living with a Windows NT 4 domain, you have my sincere condolences!

Many people have expressed surprise that I occasionally talk about Win32 APIs and refer to Win32 header files in a book for .NET programmers. I wish I didn't have to do this, but as anyone who has experience with the .NET Framework knows, the framework class library wraps only a fraction of the functionality of the Windows platform as of this writing. The coverage will get better over time, but to do many things in Windows (including security programming), you often need to call native Win32 APIs. Even as version 2.0 of the framework is being revealed in beta 1, you can see that coverage increasing, but it's still not complete. In any case, I've tried to make it clear in the prose when I'm talking about a Win32 API versus a .NET Framework class, and I've provided lots of sample code and helper classes written in Managed C++ that you can leverage to avoid having to call those APIs yourself.

This book can be found online (in its entirety) in hyperlinked form on the Web at *winsecguide.net*, where I believe you'll find it to be a great reference when you're connected. I plan to continue filling in more items over time, so subscribe to the RSS feed on the book for news. You can also download samples and tools that I mention in the book from this Web site. Errata will be posted to this site as well, so if you find a problem please let me know.

Good luck in your endeavors!

Keith Brown
Highlands Ranch, CO
http://www.pluralsight.com/keith

Acknowledgments

THANKS TO MY TECHNICAL REVIEWERS: John Lambert, Peter Partch, and Bill Moseley. The book wouldn't be the same without your efforts.

I'd like to say a special thank you to Don Box, who jump-started my writing and teaching career back in 1997 when he invited me to teach COM for the training company he founded. It was Don who helped me land a column with *Microsoft Systems Journal.* He encouraged me to work on security back when nobody seemed to care about the topic. I'm still using his Word template when I write articles for *MSDN Magazine.*

Thanks to all of the people who read the online version of the book before it was published and took the time to e-mail in suggestions. Lots of the tips in the section on running as non-admin came from these folks.

Thanks to Chris Sells for his simple suggestion before I even started writing. "Please give me something practical," he asked.

Thanks to all of my students over the years. Your questions and insights have challenged and strengthened me. Please come up and say hello if you see me at an event. Stay in touch!

Thanks to the folks at Addison-Wesley for their help in getting this book off the ground. Karen Gettman, my editor, didn't let me slip (well, not much at least). Thanks for giving me the leeway I needed to find this rather off-the-wall format for the book. Thanks to Elizabeth Ryan at Addison-Wesley for her coordination of the book through production and to

Connie Leavitt at Bookwrights for managing the production process, even as I submitted entirely new content after beta 1 shipped.

Thanks to Curt Johnson and his staff who somehow figured out how to sell all these paperweights I've been writing over the years.

PART I
The Big Picture

■ 1 ■
What Is Secure Code?

O NE OF THE MAJOR GOALS of this book is to help clarify how Windows security works so you'll be able to use it effectively in your applications and also in your everyday life. But even if you have a perfect understanding of all the security features of the platform, and make all the right API calls and configure security policy very carefully to keep out attackers, if you don't write your code with security in mind, none of that will matter because you'll still be vulnerable to attack.

Look at the following C# method and count the number of security APIs that it uses.

```
// this code has a really nasty security flaw
void LogUserName(SqlConnection conn, string userName) {
    string sqlText = "insert user_names values('" + userName + "')";
    SqlCommand cmd = new SqlCommand(sqlText, conn);
    cmd.ExecuteNonQuery();
}
```

That's right, it doesn't call any security APIs. However, if we assume the userName parameter has been given to us by someone we don't fully trust (aka a user of our application) then this benign-looking code has a horrible security flaw. If the above function had been written with security in mind, here's how it might have looked instead:

```
// much more secure code
void LogUserName(SqlConnection conn, string userName) {
```

```
    string sqlText = "insert user_names values(@n)";
    SqlCommand cmd = new SqlCommand(sqlText, conn);
    SqlParameter p = cmd.Parameters.Add("@n",
        SqlDbType.VarChar, userName.Length);
    p.Value = userName;
    cmd.ExecuteNonQuery();
}
```

Note the difference in the coding style. In the first case, the coder appended untrusted user input directly into a SQL statement. In the second case, the coder hardcoded the SQL statement and encased the user input in a parameter that was sent with the query, carefully keeping any potential attackers in the data channel and out of the control channel (the SQL statement in this case).

The flaw in the first bit of code is that a user with malicious intent can take control of our SQL statement and do pretty much whatever he wants with the database. We've allowed an attacker to slip into a control channel. For example, what if the user were to submit the following string as a user name?

```
SeeYa');drop table user_names--
```

Our SQL statement would now become

```
insert user_names values('SeeYa');drop table user_names--')
```

This is just a batch SQL query with a comment at the end (that's what the "--"sequence is for) that inserts a record into the user_names table and then drops that same table from the database! This is a rather extreme example (your database connection should use least privilege so that dropping tables is never allowed anyway; see Item 4), but it dramatically emphasizes that the attacker has taken control of your SQL statement and can submit arbitrary SQL to your database. This is really bad![1]

There are many examples where malicious user input can lead to program failure or security breaks. If you're not familiar with things like cross-site scripting, buffer overflow vulnerabilities, and other attacks via

---

1. For more information on exploiting a SQL injection vulnerability, see *http://www. issadvisor.com/columns/SqlInjection3/sql-injection-3-exploit-tables_files/frame.htm.*

malicious user input, please stop reading now and go buy a copy of a book (for example, Howard and LeBlanc 2002 or Viega and McGraw 2002) that focuses on these sorts of vulnerabilities. Study it, seriously. Perform regular code reviews to keep your software free from such bugs. These bugs aren't the focus of this book, but so many developers are unaware of them that I'd be remiss not to mention them here.

It's not enough to know how about security technologies. You need to be able to write secure code yourself.

/

◾ 2 ◾
What Is a Countermeasure?

I N HIS BOOK *Secrets and Lies,* Bruce Schneier talks about counter-measures in three categories: **protection**, **detection**, and **reaction**.

In a military office, classified documents are stored in a safe. The safe provides protection against attack, but so does the system of alarms and guards. Assume the attacker is an outsider: someone who does not work in the office. If he is going to steal the documents inside the safe, he is not only going to have to break into the safe, he is also going to have to defeat the system of alarms and guards. The safe—both the lock and the walls—are protective countermeasures, and the guards are reactive counter-measures.

If guards patrol the offices every 15 minutes, then the safe only has to withstand attack for a maximum of 15 minutes. If the safe is in an obscure office that is only staffed during the day, then the safe has to withstand 16 hours of attack: from 5 P.M. until 9 A.M. the next day (much longer if the office is closed during holiday weekends). If the safe has an alarm on it, and the guards come running as soon as the safe is jostled, then the safe only has to survive attack for as long as it takes for the guards to respond.

Can you see the synergy of the three types of countermeasure employed in the scenario Bruce describes here? First we have the safe, which is purely a protection countermeasure. The alarms on it provide detection, and the guards provide reaction. Imagine that we didn't have the alarms or guards: The safe would have to be perfect. But as we strengthen the detection and reaction countermeasures, we can rely less on the protection counter-measure. The safe is needed only to buy time for detection and reaction to kick in. Underwriters Laboratories publishes a standard burglary classification for safes[1] that ranges from TL-15, "tool-resistant," to TXTL-60X6, "torch-, explosive-, and tool-resistant." But notice the numbers. A TL-15 safe isn't designed to withstand attack forever. It's designed to withstand 15 minutes of sustained attack by someone who knows exactly how the safe is constructed. The TXTL-60X6 rating provides 60 minutes of protection.[2] You're literally buying time.

Think about protection, detection, and reaction in a typical computer system. You might have to think hard to come up with any detection and reaction countermeasures because the focus is almost always on protection. The hardware of the machine provides isolation between processes. This is protection. Cryptography is the basis for even more protection: data integrity protection, authentication, protection from eavesdropping, and so on. Further protection is on the horizon with Microsoft's proposed Next Generation Secure Computing Base (NGSCB).

Intrusion detection systems (IDSs) like Snort (*http://www.snort.org*) and integrity management systems like Tripwire (*http://www.tripwire.com*) are examples of detection countermeasures in computer systems, and the latter has some automated reaction built into it, automatically restoring files that have been corrupted. But generally reaction is provided by a human. When the IDS sends an alert to an administrator, someone's got to be on duty to notice and react.

Reaction is an interesting idea, and sometimes we can build it into systems automatically. For example, a domain controller can lock out an account after several failed login attempts, automatically foiling password-guessing attacks (note that this also introduces the potential for a denial-of-service attack). One way to think about reaction is that it allows you to dynamically change the balance between security and usability. The Windows TCP stack is another good example of automatic reaction. It can

---

1. *http://ulstandardsinfonet.ul.com/scopes/0687.html*

2. The "X6" designation indicates that all six walls of the safe provide the same level of protection. This is a very expensive safe!

detect when a SYN-flood attack[3] occurs and react by reducing timeout durations for half-open TCP connections. Thus the system becomes a little bit harder to use (the timeout for acknowledgment is shorter) but is more resistant to attack.

I fear we may have been lulled into designing systems that are based on protection countermeasures alone, and that's not a good idea because we'll never achieve perfect protection and still have systems that are accessible. For example, because we have such great cryptography technology today, people are often lulled into a false sense of security. It often doesn't matter what cryptographic algorithm you happen to be using; as long as it's a reasonably trustworthy algorithm that's been looked at by the cryptographic community, it's probably going to be the strongest link in your security chain. The attacker isn't going to go after the strongest link. He'll look for a weaker point instead.

So, when you design secure systems, try to think of protection countermeasures as a jeweler thinks of a safe. They exist to buy you time. Design detection and reaction into your systems as well. For example, you could instrument your server processes with WMI (Windows Management Instrumentation) (Turstall and Cole 2003) and then use WMI to report security statistics directly to an administrator. You could further build WMI consumers that analyze statistics and automatically react, or provide further alerts to the administrator. This is an area we all need to be working harder to perfect.

---

3. A SYN-flood attack is denial of service by repetitively sending the first leg of the TCP handshake (a "SYN" packet) with a spoofed source IP address. The victim thinks someone is trying to open a connection and sends an acknowledgment, then waits for a final acknowledgment from the sender. By flooding the victim with SYN packets from random spoofed IP addresses, the attacker keeps the victim's kernel so busy it can't process legitimate connection requests.

3

What Is Threat Modeling?

S ECURITY IS A LOT ABOUT tradeoffs. Rarely can you apply a security countermeasure to a system and not trade off convenience, privacy, or something else that users of that system hold dear to their hearts. Bruce Schneier talks a lot about these tradeoffs in real-world systems such as airports (Schneier 2000). In computer systems, the same tradeoffs apply. Forcing users to run with least privilege (as opposed to administrators) is a huge hurdle that many organizations cannot seem to get past, for example, simply because it's painful for users. Most software breaks when run without administrative privileges (which is stupid and should be fixed, as I discuss in Item 8).

It stands to reason that when designing secure systems you should not simply throw random countermeasures at the design, hoping to achieve security nirvana, but you'd be surprised how often this happens. For example, there's something magical about the acronym RSA. Just because your product uses good cryptographic algorithms (like RSA) doesn't mean it's secure! You need to ask yourself some questions.

- Who are my potential adversaries?
- What is their motivation, and what are their goals?
- How much inside information do they have?
- How much funding do they have?
- How averse are they to risk?

This is the start of a threat model. By sitting down with a small group of bright people who span a product's entire life cycle (product managers, marketing, sales, developers, testers, writers, executives), you can brainstorm about the security of that product. Once you figure out the bad guys you're up against (Schneier 2000 has some guidance here), you can start to think about the specific threats to your system. Now you'll be asking questions like these.

- Is my system secure from a malicious user who sends me malformed input?
- Is my database secure from unauthorized access?
- Will my system tolerate the destruction of a data center in a tactical nuclear strike?

I'm not being facetious here. Someone who asserts an unqualified "My system is secure" either is a fool or is trying to fool you! No one can say a system is "secure" without knowing what the threats are. Is your system secure against a hand grenade? Probably not. You can have security theater or you can have real security, and if you want the latter, you'll need to think about the specific threats that you want to mitigate. As you'll see, you will never be able to eliminate all threats. Even if you could, you'd be eliminating all risk, and businesses rarely prosper without a certain margin of risk. Heck, if you disconnect a computer and bury it in 20 feet of freshly poured concrete, there's very little risk that anyone will steal its data, but accessing that data yourself will be a bit challenging. Real security has a lot to do with risk management, and one of the first steps to achieving a good balance between threat mitigation and ease of use is to know the threats!

But how can you possibly analyze all the threats in a nontrivial system? It's not easy, and you'll likely never find them all. Don't give up hope, though. Due diligence here will really pay off. Most threat models start with data flow diagrams that chart the system. Spending the time to build such a model helps you understand your system better, and this is a laudable goal on its own, wouldn't you say? Besides, it's impossible to secure a system that you don't understand. Once you see the data flows, you can start looking for vulnerabilities.

Microsoft has an acronym that they use internally to help them find vulnerabilities in their software, STRIDE (Howard and LeBlanc 2000):

- Spoofing
- Tampering
- Repudiation
- Information disclosure
- Denial of service
- Elevation of privilege

Spoofing is pretending to be someone or something you're not. A client might spoof another user in order to access his personal data. Server-spoofing attacks happen all the time: Have you ever gotten an e-mail that claims to come from eBay, and when you click the link, you end up at a site that looks a lot like eBay but is asking you for personal information that eBay would never request (like your Social Security number or PIN codes)? This attack is now so common that it's earned a specific name: phishing.

Tampering attacks can be directed against static data files or network packets. Most developers don't think about tampering attacks. When reading an XML configuration file, for example, do you carefully check for valid input? Would your program behave badly if that configuration file contained malformed data? Also, on the network most people seem to think that encryption protects them against tampering attacks. Unless you know that your connection is integrity protected (Item 58), you're better off not making this assumption because many encryption techniques allow an attacker to flip bits in the ciphertext, which results in the corresponding bits in the plaintext being flipped, and this goes undetected without integrity protection.

Repudiation is where the attacker denies having performed some act. This is particularly important to consider if you plan on prosecuting an attacker. A common protection against repudiation is a secure log file, with timestamped events. One interesting consideration with these types of logs is the kind of data you store in them. If the log file were to be included in a court subpoena, would it be more damaging to your company to reveal it? Be careful what you put in there!

Information disclosure can occur with static data files as well as network packets. This is the unauthorized viewing of sensitive data. For example, someone running a promiscuous network sniffer such as **NETMON.EXE** can sniff all the Ethernet frames on a subnet. And don't try to convince yourself that a switch can prevent this!

Denial of service (DOS) is when the attacker can prevent valid users from receiving reasonable service from your system. If the attacker can crash your server, that's DOS. If the attacker can flood your server with fake requests so that you can't service legitimate users, that's DOS.

Elevation of privilege allows an attacker to achieve a higher level of privilege than she should normally have. For example, a buffer overflow in an application running as SYSTEM might allow an attacker to run code of her choosing at a very high level of privilege. Running with least privilege is one way to help avert such attacks (Item 4).

Another technique that is useful when rooting out vulnerabilities is something called an attack tree. It's a very simple concept: Pick a goal that an attacker might have—say, "Decrypt a message from machine A to machine B." Then brainstorm to figure out some avenues the attacker might pursue in order to achieve this goal. These avenues become nodes under the original goal and become goals themselves that can be evaluated the same way. I show a simple example in Figure 3.1. You can continue the analysis by drilling down into each new goal (Figure 3.2).

The beauty of attack trees is that they help you document your thought process. You can always revisit the tree to ensure that you didn't miss something. Entire branches of an attack tree can sometimes be reused in different contexts.

Once you have a list of vulnerabilities, you need to prioritize them. Remember that, just like in business, good security really comes down to

```
GOAL: Decrypt a message from machine A to machine B.
1. Break the encryption algorithm and decrypt the message, or
2. Acquire an encryption key and decrypt the message, or
3. Read the message before it's encrypted on A, or
4. Read the message after it's decrypted on B.
```

Figure 3.1 Building an attack tree

```
GOAL: Decrypt a message from machine A to machine B.
1. Break the encryption and decrypt the message, or
2. Acquire an encryption key and decrypt the message, or
   2.1. Perform a brute force attack against the key, or
   2.2. If the key was derived from a password,
        perform a dictionary attack against the key, or
   2.3. Use social engineering to steal the key, or
        2.3.1 Phone someone in the organization, or
        2.3.2 Befriend an employee outside work
   2.4. Threaten someone to get the key
3. Read the message before it's encrypted on A, or
   3.1. Compromise the FOO service on A, and
   3.2. Elevate privilege by exploiting a bug in the BAR service, and
   3.3. Read the process memory of the sending process on A.
4. Read the message after it's decrypted on B.
   ...
```

Figure 3.2 Further developing an attack tree

good risk management. The simplest way to prioritize threats is with two factors: damage and likelihood. Rate each vulnerability on a scale of one to ten based on the amount of damage a successful exploit might cause (financial damage, reputation damage, or even physical damage to persons or property). Calculate a second rating on the likelihood of someone being able to pull off the attack. To prioritize, calculate the overall risk factor for each vulnerability: Risk = Damage × Likelihood. Sort your vulnerabilities into a list of decreasing risk, and address the highest risk items first. This is a highly subjective analysis, so you'll be glad you built a well-rounded threat modeling team when it comes time to rank the threats.

Now you need to figure out how you're going to manage the risk for each vulnerability. You've got four choices.

- Accept the risk.
- Transfer the risk.
- Remove the risk.
- Mitigate the risk.

Accepting risk is part of everyday life in business. Some risks are so low and so costly to mitigate that they may be worth accepting. For example,

accepting the threat of a nuclear strike that destroys two data centers in two different locations simultaneously might just be the cost of doing business. But each threat model is different: For a military system, this might be worth mitigating.

Transfer of risk can be accomplished many ways. Insurance is one example; warnings are another. Software programs often transfer risk to the users via warnings. For example, try enabling Basic Authentication in IIS and you'll be warned that passwords will be sent in the clear unless you also enable SSL.

Remove the risk. Sometimes after analyzing the risk associated with a feature, you'll find that it's simply not worth it and the feature should be removed from the product. Remember that complexity is the number-one enemy of security. In many cases this simple approach is the best.

Mitigating a risk involves keeping the feature but reducing the risk with countermeasures (Item 2). This is where designers and developers really need to be creative. Don't be surprised if this means reshaping the requirements, and perhaps the user's expectations, to allow the feature to be secured.

Threat Modeling (Swiderski and Snyder 2001) is an entire book dedicated to this important topic. The second edition of *Writing Secure Code* (Howard and LeBlanc 2002) also has a chapter on threat modeling, and *Secrets and Lies* (Schneier 2003) is an invaluable resource as well. To learn more about social engineering, check out *The Art of Deception* (Mitnick 2002). And the next time someone claims that her feature is secure, ask to see her threat model!

■ 4 ■
What Is the Principle of Least Privilege?

T HE PRINCIPLE OF LEAST PRIVILEGE was originally defined by
Saltzer (1975):

> Every program and every user of the system should operate using the
> least set of privileges necessary to complete the job. Primarily, this prin-
> ciple limits the damage that can result from an accident or error. It also
> reduces the number of potential interactions among privileged programs
> to the minimum for correct operation, so that unintentional, unwanted, or
> improper uses of privilege are less likely to occur. . .

I sometimes like to think about this principle in reverse. Imagine if you
ignore it entirely and run all your code with full privileges all the time.
You've basically turned off a whole raft of security features provided by
your platform. The less privilege you grant to a program, the more walls
are erected around that program by the platform. If a program misbehaves
because of a coding error, perhaps one that was tickled by a malicious user
providing malformed input (Item 1), you'll be glad those walls are in place.

Security compromises usually occur in stages: The attacker gains a certain level of privilege via one security hole and then tries to elevate his privilege level by finding another hole. If you run programs with more
privilege than they really need, the attacker's life is much easier.

This principle can be applied in many different places; it really is a mindset that you should follow as you design and build systems. The following paragraphs describe some examples that are relevant to .NET programmers working on Windows. The examples are by no means exhaustive, but they will give you some concrete ideas that will help you get into the right mindset.

Daemon processes on servers should be designed and configured to run with only the privileges they need to get the job done. This means that you should absolutely avoid the SYSTEM account when configuring an ASP.NET worker process, Windows Services, COM+ servers, and so on (Item 28).

Desktop applications should be designed to conform to the Windows Logo guidelines[1] to ensure that they don't attempt to write to protected parts of the file system or registry. When you ship programs that don't follow these guidelines, they break when users attempt to run with least privilege (under normal, nonadministrative user accounts). If you don't want your Mom browsing the Web as an administrator, then start writing programs that she can use as a normal user (Item 8)!

When opening files or other secure resources, open them only for the permissions you need for that session. If you plan on reading a file, open it for read-only permissions. Don't open it for read-write permissions thinking, "Someday I may want to write to that file." Open resources for the permission you need at that particular moment.

Use the least privileged form of state management you can for your application. In the .NET Framework, storing application state via Isolated Storage requires less privilege than using a named file, and it has the added benefit of ensuring that your data is written to the user profile (Item 19), which is one of the Windows Logo guidelines I alluded to earlier.

Close references to files and other resources as soon as possible. This is especially important if you use impersonation (Item 31), as these resources can "leak" from one security context (Item 15) to the next if you're not careful. Remember that Windows and the .NET Framework tend to check permissions only when resources are first opened. This is a performance

---

1. *http://www.microsoft.com/winlogo.htm*

enhancement, but it can also lead to security holes if you don't close those resources promptly when you're finished using them.

And, finally, choose to run with least privilege whenever you log in to your computer, whether you're at home or at work. Item 9 provides tips for software developers trying to run with least privilege.

■ 5 ■
What Is the Principle of
Defense in Depth?

D
URING THE COLD WAR, the United States wanted to learn more about Soviet submarine and missile technology. How fast were the Soviets progressing? What were the results from their ICBM tests? Even more important, were the Soviets working toward a first strike capability? In October of 1971, the United States sent its most advanced nuclear spy submarine, the USS *Halibut*, deep into Soviet territory in the Sea of Okhotsk. It's mission? Find the undersea telephone cable that connected the Soviet submarine base at Petropavlovsk to the Soviet Pacific Fleet headquarters on the mainland at Vladivostok (Figure 5.1). The mission was a success, and you can imagine the mood of the divers as they eavesdropped on the wire with an instrument that measured electromagnetic emanations. What they heard was easily understandable Russian conversations—no encryption. The following year, the *Halibut* installed a permanent tap on the line to record the conversations, with a plan to return in about a month to retrieve the records. Eventually more taps were installed on Soviet lines in other parts of the world—the more advanced instruments could store a year's worth of data. All in all, the intelligence gathered from these exercises helped end the Cold War, as it gave the United States a window directly into the Soviet mind (Sontag and Drew 1998).

What does this story have to do with computer security? It demonstrates what can happen when systems are designed without redundant

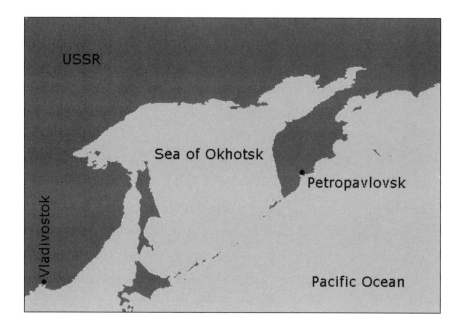

Figure 5.1 The Sea of Okhotsk

security measures. The Soviets assumed that their conversations were secure simply because they were being carried on phone lines that were protected by perimeter defenses (the entrance to the Sea of Okhotsk is much more narrow than my map might first indicate and could easily be defended by the Soviet Navy).

Companies rely on firewalls for perimeter security. Most developers assume that if they are behind the firewall they're safe. But think how easy it is for an attacker to slip behind a firewall. Want some information from an internal company database? Just pick up the phone and call someone in the company and ask for it (Mitnick 2002). Or use a modem to contact some-one's computer inside the company. Or park your car in the company's underground parking garage and surf onto the company intranet via an insecure wireless connection set up by the employees for convenience. Feel-ing cocky? Walk into the company's headquarters and ask if you can do some work in an empty conference room while you wait for an employee to meet you. Then plug into the Ethernet jack in the room and party on. You'll be surprised how far you get once you find out the names of a few employees. Don't want that much risk? Then compromise an employee's home computer and use his VPN connection to access the network.

These examples assume you are worried only about outsiders getting behind the perimeter. What about the employees who are authorized to work behind the firewall each and every day? I'm not trying to insult you or your colleagues, but you should know that your fellow employees aren't always thinking about the good of the company when they're on the job.

Defense in depth is all about building redundant countermeasures into a system. Don't assume a perimeter defense will protect you. Don't assume someone else's code will protect you. When you write a component, validate the input assuming it can be purposely malformed. Just because your component is currently used only by other trusted components doesn't mean those other components were written by people who know how dangerous malformed input can be (Item 1). Besides, components are designed for reuse, so a component that's used by trusted components today may be deployed in a less trusted environment tomorrow. And never assume that because you're behind a firewall, your internal network conversations are automatically secure. Make sure internal server-to-server communication is protected (Item 58).

Always think about failure. Secure systems should not fail badly; rather, they should bend and flex before they break (Schneier 2000). Using a mixture of countermeasures that overlap can provide a synergy that makes the resulting system more secure than its individual parts (Item 2).

■ 6 ■
What Is Authentication?

A UTHENTICATION ANSWERS THE question, Who are you? When `Alice` logs in to a machine, the machine challenges her to prove her identity by asking for a password (or something else, like a smartcard). This is one example of authentication. Another is when `Alice` is already logged in to a machine and requests a file from another machine via a file share. Even though she's already logged in to the local machine, that doesn't help the remote machine at all. The remote machine wants proof that this is really a request from `Alice` as opposed to some attacker on the network just pretending to be her. Kerberos (Item 59) is an example of a network authentication protocol that protects most Windows systems.

It sometimes helps to break down the question Who are you? into three, more specific questions.

- What do you have?
- What do you know?
- What are you made of?

Asking one or more of these questions can help you infer the identity of a user. For example, a password is something that only the named user should know, whereas a smartcard raises two questions: What do you have (the card) and What do you know (the PIN code on the card). This is referred to as "multifactor" authentication and can lead to considerably more secure systems. The last question queries biometric data such as hand geometry, retinal patterns, thumbprints, and so on. Schneier (2000) talks a bit about the pros and cons of biometrics, pointing out that they often aren't all they are cracked up to be. For example, thumbprint readers have been shown to be incredibly easy to fool (Smith 2002).

Network authentication can happen in one of three ways. The server can ask the client to prove her identity (the default mode in Kerberos). The client can ask the server to prove his identity (the default mode in SSL), or we can have mutual authentication, where both client and server are assured of each other's identities (both Kerberos and SSL support this as an optional mode). Usually you should prefer mutual authentication wherever possible, unless anonymity is an important feature of the service you happen to be providing. I find it interesting that, in many cases where it seems as though you're getting mutual authentication, you really aren't. For example, when you log in to a Web server over SSL by typing a user name and password into a form, logically you'd think you've established mutual authentication. You've proven your identity with a user name and password, and the server has proven its identity with a certificate and its private key. But did you double-click the lock to actually *look* at that certificate? Did you look closely at the URL in the browser address bar? Probably not. For all you know, the server is being spoofed by a bad guy who has simply duplicated the look and feel of the real server. The same problem exists in some of the built-in security mechanisms in Windows. For example, COM has always claimed to use mutual authentication. But the dirty little secret is that, unless you set up a server principal name (Item 60) and specify it in the client code, you're not really authenticating the server; you're just trusting the server to tell you whom it's supposed to be running as. But nobody does this, just as nobody checks the certificates of sites they visit. One of the goals of this book is to make you aware of how these security mechanisms work so that you know what you're really getting!

■ 7 ■
What Is a Luring Attack?

T HE LURING ATTACK IS a type of elevation-of-privilege attack where the attacker "lures" a more highly privileged component to do something on his behalf. The most straightforward technique is to convince the target to run the attacker's code in a more privileged security context (Item 15).

Imagine for a moment that you normally log in to your computer as a privileged user, perhaps as a member of the local Administrators group. An acquaintance sends you a zipped executable file and asks you to run it. You unzip the file to your hard drive and see a program called **gophers.exe**. Now let me state up front that you should never run code on your machine that you don't trust. The following example shows that even the precaution of running untrusted code under a low-privilege user account often won't save you.[1]

Say you add a new local account to your machine called Untrusted-User: a normal, restricted user account. Then you use the secondary logon service (Item 30) to run **gophers.exe** under the restricted account, thinking to yourself what a great little sandbox Microsoft has provided with the **runas** command. Because you keep all of your personal files under your profile directory, **gophers.exe** won't be able to access them because of the

---

1. Programs are a lot like hamburgers: If someone off the street handed you one, would you feel safe eating it? Ask yourself this question next time someone gives you a program to run!

ACLs that restrict access to your user profile (Item 19). Because your mail settings are under your profile as well, **gophers.exe** won't be able to send malicious e-mail to anyone in your name. The program runs fine, and you laugh as you watch it animate 500 dancing gophers and play a silly tune.

The next day you receive hate mail from a few of your friends who wonder why you sent them e-mails with embedded images of gopher porn. You also discover that some new files have been added to your System32 directory! What the heck happened? You just got suckered by a very simple luring attack. When **gophers.exe** started up, it checked to see if it was running in a privileged security context by peeking at the groups in its token (Item 16). On discovering its lack of privilege, it took a gamble that the interactive user might actually be logged in with more privileges, so this obnoxious little program simply lured **explorer.exe** into launching another instance of **gophers.exe**. It did this by calling a few functions in **user32.dll**. First it sought out Explorer's Start button and posted a WM_LBUTTONDOWN message to it; then, with a little SendKeys magic, it brought up the "Run..." dialog from the Start menu, entered the full path to **gophers.exe**, and simulated pressing **Enter**. Explorer was happy to launch the program, as it had no idea that the interactive user wasn't really in control anymore, and when the new copy of **gophers.exe** started up it inherited a copy of Explorer's token (Item 16). Through this simple luring attack (which is just a few lines of code), the attacker not only compromised your documents and e-mail, but, since you were logged in with high privilege, also compromised your operating system. What fun! Figure 7.1 shows a picture of this attack.

Look for luring attacks whenever you try to create a sandbox for code that you don't fully trust. The CLR's code access security infrastructure is a great example of a place where luring attacks are taken very seriously. Because managed code from different assemblies can run in the same process with varying degrees of trust, any partially trusted assembly must be verified for type safety, and each full-permission demand performs a stackwalk to ensure that a less trusted component isn't luring a more trusted component into doing its dirty work. Window stations (Item 18) were invented way back in Windows NT 3.5 to prevent luring attacks from daemons (Item 27) against the interactive user.

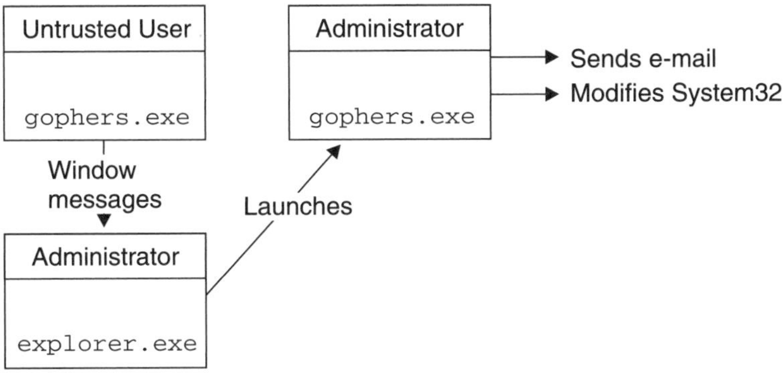

Figure 7.1 A luring attack mounted by evil gophers

Given luring attacks, you might wonder why I suggest in Item 9 that as a developer you should log in using a low-privilege account while keeping a high-privilege Explorer window and/or a command prompt open so you can administer the machine when necessary without having to log out. This clearly exposes you to luring attacks, but if you were simply running as admin all the time before you read my chapter and changed your evil ways (grin), you would certainly be no less secure now than you were before. No luring attack was necessary before—you were running all programs with high privilege directly. As with any security decision, you always need to balance productivity with the threat level (Item 3). Someday you may find yourself on a development machine so sensitive that you aren't even allowed to *know* an admin password for the machine.

■ 8 ■
What Is a Nonprivileged User?

I F YOU'RE A WINDOWS programmer today, depending on your age most likely you got your start programming one of Microsoft's early platforms: DOS, 16-bit Windows, or Windows 9X. Some of today's Windows programmers came from UNIX, but I'd say the vast majority grew up in the ghetto (as I did). None of these early platforms had any support for security. There wasn't much need for security back then as DOS and Windows were not multiuser networked platforms. Programmers quickly learned that Windows was a single-user system, and security wasn't part of the picture.

When Windows NT arrived, things changed. The platform suddenly sprouted a new feature called user security and supported things like multiple logons, user profiles, and access control. However, most Windows programmers paid little attention to these new features and kept hacking up single-user programs. You really can't blame them, as Windows NT didn't encourage anyone to create normal user accounts and experience this new feature called security. Running with admin privileges gave people the illusion that they were running on a single-user, isolated system as before.

Eventually corporations started using the networking and security features of Windows NT and began implementing security policies that forced their users to run under nonprivileged accounts. However, developers did not follow suit for one of two reasons. Most developers simply didn't have the time or the inclination to learn how to navigate the barriers in a non-privileged world. Others who tried to run as non-admins failed miserably because their tools broke when run under nonprivileged accounts (take the classic Visual Basic 6 example, which updates protected parts of the registry each time you compile). Developers took this as a sign that they were meant to always run as administrators on Windows, which was the beginning of the vicious cycle that we're stuck in today.

Today we have hundreds of thousands of Windows developers who know little about security, building programs that often must be run on secured computers. Because the typical Windows programmer still runs as an admin, she tends to build code that breaks in a nonprivileged environment. I've heard arguments from people I respect that the solution is to test in a nonprivileged environment. Yet these same people fail to produce software that can run correctly in a nonprivileged environment. It would be funny if it weren't so sad a state of affairs.

> *Security Is a Process, Not a Product*
> —Bruce Schneier (Schneier 2000)

Security is not something you can buy or even build. It's much more than that—it's a process, and in many ways, a state of mind. Developers running as admins continue to produce software that breaks for non-admins. When asked to stop running as admin, the developer complains that stuff breaks when he does that. This is the quagmire we're in today. Figure 8.1 shows an example of a popular music jukebox (which shall go unnamed) that forces its users to run as administrators. At least this application warns the user that it's got a problem. Most broken applications simply fail at random places, leaving the user utterly mystified.

Figure 8.1 This is pathetic.

It's obvious that Windows programmers need to learn how security works on their platform. I believe that a great way to start is to run from day to day as a normal, nonprivileged user. Why? Because I did it myself. I stopped running as an administrator, and I immediately began to spot problems in my own code and in other products that I used to use on a daily basis. I was shocked to see how many programs failed miserably when run nonprivileged, but at the same time I was learning how to avoid these failures in my own code. I felt like I'd taken the red pill (apologies to *The Matrix*) and was seeing the real world for the first time.

I truly believe that the security revolution on this platform must be organized at the grassroots level with programmers like you and me. For example, if you're building developer tools (compilers, profilers, source control tools, UML tools, etc.), you have a special responsibility to the community to make sure these tools can be run by nonprivileged users. We all need to work toward a development environment that supports nonprivileged users so that we can change the culture for new programmers on this platform.

The best way to build software that can be run by nonprivileged users is to run as a nonprivileged user while you write and test the code. This is known as eating your own dog food, a technique that has been used for years by good coders.

I have a dream. In this dream I can run as a normal user and all the software I install runs flawlessly. I can develop code easily as a non-admin, and I'm not constantly distracted by security barriers. I believe we can get there, but we need to work together to make it happen. Item 9 will show you how easy it is to join the growing revolution yourself.

9

How to Develop Code as a Non-Admin

T HE TRICK TO DEVELOPING code in a nonprivileged environment is to have your main interactive logon be nonprivileged but to keep an admin logon in your pocket for those times that you need it. Look, it doesn't take administrative privileges to edit a text file, and that's what you're doing most of the time when you're programming, right? And you don't want your programs to require admin privileges to run, which is the point of this whole exercise. So your main logon, where you write, compile, link, and test your code (and where you surf the Internet, of course) should be nonprivileged. However, during development you will occasionally need to create a virtual directory in IIS, add a user account, or add an assembly to the global assembly cache, and that's where your secondary logon comes in handy.

By far the easiest and cleanest way to get a second logon is through Terminal Services. For example, if you develop code on Windows Server 2003, just run the command **mstsc** to bring up the remote desktop connection dialog; then press the Options button, fill out the form as I've done in Figure 9.1, and press "Connect." You'll get a window running in a second terminal services session, with a new desktop, running as whomever you specified when you filled out the form. Just minimize this window and bring it up whenever you need to do something as an administrator! If this doesn't work for you at first, then bring up the System control panel applet

Figure 9.1 TermServ into your own computer!

as an administrator. On the Remote tab, check the box that says "Allow users to connect remotely to this computer."

Unfortunately, as of this writing this trick only works on Windows Server 2003, not on older platforms like Windows XP, because of licensing restrictions. With the version of Terminal Services that's built in to the operating system, you're allowed only a single connection to the console on Windows XP. Even on Windows Server 2003, you may not be able to use this feature because it's mutually incompatible with the "offline files" feature, which you may already be relying on. If for some reason you can't use this mechanism, don't give up hope. You can use the Secondary Logon Service instead. Read on.

The Secondary Logon Service

This service, introduced in Windows 2000, allows you to easily run with multiple logons. If you're familiar with UNIX, this facility is similar to the

su command, at least in spirit. The secondary logon service can be accessed three ways:

- Programmatically (via `CreateProcessWithLogonW`)
- From the command line (via the **runas** command)
- From Explorer (via the "Run As" context menu item)

If you're not familiar with this service, try the following experiment. Running as an administrator, log out and log back in as a non-admin (create a normal user account locally if necessary). Once you're running as a normal user, press the Start button in Explorer and navigate into All Programs, Accessories, and select (but don't click) the Command Prompt shortcut. Once it's highlighted, right-click it to bring up the context menu (if you're running Windows 2000, you'll need to hold down the Shift key while you right-click—for some screwy reason this feature was hidden in that operating system). When the context menu appears, you should see a menu item called "Run As." Click it to bring up the Run As dialog. Select the radio button that says "The following user:" and notice that the built-in local administrator account is selected by default. Type the password for the admin account and press OK. You should see a new command prompt appear—this one running as the administrator. Verify this by running the command **whoami**[1] from this new command prompt or, if that's not available, just type **set username** instead. Now, imagine keeping a little command prompt like this down at the bottom of your desktop, always open, always waiting to execute your commands in a privileged security context. Any program you start from this command prompt will run as administrator. Nifty, eh? But we're nowhere near being done yet. Read on.

But I Hate the Command Prompt!

Many developers are comfortable using the command prompt to get tasks done. For example, I much prefer **netsh** for configuring my IP settings over messing around with the GUI. But for some tasks in Windows, using a GUI

---

1.   If you don't have this tool, I show where to get it in Item 21.

is pretty much unavoidable. For example, the command-line ACL editor,[2] `cacls,` doesn't correctly propagate inheritable ACEs (in English this means it can screw up your file system ACLs over time), so I prefer to use the GUI to modify my file system ACLs. You really need a special Explorer window for performing administrative tasks. Unfortunately, simply typing `explorer` from your admin command prompt will very likely not do what you want. `explorer.exe` normally uses a single process, and when the new process starts it simply sends a message to the earlier instance and terminates. This means that the new window you get is not running in a different security context. There is an option to force every Explorer window to run in its own process, however I've never managed to get it to solve this problem. On the other hand, there is another facade that you can use to start an Explorer window in its own process: `iexplore.exe`. If you type `\program files\internet explorer\iexplore.exe` from your admin command prompt, the new Explorer window will run in its own process, with admin privileges. If you type "Control Panel" into the address bar, you'll quickly see that there's not much you can't do from here. One odd thing that I've noticed, and that you should watch out for, is that this copy of Explorer won't refresh things automatically. For example, if you create a new file, it might not show up in your admin Explorer window. Don't fret, though, just press `F5` to force a refresh.

Take a close look at this new window. You likely can't distinguish the admin Explorer window from any other Explorer window, and you will make a royal mess of your system if you leave things this way. For example, you might accidentally create a directory with your admin Explorer when you really intend to have your normal account own and manage that directory. Take it from my own painful experience: You don't want to stop here. The trick is to use per-user customization to make the admin window stand out so you can't miss it. There's an utterly cool way to do this, too. Skin it! Run `regedit` from your admin command prompt and drill down to the following registry key: `HKEY_CURRENT_USER\Software\Microsoft\ Internet Explorer\Toolbar`. Add a named string value, `BackBitmap`, whose value is the path to a bitmap file. At the moment, I use a boring lit-

---

2. If you're not sure what an ACL or ACE is, be sure to read Item 43.

tle red 32×32-pixel bitmap, but you can get more fancy if you like. Since Explorer tiles this all over the toolbar, this means my admin Explorer ends up with a bright red toolbar that I can't miss. The `Toolbar` key has a sibling called `Main`. Surf over there and add a named string value, `Window Title`. Set this to "ADMIN" or whatever you like. This will help you see which window is which when you press Alt-Tab repeatedly to switch between programs.

Network Credentials

The only problem with our setup so far is that our admin prompt lacks domain credentials. This may not be a big deal if you're not in a domain, but if you are it's really annoying to be prompted for domain credentials when you're simply trying to administer your local machine. Try to edit an ACL (Item 43) on a file using your admin Explorer window, for example. At some point the GUI will contact the domain asking for a list of users and groups, and you'll be prompted for domain credentials because your local admin account can't be authenticated by the domain. To avoid your fingers falling off from typing your domain, user name, and password over and over, use this nifty trick to impart a set of domain credentials to a local admin command prompt: **runas /netonly /u:MyDomain\MyUser-Account cmd**. After prompting you for a password, the system creates a new command prompt that has a split personality. On your machine it's running as your local administrator, but on the network it will be authenticated using your domain credentials. Close your old admin command prompt. That was yesterday's news!

A Sample Setup for a VS.NET Developer

To be productive, it's important to have an admin command prompt ready at all times, so I find it useful to automate as much as possible the process of getting one. I suggest creating a couple of batch files to help (I call mine **adminShell.cmd** and **adminShellInit.cmd**). Use the first batch file to house two **runas** commands, the first initializing a local admin shell and the second creating a new shell that has your domain credentials. Here's my **adminShell.cmd**. Note that XYZZY\la is the local admin account on my box (I always rename the Administrator account to annoy potential hackers).

```
REM adminShell.cmd
REM Starts a command prompt running as the local admin (XYZZY\la)
REM but with my domain credentials (ps\kbrown)
runas /u:xyzzy\la "runas /netonly /u:ps\kbrown \"cmd /K
c:\etc\utils\adminShellInit.cmd\""
```

I've heard reports that, on some systems, allowing the first command prompt to exit results in painting problems for applications. I've not personally run into this, but if you do you might find **knowledge base article 322906** helpful. In short, the workaround is to modify the batch file just shown so that the second reference to **runas** becomes **cmd /K runas.**

My second batch file initializes the environment and makes the command prompt stand out by changing its color to black on red and setting an obvious title. Because the current directory of the admin prompt will be SYSTEM32, I change to a less dangerous directory by default. I don't want to accidentally modify anything in there!

```
REM adminShellInit.cmd
@echo off
title *** ADMIN ***
color C0
call  "c:\program files\microsoft visual studio .net
2003\common7\tools\vsvars32.bat"
cd "%USERPROFILE%\My Documents"
cls
```

Figure 9.2 shows what my desktop looks like with my normal and admin command prompts running.

Debugging

Contrary to popular belief, you don't normally need any special privileges to debug programs on Windows. If you start a process, you own it and thus have full permissions to it. That's all a debugger needs. However, if you want to debug processes running in other logon sessions (services, for

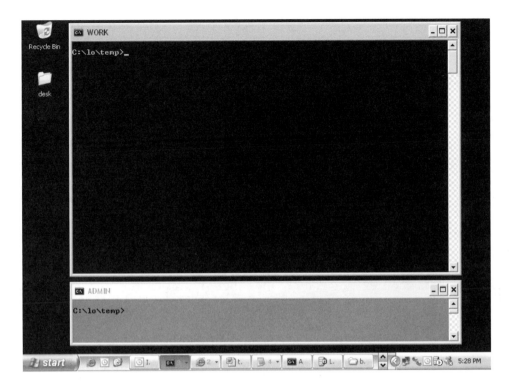

Figure 9.2 An admin secondary logon

instance, or IIS worker processes) you'll need the Debug privilege. This privilege allows you (and therefore your debugger) to open any process on the machine for full permissions, even operating system services. It's a really powerful privilege normally granted to the local Administrators group, so instead of granting this to my account I simply start the debugger from my admin prompt (if you've set up your environment like I do for .NET, you can just type **devenv** to get it started).

If you're running Visual Studio .NET, you must add your low-privilege developer account to the local Debugger Users group. This is not an operating system requirement, rather it's a policy enforced by Visual Studio .NET. If you aren't a member of this group, you aren't allowed to do JIT debugging, remote debugging, or pretty much debugging of any kind using Visual Studio .NET.

Creating Web Projects in VS.NET

The Visual Studio .NET Web Project wizard doesn't work very well if you're not running as an administrator. I've found the easiest way to get a Web project started as a non-admin is to first create the virtual directory using the IIS admin tool from the computer management console[3] and then run the wizard and point it to the URL I just created. You can also add yourself to the VS Developers group, which grants you write access to \inetpub\wwwroot and seems to make the wizard a lot happier.

Writing Code That Can Be Used by a Non-Admin

One result of developing code as a nonprivileged user is that you'll be more likely to produce programs that run without requiring elevated privileges. So this item would not be complete without pointing out the most common reasons that programs break for nonprivileged users, and helping you do better.

If there were only one bit of advice I could give on this topic, it would be this: Separate program files (executables, DLLs, etc.) from data files! Normal users don't have write permission under the Program Files section of the file system,[4] which means that your program won't be able to write here either, so don't try (this is an example where running as a normal user can help you catch silly mistakes early). This is by far the most common bug that causes programs to require elevated privileges in order to run.

As part of the Windows Logo program, Microsoft provides guidelines on where to store data files. The .NET Framework has methods that allow your program to discover the appropriate location for data files at runtime, so there's really no excuse for the plethora of apps that insist on writing data to their install directories. Figure 9.3 shows the various types of data, the recommended locations, and the enumerations in the .NET Framework used

---

3. The quickest way to run this very useful console as an administrator is to launch **compmgmt.msc** from your admin command prompt. But if you are a mouse clicker, you can also navigate from your admin Explorer window into Control Panel | Administrative Tools | Computer Management.

4. There's a good reason for this: On a multiuser system, you wouldn't want a malicious program overwriting **WINWORD.EXE** with a Trojan horse, for example.

Description	Recommended Section of File System	Environment.Special Folder enum
Static, read-only data files	c:\Program Files	`ProgramFiles`
Writable data files shared by all users of the application	c:\Documents and Settings\All Users\ Application Data	`CommonApplicationData`
Writable data files specific to a single user	c:\Documents and Settings\username\ Application Data	`ApplicationData`
Writable data files specific to a single user and machine	c:\Documents and Settings\username\ Local Settings\Application Data	`LocalApplicationData`
User documents	c:\Documents and Settings\username\ My Documents	`Personal`

Figure 9.3 Recommended data file locations

to look up these locations at runtime, because the actual paths I provide here may be different on each machine. Here's a link to the Logo requirements.

http://www.microsoft.com/winlogo/

I strongly recommend reading the section on data and settings management, as it provides further tips on using these common directories.

Note that I'm not recommending writing directly into any of these directories. Rather, you should create a subdirectory that's unique to your application and store your data files under it. The Logo requirements specify the directory structure as follows: `[company name]\[product name]\ [version]`. Here's some C# code that prints out the recommended directory for the second item in Figure 9.3.

```
using System;

class App {
  static void Main() {
    string path = Environment.GetFolderPath(
      Environment.SpecialFolder.CommonApplicationData
    );

    Console.WriteLine(path);
  }
}
```

If you're building a Windows Forms application, your life is even easier, because the Logo requirements for forming your product's subfolders are implemented for you via the following properties on the `Application` class.

- `UserAppDataPath`
- `LocalUserAppDataPath`
- `CommonAppDataPath`

Here's a program that prints out these paths. Compile and run it; then go look at your user profile directory (Item 19)! The subfolders for your product are created automatically. The first time you read one of these properties, the `Application` class creates the folder on your behalf (if it doesn't already exist), using the metadata provided by the three assembly-level attributes shown in the following code sample:

```
using System;
using System.Windows.Forms;
using System.Reflection;

[assembly: AssemblyCompany("ACME")]
[assembly: AssemblyProduct("WidgetManager")]
[assembly: AssemblyVersion("1.1.0.0")]

class App {
  static void Main() {
    // simply accessing these properties creates
    // subfolders based on company/product name
    // and version, according to logo requirements!
    Console.WriteLine("Roaming Settings Folder: {0}",
      Application.UserAppDataPath);
    Console.WriteLine("Local Settings Folder: {0}",
      Application.LocalUserAppDataPath);
    Console.WriteLine("Shared Settings Folder: {0}",
      Application.CommonAppDataPath);
  }
}
```

Isolated Storage

For storing per-user settings (as opposed to documents that the user might want to manipulate directly in the file system), you should consider using the .NET Framework's isolated storage system. This is really just another way to access files stored under the user profile directory, but the .NET Framework manages the location of the storage so that each assembly gets its very own private root directory where files can be stored. Once you realize that an isolated storage file is just a real file in the file system, you'll see how easy it is to use. Because `IsolatedStorageFileStream` derives from `FileStream`, if you've used the `FileStream` class, using a file from Isolated Storage isn't any different. Here's an example that creates a text file using `IsolatedStorage`.

```
using System;
using System.IO;
using System.IO.IsolatedStorage;

class App {
  static void Main() {
    IsolatedStorageFile myRoot =
      IsolatedStorageFile.GetUserStoreForAssembly();
    using (FileStream media =
      new IsolatedStorageFileStream("myFile.txt",
          FileMode.Create, FileAccess.Write,
          FileShare.None, myRoot))
    using (StreamWriter w =
      new StreamWriter(media)) {
      w.Write("Hello, isolated storage!");
    }
  }
}
```

There is now a file called `myFile.txt` somewhere on your hard drive. To find it, configure Explorer to show hidden files and drill down into your user profile directory a bit: `c:\Documents and Settings\ [user name]\Local Settings\Application Data\IsolatedStorage`. From here names are mangled, but just keep drilling down and you'll eventually find your file. Open it in Notepad and see that there's nothing magical happening here. To see how your assembly's storage location is identified, use **storeadm /list**. You'll notice that by default your storage is indexed by your assembly's URL. This means that, if your assembly is loaded from a different location, it will be looking at a new storage location. If this is a problem, give your assembly a strong name. Now the storage location will depend only on your assembly's strong name, which means that, if the version of your assembly changes, it will be looking at a new storage location, but this is usually acceptable if you plan ahead. Run **storeadm /list** after giving the previous example a strong name and see how things change.

Installation Tips

Even well-written programs that don't require special privileges are usually installed by administrators. Let me say this another way, with emphasis: **You must assume that your program will be run by one person and installed by another!** This means that there's no point messing with per-user settings during an installation. For all you know, an administrator is setting up a machine for a new user who doesn't even have an account in the domain yet, let alone a user profile on the machine. So wait until your program is launched the first time to initialize per-user settings. Also consider that your program may be installed on a machine where more than one user normally logs in (think of the front desk at your company). Test for this! Use **runas** as a quick way to launch your app under different security contexts and ensure that it works properly.

Strive for a power user installation. Power Users is a special group granted read-write access to the Program Files directory tree. Unless you need to install an NT service or COM+ component, or put assemblies in the GAC, it's very likely that the person installing your software doesn't even need full admin privileges, which is a very good thing. When someone installs your app as a power user instead of an admin, she can rest assured that your installer won't be allowed to do nasty things such as overwrite parts of the operating system, install kernel-mode code like device drivers, which can do anything they want, and so forth. Even better would be an xcopy deploy that doesn't require any privilege at all, or a "no-touch" deployment over the network. Remember the principle of least privilege (Item 4) when designing your installer as well as your app!

10

How to Enable Auditing

U NFORTUNATELY, WINDOWS DOES NOT have a lot of detection countermeasures (Item 2) built into it, but one of the features that comes close is auditing. On a secure production system, auditing is one way an administrator can detect that an attack has occurred or is in progress. A good sysadmin will turn on auditing to detect password-guessing attacks, attempts to access sensitive resources, null session connections (Item 35), and so on.

The security audit log can also be helpful to a developer in tracking down security problems where an authorized user is accidentally denied access. For example, I've always recommended auditing of logon events on all lab machines. A logon event occurs when a new logon-session (Item 17) is created on the machine, which means that some user successfully authenticated. But it also occurs when authentication fails for some reason—and there are loads of reasons. A classic example is where a developer recently created a new user account for a daemon but forgot to uncheck the option "User must change password at next logon." Countless hours are spent trying to track down silly misconfigurations like this one, when the security audit log often gives you all the detail you need (see Figure 10.1 for another typical example). But these audit entries won't show up unless you've turned on auditing on the machine!

Let me show you how to turn on auditing in Windows. Auditing is part of security policy, and you can get to the machine's security policy by

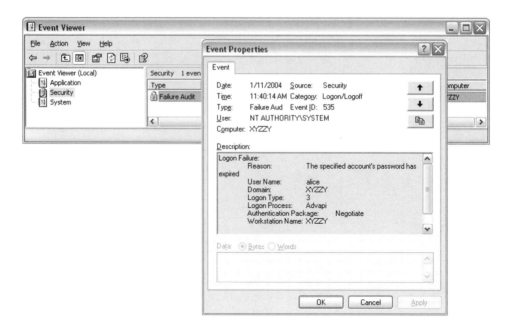

Figure 10.1 Auditing: It's a developer's best friend.

looking in the **Administrative Tools** folder for "Local Security Policy." To launch this from your admin command prompt (Item 9) just run **secpol.msc**. I've shown how to find the auditing settings in Figure 10.2. In a lab setting, I recommend at least turning on auditing of failed logon events; on a production server, you'll want to audit failed object access as

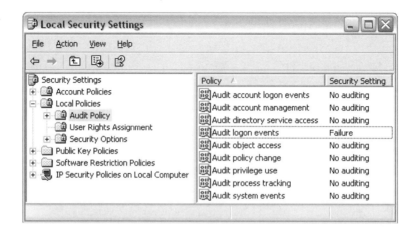

Figure 10.2 Finding the auditing settings

well. You'll also need to put a SACL on any file or registry key you want to watch (see Item 11 for details).

In many scenarios, the administrator uses group policy to control the auditing settings for a particular machine. In that case, changing the local policy for the machine may have no effect because it's being overridden by upstream group policy. To learn more about group policy, see Item 74.

11.
How to Audit Access to Files

T O ENABLE AUDITING FOR a file (or folder), you need to edit the security descriptor (Item 42) for it and give it a SACL (Item 43). This is easy to do with Explorer. Just find the file you want, bring up its property sheet, and choose the Security tab. From there, press the Advanced button. The dialog that pops up will have an auditing tab that you can use to edit the SACL. If you normally run with least privilege as I do, note that Explorer will hide this tab unless you have the `SeSecurityPrivilege`, which administrators have by default. Therefore, log in as an administrator (or run another copy of Explorer, as I suggested in Item 9) before you attempt this.

When you edit the SACL you're specifying the conditions for an audit to be generated. Take Figure 11.1 as an example. In this case, an audit will be generated if someone attempts to open the file called **sensitive.txt** for read permission and fails. If the request to open the file for read access succeeds, no audit will be generated. It's possible for someone to try to open the file for write-only permission; even if the request fails, no audit will be generated because you didn't say you wanted to audit the write permission. For this reason, think carefully about the permissions you want to audit. It's safest to start by auditing all of them—that way you won't miss anything—but your signal-to-noise ratio in the audit log may suffer if you cast too wide a net.

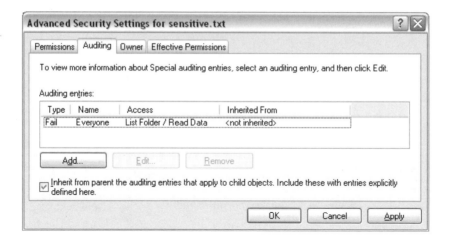

Figure 11.1 Turning on auditing for a file

You can enable auditing of registry keys the exact same way: Just use **regedit** to bring up the security dialog via the Edit menu. It will look similar to the file dialog although the types of permissions listed will be registry related as opposed to file related.

For both registry keys and files (and directory service objects, while we're at it), you can audit entire trees using ACL inheritance, which I cover in more detail in Item 45. So, if you've got a directory full of sensitive files, you can enable auditing on the entire directory by bringing up this same property sheet on the directory itself. Just make sure that, when you add any audit entries, the "Apply onto" selection is set to enable inheritance (see Figure 11.2). It should be set this way by default: "This folder, subfolders and files," which is usually your safest bet.

If you want to audit anything at all, you'll need to throw a switch in security policy because auditing is completely disabled by default. See Item 10 for more detail, but the type of auditing you'll want to turn on in this case is "Object Access." This covers not only the file system but the registry and any secured object in Windows that has auditing support, even transient kernel objects like processes and mutexes, although these don't have a user interface for setting up auditing (you must programmatically set the SACL for these more obscure auditing scenarios).

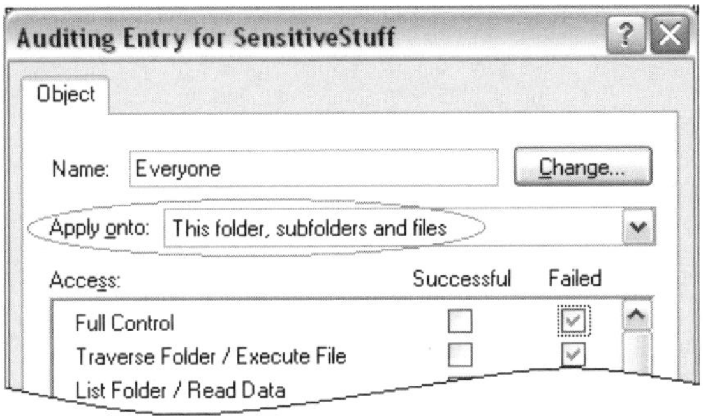

Figure 11.2 Auditing an entire folder

To audit access to a registry key, just select a key in the registry to bring up the permissions editor (Edit:Permissions) and follow the same procedure. Just as with a folder in the file system, you can audit an entire tree of registry keys by using inheritance.

Auditing Active Directory objects works similarly. From the Active Directory console, bring up the property sheet for the object and flip to the Security tab. You'll find that process is very similar, although in Active Directory it is possible to audit access to individual properties of an object as well as the object as a whole.

PART II
Security Context

12

What Is a Security Principal?

A SECURITY PRINCIPAL IS AN entity that can be positively identified and verified via a technique known as authentication (Item 6). Usually when people think of security principals, they think of users, but there's a bit more to it than that. I like to think of three different types of principals:

- User principals
- Machine principals
- Service principals

Here's an example. Imagine that we have two machines in a domain called DOM, named MAC1 and MAC2. DOM\Alice is logged into MAC1 interactively. Now a bunch of network requests that originate from MAC1 are serviced by MAC2. If those requests are authenticated, which security principal will MAC2 see for any given request?

The answer is that I've not given you enough information! Just because Alice is logged on interactively doesn't mean that all requests from that machine will go out using her credentials. Security principals in Windows are assigned on a process-by-process basis, via a little kernel object called a token (Item 16). So it depends on which process made the request. Take a look at Figure 12.1 for an example. Here we have three different

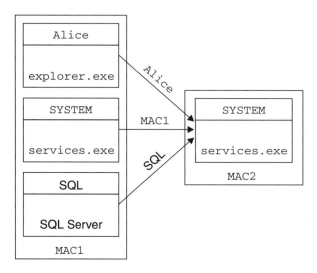

Figure 12.1 Security principals and processes

processes running on the machine where `Alice` is working. The first is
explorer.exe, which is `Alice`'s shell program. When `Alice` uses
Explorer to connect to a share on `MAC2`, her request is authenticated
between **explorer.exe** on `MAC1` and **services.exe** (the process that
implements file and printer sharing) on `MAC2`. Because **explorer.exe** is
running as `Alice`, her credentials are used for that request.

We also see the operating system itself (some service hosted in
services.exe on `MAC1`) making a request to `MAC2`. It's not `Alice`, though!
It's the operating system of `MAC1` (that's what `SYSTEM` represents), so this
request will use `MAC1`'s domain credentials and will be seen as `DOM\MAC1` by
the server. Finally, `MAC1` is running SQL Server under a custom service
account called `DOM\SQL`, so any requests from that process will be seen as
`DOM\SQL`. Bear in mind that at any given time there will very likely be several different principals operating on any given machine. Oh, and if you've
heard that `SYSTEM` has no network credentials, please check out Item 28 for
clarification.

Each security principal is issued an account via an authority. An authority is an entity that maintains an account database, which includes such
basic information as the name of the principal, the groups (Item 20) in

which the principal is a member and, arguably the most important thing of all, a master key for the principal calculated by hashing the password for the account. To learn more about how the master key is used during authentication, check out Item 59.

There are two types of authorities in Windows: local and domain. In the example just described, we were using a domain. A domain authority stores the accounts database in Active Directory, and each domain controller for a given domain has a replicated copy of that database. A local authority (called the Local Security Authority, or LSA for short) exists on each machine and stores its account database in the registry (this is sometimes referred to as the SAM, or Security Accounts Manager).

Local accounts aren't used much in domain environments, but on a standalone machine that isn't part of a domain they're the only security authority you've got and they work quite well protecting the local machine. Local accounts can even be used (some would say "abused") to authenticate network requests between machines by adding the same local account (user name and password) to several machines. Windows will use an older authentication protocol called NTLM (you may have heard it called challenge-response) to authenticate these principals over the network (Brown 2000b), but it's a bad idea to rely too much on this because the master key for the account must be kept on every machine that needs to authenticate that principal. This makes administration tough (just try to change your password!) and exposes the key to offline brute force and dictionary attacks from anyone who administers any of the workstations on which the account exists. Domain accounts, on the other hand, centralize these keys in Active Directory, which is hosted only by domain controllers and can therefore be more easily secured from physical attack. You can lock up your domain controller in a closet, but that won't fly for the secretary's workstation.

To see a list of security principals in a domain, you'll need to use an MMC snap-in called "Active Directory Users and Computers." If you drill down into a domain and into a folder called Users, you'll see a list of user principals and domain groups. If you sidestep over into a folder called Computers, you'll see a list of machine principals. These are first-class security principals, each with its own master key. Machines can be made members of groups just like users can. They log in to the domain just as users do by proving knowledge of their master key, which each machine that is a member of a domain stores in its registry.[1]

I cover service principals in Item 60.

---

1. If you don't believe me, run the registry editor as SYSTEM. (The easiest way to do this is from an administrative command prompt. Type **at 9:23am /interactive regedit.exe**, substituting whatever time is appropriate: Make it one minute in the future.) Once regedit fires up, carefully look at the subkeys under HKLM/Security/Policy/Secrets. You're looking at the machine's password stash, more formally known as the LSA private data store, and if the machine is a domain member, you should see a subkey called $MACHINE.ACC, where the machine's master key lives. You won't be able to view the key with **regedit.exe**, but at least now you have some evidence that it exists. Now close that copy of **regedit.exe** before you break something!

■ 13 ■
What Is a SID?

S ECURITY IDENTIFIERS, OR SIDs for short, are used to uniquely identify user and group accounts in Windows. They can be found in tokens (Item 16), in ACLs (Item 43), and in security account databases (Item 12). Most Windows programmers are already familiar with another unique ID, the GUID (or UUID), which is a 128-bit randomly generated identifier used extensively in COM programming. A GUID generated on any machine at any time will be unique from any other GUID because of the large random space from which GUIDs are generated.

The SID is conceptually similar to the GUID in that it also provides uniqueness in space and time. Uniqueness in space is achieved by a 96-bit machine identifier generated at the time the Windows OS is installed. Its value is tucked away in the registry and is combined with a persistent monotonically increasing counter to create new SIDs that are unique in space and time. However, this is where the similarity ends. SIDs are variable-length data structures, which makes using them more difficult for programmers (at least prior to version 2.0 of the .NET Framework, when there was no managed representation of a SID). On the flip side, SIDs allow more flexibility because they have structure that a programmer can depend on. A SID is composed of several parts, which combine to form a hierarchical naming structure that is quite useful in many cases at runtime.

This hierarchical structure becomes most apparent in the text form in which SIDs are often represented: S-R-I-SA-SA-SA, where S is the letter *S*,

R is the revision number of the SID binary format (currently 1), I is a 48-bit identifier authority value, and SA is a 32-bit subauthority. For example, S-1-5-32-547 represents the Power Users group. The numbers 32 and 547 represent subauthority values that help make the SID unique.

The identifier authority represents the outermost scope of the name, and it identifies a unique namespace via a 48-bit identifier. One can only imagine the original intended use for this field; perhaps it was designed to allow 48-bit IEEE 802 addresses to be used to give any third-party vendor its own namespace. The vast majority of SIDs, however, are issued within the NT Authority namespace, whose value is 0x000005. Other interesting namespaces include World Authority (0x000001), which is used for the well-known SID S-1-1-0, more commonly known as Everyone. In certain specialized applications, you might find other values for the identifier authority, so don't make assumptions in your code about its value.

The identifier authority is then combined with either a well-known subauthority (such as the BUILTIN domain, which is present on all Windows machines) or a set of subauthorities determined from the unique machine ID assigned when Windows was installed on the machine. As examples, here are two well-known principals that are automatically created whenever you install Windows on a machine:

- Administrator: S-1-5-21-XXXX-XXXX-XXXX-500
- Guest: S-1-5-21-XXXX-XXXX-XXXX-501

In place of XXXX, you'll find the 32-bit subauthority values that comprise the 96-bit unique ID of the machine that generated the SID. This virtually guarantees that two machines won't generate the same SIDs.[1] After the subauthority values that define a unique namespace, you'll find a number that identifies the principal within the namespace. In the above examples, the number 500 identifies Administrator and the number 501 identifies Guest.

---

1. Although if you've ever ghosted a machine in a domain, you know that it's important to run **sysprep.exe** to allow the machine identifier to be recalculated when the new image is first booted.

There is clearly a pattern that you can rely on here. For instance, the number 21 is used to prefix the three machine-specific subauthority values, and the number 501 always represents the special principal named `Guest`, no matter what machine you happen to be working on. Each of these well-known values is also called a RID (for Relative ID), and **winnt.h** includes definitions for the ones used by the core Windows OS. I've included a list of well-known SIDs in Item 14 that you might find useful, and version 2.0 of the .NET Framework has an enumeration called `WellKnownSidType` that makes it easy to specify these SIDs in an ACL. This is important when writing internationalized code: `Guest` is not spelled the same way in German as it is in Japanese, so instead of referring to well-known principals by name, it's much safer (and more efficient) to form the SIDs programmatically (Item 14).

By the way, in case you've never looked, bring up your registry editor and drill down into `HKEY_USERS`. You'll see a bunch of registry hives here, named with user SIDs. For more info on what you're looking at, see Item 19. This is yet another example of where you can find SIDs.

14

How to Program with SIDs

S UPPORT FOR PROGRAMMING with SIDs is new in version 2.0 of the .NET Framework. There are two new classes that represent a user or group account. The first, `SecurityIdentifier`, represents a machine-readable SID like I described in Item 13. The second, `NTAccount`, represents a human-readable user or group account name. The base class for both of these is `IdentityReference`, and you can easily translate back and forth between SID and name. Under the covers, the `Translate` method calls a low-level function in the local security authority (LSA), which translates names to SIDs or vice versa. If a domain controller needs to be contacted, this low-level function can batch up requests and translate many names in one round trip. It's great to see this support being built into the framework.

```
using System;
using System.Security.Principal;

class NamesAndSIDs {
  const string userAccount = @"acme\bob";
  static void Main(string[] args) {
    NTAccount name = new NTAccount(userAccount);
    Console.WriteLine(name);
    SecurityIdentifier sid = (SecurityIdentifier)
      name.Translate(typeof(SecurityIdentifier));
    Console.WriteLine(sid);
    name = (NTAccount)sid.Translate(typeof(NTAccount));
    Console.WriteLine(name);
  }
}
```

When run, this program displays the following output:

```
v-xp-vs2005\NormalUser
S-1-5-21-1409082233-1060284298-1343024091-1006
V-XP-VS2005\NormalUser
```

When you use some of the new security classes, you'll find that many of them give you the choice of whether you want human-readable names for accounts or SIDs. For example, if you wanted to enumerate a DACL (Item 43) and print out which users and groups were granted permissions, you might write code that looks like this:

```
using System;
using System.IO;
using System.Security.Principal;
using System.Security.AccessControl;

class EnumerateDACL {
  const string path = @"c:\work\test.txt";
  static void Main(string[] args) {
    FileSecurity sd = File.GetAccessControl(path);
    foreach (FileSystemAccessRule ace in
      sd.GetAccessRules(true, true, typeof(NTAccount))) {

      // since we asked for a type of NTAccount,
      // all identity references will be of that type
      // so this cast should always succeed here
      NTAccount name = (NTAccount)ace.IdentityReference;
      Console.WriteLine(name);
    }
  }
}
```

You'll see more code like this when I show how to program ACLs in Item 47, but for now, note the call to GetAccessRules. Because this is going to return a list that will contain IdentityReferences, you get to choose what form those references will take: SID or human-readable name. If you ask for names, realize that this might incur round-trips to domain controllers, but at least the requests are batched as I mentioned earlier, which will help reduce the overhead.

Another thing I really like about these new classes is the ease of representing well-known user accounts and groups. The WellKnownSidType enumeration (Figure 14.1) is very complete and makes it trivial to compute well-known SIDs without having to rely on human-readable names, which

```
AccountDomainGuestsSid
AccountDomainUsersSid
AccountEnterpriseAdminsSid
AccountGuestSid
AccountKrbtgtSid
AccountPolicyAdminsSid
AccountRasAndIasServersSid
AccountSchemaAdminsSid
AnonymousSid
AuthenticatedUserSid
BatchSid
BuiltinAccountOperatorsSid
BuiltinAdministratorsSid
BuiltinAuthorizationAccessSid
BuiltinBackupOperatorsSid
BuiltinDomainSid
BuiltinGuestsSid
BuiltinIncomingForestTrustBuildersSid
BuiltinNetworkConfigurationOperatorsSid
BuiltinPerfLoggingUsersSid
BuiltinPerfMonitoringUsersSid
BuiltinPowerUsersSid
BuiltinPreWindows2000CompatibleAccessSid
BuiltinPrintOperatorsSid
BuiltinRemoteDesktopUsersSid
BuiltinReplicatorSid
BuiltinSystemOperatorsSid
BuiltinUsersSid
CreatorGroupServerSid
CreatorGroupSid
CreatorOwnerServerSid
CreatorOwnerSid
DialupSid
DigestAuthenticationSid
EnterpriseControllersSid
InteractiveSid
LocalServiceSid
LocalSid
LocalSystemSid
LogonIdsSid
MaxDefined
NetworkServiceSid
NetworkSid
NTAuthoritySid
NtlmAuthenticationSid
```

continues

Figure 14.1 The WellKnownSidType enumeration as of version 2.0 beta 1

```
NullSid
OtherOrganizationSid
ProxySid
RemoteLogonIdSid
RestrictedCodeSid
SChannelAuthenticationSid
SelfSid
ServiceSid
TerminalServerSid
ThisOrganizationSid
WinBuiltinTerminalServerLicenseServersSid
WorldSid
```

Figure 14.1 The WellKnownSidType enumeration as of version 2.0 beta 1 (*continued***)**

change depending on the regional settings of the computer on which your program is running.

```
using System;
using System.Security.Principal;

class WellKnownSids {
  static void Main() {
    SecurityIdentifier sid =
      new SecurityIdentifier(WellKnownSidType.BuiltinAdministra-
torsSid, null);
    Console.WriteLine(sid.Translate(typeof(NTAccount)));
  }
}
```

The output from this program looks like this on my U.S. English installation of Windows XP:

```
BUILTIN\Administrators
```

Having a managed representation of a SID will make it much easier to wrap more and more of the security functionality on the Windows platform, and I'm really looking forward to that. Being able to write security tools in C# is so much more palatable than having to drop down into C or C++. The day I write my last line of C code will be a very happy day for me!

■ 15 ■
What Is Security Context?

To PUT IT SIMPLY, a security context is a bit of cached data about a user, including her SID, group SIDs, privileges, and some other stuff that I'll cover in Item 16. One of the fundamental tenets of Windows security is that each process runs on behalf of a user, so each process has a security context associated with it, like a global variable controlled by the kernel. This allows the system to audit the actions taken by a process and make access control decisions when the process acquires resources.

To be more precise, a process is just a container, and it's really threads that do things, such as open resources. But unless you're impersonating (which I'll discuss in Item 31), all the threads in your process are by default associated with the process's security context.

In Windows, a security context is represented by a data structure called a token. Each process object in the kernel holds a handle to an associated token object in the kernel. In this marriage, there's no option for divorce; once a process starts, it's associated with the same token for its entire lifetime.

The ability of a token to cache a snapshot of a user's security profile is critical for performance. But a cache is like a loaf of bread; the longer you keep it, the more stale it gets. A process that runs for a week has a security context that's at least a week old. If the user was recently added to or removed from a group, even a local one, the process won't know about it. And simply recycling the process isn't going to help because the operating system initializes each new process with a copy of the creator's token. To get a fresh security context, you must establish a fresh logon; in technical terms, you must reauthenticate. The latency caused by a stale security context can bite you not only in a long running desktop application but also in a server application that caches security contexts for each authenticated client that it services. Keep this in mind when designing your systems. You might occasionally need to throw away a client's moldy old token and ask her to reauthenticate, for example.

When building a desktop application, you should think about the different security contexts in which the app may run. Today it might be running with high privilege and be able to (heaven forbid) write data files in sensitive directories like `Program Files`; tomorrow, however, it may be running with low privilege. You should be sure to test your app under different security contexts, and make sure it doesn't fall to pieces when run by a normal user, as discussed in Item 9.

Server applications are very different. A server application normally runs as a daemon (see Item 27), and it has a well-defined security context that it needs to function. For example, a service is configured to run under a particular identity and, no matter who starts that service, the Service Control Manager (SCM) ensures that it's started in the security context with which it was configured to run. The designer and developer of a server application should know exactly what privileges (Item 21), roles (Item 38), and permissions (Item 39) the server app requires. This should be part of the documentation for the application, as it will allow an administrator to choose an appropriate identity for the server process (as opposed to running it as `SYSTEM`) and configure security policy to allow access to required resources. Note that these requirements may be different depending on which features of the server application are in use. Keep track of security requirements as you go, and document them carefully. Don't wait until the project is over to try and figure this stuff out.

Another difference with a server application is that it's normally juggling several security contexts at once. Each authenticated client presents its security context to the server (often in the form of a token), which must make security decisions based on the client's context. This is one of the most confusing things about security for newbies. Just remember that when a new client connects to your server, it doesn't change the server's security context. The server continues to run under its own preconfigured identity. It may choose to temporarily impersonate a client (Item 31) before accessing a resource, but that's its prerogative. Further food for thought on client authorization schemes can be found in Item 38 and Item 39. To learn more about how servers authenticate their clients in Windows, see Item 59.

Security Context in the .NET Framework

The .NET Framework doesn't limit itself to representing users only via tokens. Instead, two interfaces abstract security context: IIdentity and IPrincipal, which allows for a broad range of authentication options beyond those that Windows happens to implement natively.

```
namespace System.Security.Principal {
  public interface IIdentity {
    bool IsAuthenticated      { get; }
    string AuthenticationType { get; }
    string Name               { get; }
  }
  public interface IPrincipal {
    bool IsInRole(string role);
    IIdentity Identity { get; }
  }
}
```

For instance, you can roll your own user database and use Forms Authentication in ASP.NET to authenticate users. In that case, you'll end up representing your clients not with tokens but with a simpler security context (in the simplest case, just a user name) that you define. The roles simply become strings that you assign based on your own security database. With the notion of identity and roles so abstract, any code you write that makes demands of your clients, such as requiring authentication or membership in some role, can do so without being tied to any one form of authentication.

You might wonder why two interfaces are used to represent this one idea of security context. I like to think of it this way: IIdentity deals with authentication (Who are you?), whereas IPrincipal deals with authorization (What are you allowed to do?). This decoupling can be very convenient. For example, you can allow Windows to do the heavy lifting by authenticating your clients using Kerberos (Item 59), and then take the resulting `IIdentity` and drop it behind your own custom implementation of `IPrincipal`. In this way you can add a set of application-specific roles that are populated based on the user's group memberships (as shown in Figure 15.1). To make authorization decisions in your code, it's better to check for an application-defined role than for a Windows group. This is because each group name includes the name of the domain or machine where the group was defined (say, `SALESDOMAIN\Customers`), and if you've hardcoded names like these into your code, you're tightly coupled to that environment (what if you wanted to deploy your program in two different domains?). See Item 49 for a role-based approach to authorization that can help solve problems like these.

As you'll see in Item 16, when a token is providing the security context, `WindowsIdentity` and `WindowsPrincipal` provide concrete implementations for these interfaces.

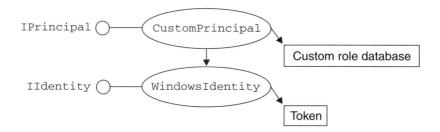

Figure 15.1 Customizing roles by implementing `IPrincipal` yourself

■ 16 ■
What Is a Token?

A TOKEN IS A KERNEL object that caches part of a user's security profile, including the user SID, group SIDs, and privileges (Item 21). Item 15 discussed the basics of how this cache is normally used, but there's a bit more to it: A token also holds a reference to a logon session (Item 17) and a set of default security settings that the kernel uses.

Tokens are propagated automatically as new processes are created. A new process naturally inherits a copy of the parent's process token. Even if the thread that creates the process is impersonating, the new process gets a copy of the parent's process token, not the thread token, which usually surprises most people who are new to impersonation (Item 31). If you want to start a new process running with some other token, see Item 30.

The .NET Framework provides two classes that allow you to work with tokens: `WindowsIdentity` and `WindowsPrincipal` (Item 24). If you ever want to look at the token for your process, call the static method `Windows-Identity.GetCurrent`. This method returns a `WindowsIdentity` instance that wraps the token that represents the thread's security context. Normally this will give you the process token, unless your thread happens to be impersonating (an exceptional case that you can read about in Item 31). This function is the way to discover your program's security context as far as the operating system is concerned: It answers the question, Who am I? which is very helpful when trying to diagnose security problems such as being denied access to ACL-protected resources like files. I'd recommend including this user name with any errors that you log.

```
// here's a simple example of a log that includes
// information about the current security context
void logException(Exception x) {
  IIdentity id = WindowsIdentity.GetCurrent();
  log.WriteLine("User name: {0}", id.Name);
  log.WriteLine("Exception: {0}", x.Message);
  log.WriteLine(x.StackTrace);
}
```

The vast majority of information in a token is immutable, and for good reason! It would be crazy to allow an application to add new groups to its token, for example. But you can change a couple things: You can enable or disable any privileges that happen to be in your token (Item 22), and you can control the default owner and DACL (Item 43). This latter feature allows your process (or another process running in the same security context, say a parent process) to control the owner and DACL that will be applied to all new kernel objects, such as named pipes, mutexes, and sections, whenever a specific DACL is not provided explicitly to the creation function. For example, these defaults will be used if you call the Win32 function `CreateMutex` and pass `NULL` for the `LPSECURITY_ATTRIBUTES` argument, which is the normal and correct procedure. If you ever need to change these default settings, call the Win32 function `SetTokenInformation`, but this will be very rare. You see, by default the operating system will set up your token so that the default DACL grants you and `SYSTEM` full permissions, which is very secure indeed. Usually the only time you want to deviate from this is if you're going to share an object between two processes running under different accounts, such as between a service process that runs as a daemon (Item 27) and a service controller process launched by the interactive user. In that case, see Item 47 to learn how to programmatically build your own DACL.

Tokens never expire. This makes programmers happy (it would be weird if all of a sudden your process terminated because its token timed out), but it can be dangerous in some cases. For example, nothing stops a server from holding onto client tokens indefinitely once those clients have authenticated. A server running with low privilege is good but keeping a bunch of client tokens in a cache negates all that goodness because an attacker that manages to take over the server process can use the cached client tokens to access resources via impersonation. Fortunately, Kerberos tickets do expire (Item 59), so if any of those tokens had network credentials (Item 62), they won't be valid forever.

Occasionally you might want to pass tokens between processes. Say you have factored a server into two processes, a low-privileged process listening on an untrusted network (the Internet) and a high-privileged helper process that you communicate with using some form of secure interprocess communication such as COM. If you've authenticated a client in your listener process and want your helper process to see the client's token, you can pass it from one process to another by calling the Win32 API `DuplicateHandle`. You can obtain the token handle from a `Windows-Identity` via its `Token` property (if you have an `IIdentity` reference, you'll need to cast it to `WindowsIdentity` first).

At some point you might think about passing a token (or its wrapper, a `WindowsIdentity`) from one machine to another. This is a big no-no in Windows security. A token only has meaning on the machine where it was created, because the groups and privileges in it were discovered based on the combination of a centralized domain security policy and the local security policy of the machine. Local groups and privilege definitions differ across machines, and domain security policy changes if you cross domain boundaries. Even if the operating system were to provide a way to serialize a token for transmission to another machine (it does not), using this "imported" token would lead to incorrect access control decisions! Thus, if a client (`Alice`, say) has authenticated with a process on one machine, and you want another machine to see `Alice`'s security context, `Alice` must authenticate with that other machine. Either she can do this directly or you can delegate her credentials (Item 62). In other words, the only way to get a token for `Alice` on a given machine is to use her credentials to authenticate with a process running *on that machine*.

While I'm on the subject of the machine sensitive nature of tokens, I should mention that you must never use a token on one machine to perform an access check on an object located on another. For example, resist the temptation to load the security descriptor (Item 42) for a remote object onto another machine and perform an access check against it using a local token. A token for `Alice` on machine `FOO` doesn't have exactly the same groups and privileges it would have if it were produced on machine `BAR`, so using a token from `FOO` in access checks against `BAR`'s resources is a very bad idea and is a gaping security hole. The correct procedure is to authenticate with a process on the machine hosting the resource and have that process perform the access check. In other words, keep the access checks on the same machine as the resources being protected.

17

What Is a Logon Session?

LOGON SESSIONS HAVE NEVER gotten much coverage in Windows documentation, but understanding them can help you get a better feel for how Windows works under the hood. A logon session is a data structure maintained by the kernel that represents an instance of a principal on a machine. It's where network credentials like your cached Kerberos tickets and the associated keys are stored (Item 59). Each token points to a single logon session, so ultimately each process is associated with a single logon session via its token, as shown in Figure 17.1.

A new logon session is produced each time a successful authentication occurs on the machine, so when you log on interactively the system creates a new logon session. When you connect to a remote machine and authenticate, say via a file share or a Web server that requires Windows authentication, a new logon session is created for you on the target machine and the server receives a token that refers to it. Logon sessions are destroyed when all tokens that refer to them are closed (their lifetime is controlled by a reference count of outstanding tokens). When you log off interactively via **explorer.exe** or call the Win32 function ExitWindowsEx, the operating system enumerates all processes tied to your logon session and asks them to close. Thus, logon sessions often help determine the lifetime of processes.

There are three built-in logon sessions that the operating system starts implicitly at boot time, and they have hardcoded logon session identifiers

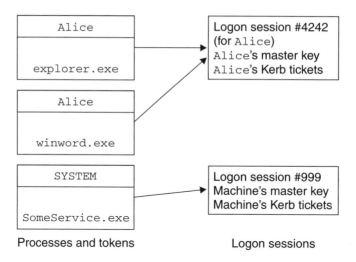

Figure 17.1 Processes are linked to logon sessions via tokens.

(there are constants defined for these numbers in the Win32 header file **winnt.h**).

- 999 (0x3e7) = SYSTEM
- 997 (0x3e5) = Local Service
- 996 (0x3e4) = Network Service

Given the hardcoded nature of these logon session identifiers, it's pretty clear that there's only one of each on a given machine at a time. If you've ever wondered what the password is for any of them, it should be clear that this is a moot question! It doesn't take a password to log these guys on—the operating system ensures that they're always present. This doesn't mean that just anyone can get a token for Network Service and start programs running under these credentials. The operating system must do this on your behalf. An administrator can configure a service, IIS worker process, COM+ server, and so forth to run as Network Service, and the operating system will construct a token for logon session 996 and launch the server process with it. These logon sessions are always present and are typically used to host daemons (Item 27). You'll never need to worry about Network

`Service` logging off, for example, unless the machine is being rebooted. See Item 28 for more on these built-in logons.

There's also a special type of logon session for anonymous users called the null session, and I've dedicated Item 35 to explaining how it's used.

Bear in mind that any code that's already running in a particular logon session can create new processes that will naturally go into that logon session. So another way to get a process running as `Network Service` (or in any of these built-in logon sessions, for that matter), is to have some code that's already there start the process for you. In a footnote in Item 12, I described an old parlor trick for starting a command prompt in the SYS-TEM logon session by asking the task scheduler (which runs in the SYSTEM logon session) to launch it for you.

This should give you pause: If you are building a server application that needs to start another process, ensure that you are under complete control of the path to the executable file that you want to launch (specify the full path). In addition, ensure that the arguments you pass are treated as arguments and not interpreted by a command shell. For example, consider the following ill-gotten attempt to run a search using an external program:

```
string cmdToExecute = "search.exe " + userInput;
```

Normal users would pass benign strings like "`butterfly`," while a malicious user could pass a string that would cause you to launch another program, "`| net user hacker P@ssw0rd /add`." Note the pipe symbol at the beginning of the malicious input. Of course **net.exe** will run in the same logon session you are running in, and if it happens to be a privileged session, the attack will succeed and you'll have a new user account on your server!

The most natural way to avoid this problem is to launch new processes using the `System.Diagnostics.Process` class, where you're forced to separate the name of the file you want to launch from the arguments that should be passed to the process:

```
Process p = new Process();
p.StartInfo.FileName = @"c:\legacy\search.exe";
p.StartInfo.Arguments = filteredUserInput;
p.Start();
```

Note that even when taking this precaution, you should still relentlessly filter any user input that you pass to the external program, because that program may itself be vulnerable to malicious input (it may never have been designed to accept input from remote, untrusted users, for example).

■ 18 ■
What Is a Window Station?

WINDOW STATIONS ARE A little-known but very important security feature designed to sandbox the windowing environment in the operating system. In order to avoid putting ACLs on each window and incurring the wrath of the performance gods by doing access checks on each window message, we simply let windows message each other without any security checks. However, we do so in a private environment known as a window station.

A window station is a secure kernel object that contains a clipboard, a private atom table, a set of desktops, and a set of windows. Each process is tied to one window station, and this association normally parallels logon session assignments. That is, for each logon session there's a corresponding window station, as shown in Figure 18.1. In fact, window station names are derived from logon session identifiers (Item 17). The window station for `Network Service`, for example, is Service-0x0-0x3e4$. Occasionally a daemon (IIS, for example) will take window station management into its own hands, but this is the exception to the rule. There is also an "interactive" window station, which always exists even when no interactive user is present. This special interactive window station, hardcoded with the name WinSta0, deserves a bit more attention.

WinSta0 is the only window station actually bound to hardware. That is, you can see windows there, and they can receive input from the mouse and keyboard. WinSta0 is also tightly secured, with an ACL that sandboxes the

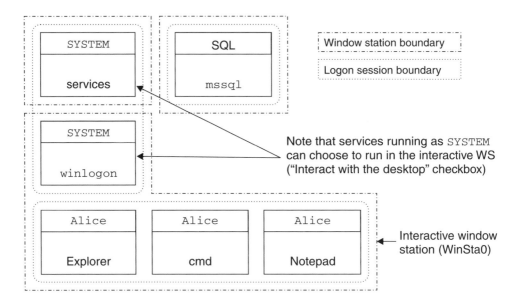

Figure 18.1 Window stations normally parallel logon session boundaries.

interactive logon session, although from Figure 18.1, you can see that some highly trusted services running in the SYSTEM logon session may also run there, such as **winlogon.exe**. The ACL on WinSta0 controls what you can do with the GUI at a very detailed level, but, practically speaking, it's an all-or-nothing grant and really only necessary to constrain which processes are allowed to attach to the window station. (It's possible to change your process's window station affiliation by calling the Win32 function SetProcessWindowStation, or to launch new programs that attach to particular window stations by tweaking the STARTUPINFO parameter to the Win32 function CreateProcess.) In this way the ACL on the window station prevents programs in other logon sessions from intruding into your windowing world.

The practical point of having window stations is to avoid luring attacks from daemons[1] against an interactive user. If a process running under a low-privilege account can send window messages to a highly privileged program, it can take control of that program. For one example of how this

---

1.   Or from interactive users in other Terminal Services sessions

can be done, see Item 7. Because window station boundaries normally parallel logon session boundaries, this helps prevent this sort of attack.

So, we have the interactive logon assigned to a window station that's bound to hardware, but what about daemons (Item 27)? Each daemon logon has its own window station, but these are noninteractive (remember, there's only one interactive window station, WinSta0[2]). A noninteractive window station is not bound to hardware, so if you're a daemon you can create legitimate windows that work just fine—but nobody will ever see them. This is important for some plumbing such as COM apartments. But imagine if, as a daemon, you put up a modal dialog and sat there waiting for someone to press the OK button? You'd be waiting an awful long time! The only way to dismiss a modal dialog in a noninteractive window station is to do it programmatically. For example you could simulate a button press by sending the dialog a WM_CLOSE or a WM_COMMAND message. Knowing this, nobody in their right mind would purposely put up a modal dialog from a daemon, but what about debug builds of C++ apps using the ASSERT macro? Or what if you buy a third party library for use in a daemon you're writing and find out later that it pops up modal dialogs from time to time? This isn't fun to deal with, so, as a library developer, carefully consider where your component may be used before putting up dialog boxes. That said, if you think you have a legitimate reason for putting up a user interface from a daemon, read Item 29.

If you come from a Win9X background, you may be surprised that a window handle isn't valid for use from any old process on the machine. If you're used to using window messages for interprocess communication, then it's time to learn another technique, such as .NET Remoting or COM.

When one process creates another, the new process is placed in the same window station as the old one, unless you write special code to do otherwise (which is extremely rare). So, just like tokens and logon sessions, a new process naturally inherits its parent's windowing environment. Note that starting a service is not the same as simply creating a new process. When a service is started, it is assigned to an appropriate logon session and window station by the operating system, as I discuss in Item 27.

---

2. Note that Terminal Services adds a twist here: In this case there is one interactive window station (named WinSta0!) in each Terminal Services session.

■ 19 ■
What Is a User Profile?

HAVE YOU EVER NOTICED that the first time a particular user logs on to a machine it takes a little while longer for the shell (typically **explorer.exe**) to start up? You can hear the disk drive whirring and clunking—obviously something is going on. Subsequent logons are much faster. What's happening is this: A profile is being created on the machine for the user.

A user profile consists of a home directory for the user, along with some standard subdirectories and files that allow the operating system to store per-user settings. If you're sitting in front of a computer, bring up Explorer and surf to the `Documents and Settings` folder, which is on the drive where the operating system was installed. You should see subdirectories for all user principals that have ever logged on interactively to the machine. If you view hidden folders (which I recommend for this experiment), you'll see one called `Default User`. It's this folder that's being copied when you first log on with a new user account. This is the seed for all new user profiles.

If you drill down into your own user profile, you'll see a couple of hidden files, called **NTUSER.DAT** and **NTUSER.DAT.LOG**, which make up the registry hive for your user profile. Bring up the registry editor and look under HKEY_USERS to see what I mean. The operating system dynamically loads the subkeys under HKEY_USERS as users log on and off interactively. To see this happen, bring up a command prompt and run the following command using a local account on your machine (I'll assume you're using a user account named `Alice`):

```
runas /u:Alice cmd
```

You'll be prompted for a password, and once you enter it you'll see a new command prompt that's running under an interactive logon for `Alice`. Refresh the registry editor, and you'll see a couple of new keys under `HKEY_USERS`. These keys point into the **NTUSER.DAT** file in `Alice`'s home directory. Close this new command prompt and refresh the registry editor again. You should see that those keys have now disappeared. The profile has been unloaded.

`HKEY_CURRENT_USER` is a very interesting key. The operating system dynamically maps it onto one of the subkeys under `HKEY_USERS` based on the security context you're running in when you open it. Thus, if I were to run the following code from `Alice`'s command prompt, I would be reading from her registry hive.

```
using System;
using Microsoft.Win32;

class ReadFromUserProfile {
  static void Main() {
    // this opens HKEY_CURRENT_USER
    RegistryKey hkcu = Registry.CurrentUser;

    foreach (string keyName in hkcu.GetSubKeyNames()) {
      Console.WriteLine(keyName);
    }
  }
}
```

On the other hand, if I were to run this same code from a command prompt as myself, I would be reading from the registry hive in my own user profile and looking at an entirely different set of data. Note that the mapping of `HKEY_CURRENT_USER` is affected by impersonation (Item 31), so if a process running as `Bob` uses a thread impersonating `Alice` to open `HKEY_CURRENT_USER`, `Alice`'s hive will be opened, not `Bob`'s. Of course, this assumes that `Alice`'s profile has been loaded, as you'll see later in this item.

Now, you might wonder why I'm spending so much time on how the registry works, given that it's being deemphasized in .NET. What you've got to keep in mind is that the operating system still relies quite a bit on the registry for tracking per-user settings. So, when you do something as simple as set the background color of a form to `SystemColors.Window`, under the covers you're actually doing a registry lookup under `HKEY_CURRENT_USER` to find out what window color the current user prefers. If you've ever worked with certificate stores,[1] you should be aware that they are stored on a per-user basis (unless you specifically request a machine-wide store). This sort of thing is important to know when you're writing server code because you often need to ensure that you actually have a user profile loaded to be able to access your certificates. But more on loading user profiles later!

When writing desktop applications, it's critical that you store your settings under the user profile as opposed to your program's installation directory. If you try to store data anywhere under the `Program Files` directory tree, your program will break when run by a nonprivileged user (Item 8). The DACL (Item 43) on `Program Files` allows only privileged users to write to that directory tree. Go see for yourself! But in `Alice`'s user profile, she's the owner of all the files and subdirectories. So no matter which user is running your program, you'll always be able to store settings under that user's profile. As I describe in Item 9, Isolated Storage works out of the user profile, so it's a great way to store application settings and it even works in most partial-trust scenarios!

Here's another experiment: Bring up a command prompt running under your own account (just start one from Explorer) and run the following command from there:

```
set u
```

This will display all environment variables that start with the letter "*u*." Do the same thing from `Alice`'s command prompt and notice how the environment variables are different there. The environment variable `USER-PROFILE` is really important, as it points applications to the appropriate

---

1. As of this writing, to access certificate stores you must use the CryptoAPI (CAPI), but version 2.0 of the .NET Framework is slated to include this support directly.

place to store per-user settings. You'll never need to look at this variable directly because the programs you write will use .NET Framework classes to figure out where various user profile directories are located. To see how this works, compile the following C# console application and run it in your two command prompts to see how the output changes depending on the user running it.

```csharp
using System;

class WhereIsMyUserProfile {
  static void Main() {
    string myDocuments = Environment.GetFolderPath(
      Environment.SpecialFolder.Personal);
    string desktop = Environment.GetFolderPath(
      Environment.SpecialFolder.DesktopDirectory);
    string localAppData = Environment.GetFolderPath(
      Environment.SpecialFolder.LocalApplicationData);

    Console.WriteLine("My Documents: {0}", myDocuments);
    Console.WriteLine("Desktop: {0}", desktop);
    Console.WriteLine("Local App Data: {0}", localAppData);
  }
}
```

I show an even more compelling example for Windows Forms programmers in Item 9.

There's a special user profile called All Users, where you should store state shared by all users of your application (note that Isolated Storage never uses this shared profile, so you can't use Isolated Storage to store shared state for an application). Be very careful with shared state. Remember that all users of the machine are granted read-write permissions to the All Users folder. This means that a malicious user can write malformed data to one of your shared files, causing your application to malfunction the next time some other, innocent user runs it. Frankly, though, you should consider all data coming from any of your users to be untrusted, regardless of which user profile it comes from (Item 1). You don't ever want to crash or, even worse, lose control of your application because some user tweaked one of the files in her user profile!

The last point I want to make has to do with daemons (Item 27). You see, loading a user profile (setting up the environment, loading a new registry hive under HKEY_USERS, etc.) takes a nontrivial amount of time. For example, compare the time it takes to run the following two commands (first close any programs you might already be running as Alice to ensure that her user profile is unloaded).

```
runas /u:Alice /noprofile cmd
runas /u:Alice cmd
```

If you use the first command, you will see that no registry hive is loaded. Although this allows the new program to launch quicker, it also means that the program won't have access to Alice's user profile. In fact, run the following command from the noprofile command prompt for Alice:

```
set u
```

The USERPROFILE points to the Default User folder. It would be a mistake to try writing to this profile because it's not the right one for Alice. In fact, this is the profile used by SYSTEM. If Alice isn't an administrator, she won't be allowed to write to this profile (look at the DACL on the Default User home directory to see what I mean, and note that it's a hidden folder).

Normal desktop applications won't need to worry about this because Windows will always load a user profile for a user who logs on interactively via **winlogon.exe**. But some daemons won't have their user profiles loaded for them, as I mention in Item 27, and this can cause you major headaches if you're not prepared for it. The most notable case is for COM servers because the COM SCM doesn't load profiles for a COM server configured to run as a particular user.

It's possible to load a user profile programmatically using the Win32 API LoadUserProfile, but this is a privileged operation so a well-configured daemon that runs with least privilege (Item 4) won't be able to load its own profile. For that reason, when working with operating system functionality such as the certificate stores I mentioned earlier, or even the DPAPI (Item 70), you'll need to use machine-level as opposed to user-level functionality if you know you won't have a profile loaded.

■ 20 ■
What Is a Group?

M OST DEVELOPERS HAVE A basic idea of what a security group in Windows is all about. It's a way to simplify administration by grouping users together. In a large system, a clearly defined group can allow an administrator to assign permissions for hundreds of files, registry keys, directory objects, and so on, without having to think about each individual user that will be in the group to which he's granting permission. Similarly, when managing the group membership list, the administrator doesn't have to remember each and every resource to which the group has access. By clearly defining the semantics of the group, he can manage a more complex system than would otherwise be possible.

It would be nice if that were all there was to it, but in Windows there are four types of group and each has a different scope, overhead, and latency. Developers who care about security should know how they differ. Figure 20.1 summarizes the differences between them.

The first three group types are housed in Active Directory and are always defined within a domain. The first two, universal and global, are pretty much equivalent as far as most developers are concerned. They are normally used by an administrator to categorize her enterprise. For example, she might create groups called `SalesDept` and `EngineeringDept` to track people based on their department. If this is a small business, it's likely that the entire sales force has accounts in a single domain, say `DomA`. In this case, she should create a single global group called `DomA\SalesDept`.

Group Type	Defined In	Scope	Global Catalog Usage
Universal	Domain	Forest	High
Global	Domain	Forest	Low
Domain local	Domain	Domain	None
Local	Machine	Machine	None

Figure 20.1 The four group types in Windows

Because global groups have forest scope, they can be used in any domain in the forest.[1] This means that our administrator can now use a single group to grant access to the entire sales department, and she can do so on any resource in the entire forest. This is goodness!

Unfortunately global groups don't scale to a larger organization. You see, they have a very tight restriction on them. Take DomA\SalesDept. Only principals from DomA are allowed to be members of this group. If our administrator were working for a large company with many different offices, the sales department would be spread across many domains (domain boundaries are often decided based on geography to allow each region some autonomy of administration). To continue using global groups, she would need to create a SalesDept group in every domain that had salespeople. In a Windows NT 4 domain, this would be her only choice, and in order to grant access to the entire sales force, she would have to grant access to each of these groups. Imagine her agony each time a new domain was added or removed! Each resource that granted access to all of sales would have to be visited and its ACLs adjusted.

Windows 2000 solved this problem with the introduction of the universal group. Unlike global groups, universal groups make extensive use of the Global Catalog (GC) in Active Directory, allowing their entire membership list to be replicated among all domain controllers in the forest. A naïve system administrator might very well just create a single universal group

---

1. Technically, groups I've labeled with "forest" scope can be used in any domain that trusts the domain in which the group is defined. You see, some external domains may be linked to the forest via manual trusts.

to house all salespeople across all domains. This would work, but it wouldn't be very efficient, and the latency would be very high when adding or removing group members.[2] A better approach would be to use a global group in each domain to gather together the individual salespeople and then use a single universal group to unify the global groups, as shown in Figure 20.2.

Groups defined in Active Directory can be nested. This method of "fanning out" group membership is more efficient because the universal group's membership list consists of only three SIDs: the three global groups. This reduces overhead in the GC and also reduces latency because adding a user to a global group can take effect immediately, assuming the user logs out and logs back in to get a new ticket (more on that later). For this reason global groups and universal groups are often used together by administrators to efficiently manage large groups of users, and because they have the same scope they can be regarded by application developers as largely the same.

Let me skip ahead to the lowly local group. Local groups are a remnant from Windows NT 4, but they can be quite useful for developers, even on modern versions of Windows. You see, local groups are defined and scoped to a single machine; they aren't defined at the domain level. This means

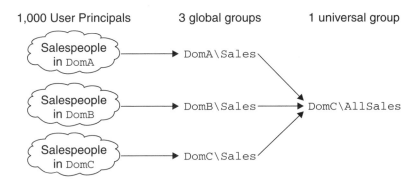

Figure 20.2 Fanning out using universal and global groups

---

2. For example, if she makes the change to a universal group defined in Chicago, it may take quite a bit of time before the change is replicated to a domain in New Zealand.

they can be easier to deploy for an application developer without much clout with the domain administrator, and they're well suited to enabling role-based security in an application (Item 38). Because they're expanded last (more on this later), they're nicely flexible: Although they can't be nested inside each other as domain groups can, they can hold principals and domain groups from any domain in the forest.

Finally we come to the domain local group, another idea introduced in Windows 2000. The domain local group is a lot like a local group in that it is expanded pretty late in the game and therefore can contain universal and global groups and principals from any domain. However, because it makes no use at all of the GC, its name and membership list are known only by the domain in which it is defined, making it a nice choice for implementing role-based security in a larger, distributed application such as a Web farm. It's a lot easier to convince a domain administrator to create a few domain local groups for your application than to get her to create any global or universal groups, as the latter have a much broader impact on the forest. You can think of a domain local group as the big brother of the local group. A local group is scoped to a single machine whereas a domain local group is scoped to a single domain. A domain local group can be used to regulate access to resources throughout the domain where it's defined.

The Mechanics of Group Expansion

So far I've focused on the practical use of each group type. Now I want to focus on why groups work the way they do. Why do global groups have such onerous restrictions? What is this "scope" I keep referring to? Once I figured out the mechanics of how groups are expanded, a light turned on in my head and things really fell into place. I hope you'll have the same experience. Read on.

Group membership is discovered during authentication (I need to talk about Kerberos a bit to explain this, so you may want to read Item 59 if you haven't already). Figure 20.3 shows a typical authentication scenario where a client (Alice) in one domain wants to access a resource on a machine (BobsMachine) in another domain. The way Kerberos works with cross-domain authentication is as follows: Alice needs to transit the trust path

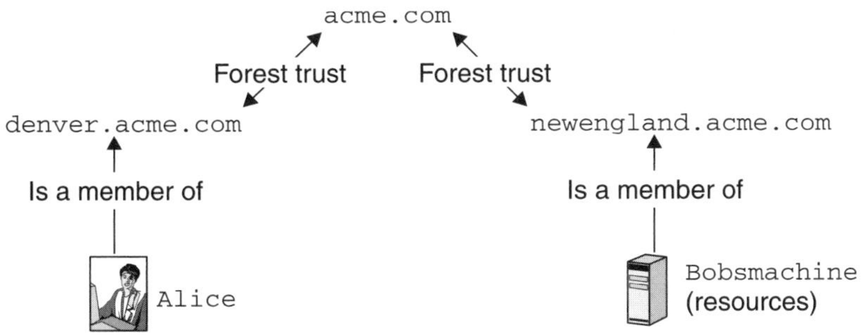

Figure 20.3 A scenario for exploring group expansion

from her domain to the resource domain,[3] obtaining tickets along the way. Groups are communicated via tickets, so it's possible for each domain controller in the trust path to actually contribute groups. However, as of this writing only the client's domain (Denver) and the resource domain (NewZealand) will do so. The client's first stop is at her own domain controller (Denver). This is where global and universal groups are expanded, in that order. You see, global groups are designed to have low impact on the GC. Only the name of each global group is replicated in the GC for distribution throughout the forest, whereas the actual membership list is known only by the domain where the group is defined. This is why we must have Alice's domain authority (Denver) expand her global groups—it's the only domain that knows whether she's a member of these groups or not! And while Denver is at it, it may as well also expand all of Alice's universal groups, because the name and entire membership list for each universal group is replicated in the GC (thus the "high" impact I mentioned in Figure 20.1). Because all domain controllers have a replicated copy of the names and membership lists for all universal groups, Denver performs this expansion after expanding Alice's global groups. It then places the list of resulting groups (global and universal) in the ticket that it issues to Alice.

---

3. I use the term *resource domain* to indicate the domain that hosts the server machine holding the resources (files, services, and so on) that a client wants to access. The distinction is purely temporal—any domain can play this role. We just need a way to identify the domain that hosts the server machine for a given request.

Alice sends this ticket to the next domain controller in the trust path, which copies the groups into the new ticket it issues for the next domain in the path. This continues until Alice reaches the resource domain (NewZealand). The resource domain is responsible for expanding any domain local groups because, just like Denver with its global groups, NewZealand is the only domain that knows the membership list of the domain local groups in use in the NewZealand domain. Heck, NewZealand is the only domain that knows *anything* about the domain local groups in it because domain local groups make no use at all of the GC. After expanding these groups, the entire group list is placed in the last ticket issued to Alice: This is the ticket that will authenticate her to the server process on BobsMachine.

So this final ticket has all of Alice's domain groups nicely flattened out in a list. When she sends this ticket to BobsMachine, the authentication plumbing in the server process hands it off to the local security authority on BobsMachine, which proceeds to expand local groups. Once all the groups are known, privileges (Item 21) can be expanded. The user SID, group SIDs, and privilege identifiers are then tucked away into a token (Item 16), which references a brand-new logon session (Item 17) for Alice.

At each step of this process, groups are expanded by looking at all previously expanded groups (and the user principal SID, of course), which leads us to the following rules that you'll find documented in the Windows help system.

- A local group may contain any[4] domain (or local) principal or domain group.
- A domain local group may contain domain local groups from the domain where the group is defined, universal and global groups from any domain, and principals from any domain.
- A universal group may contain universal and global groups as well as domain principals, all from any domain.

---

4. Note that in this list, when I say "from any domain" or "any domain user or group," I'm talking only about domains with which there is a trust relationship. This covers all domains in the forest and any domains that are linked to the forest via manual trusts.

• A global group may contain global groups and principals from the domain where the group is defined.

The rule of thumb is that a group can have as a member any other type of group that has already been expanded. For example, the local group is the most flexible because it's expanded last. Pretty much anything can be a member of a local group because by the time the server's authority expands it, all the other group memberships are known. Global groups, on the other hand, because they're expanded first, are heavily restricted. At the time they're expanded, we know very little: The client's domain starts with the user's SID and begins expansion from there.

After seeing where the expansions occur, scoping becomes much more obvious. Why do global and universal groups "follow" you around the entire forest, no matter which server machine or domain is the target of your request? I hope Figure 20.4 helps answer this. No matter where the client looks for resources she always gets her initial ticket from her own domain, which expands global and universal groups. Global groups take advantage of this by not bothering to replicate their membership list in the GC. There's no need because the client must first request a ticket from her own domain before authenticating with any other principal. In other words, she'll always be talking to the one domain controller who knows the exact set of global groups in which she's a member. On the other hand, each server machine will define its own set of local groups and each domain will define its own set of domain local groups. If `Alice` decides to

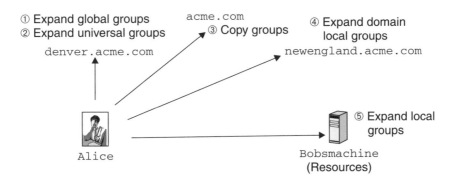

Figure 20.4 Domain and local authorities expand groups during authentication.

authenticate with a machine in the `CentralAmerica` domain, there's no need to talk to the `NewZealand` authority. The domain local groups come from `CentralAmerica` in this case.

But What about NTLM?

In case some of you are wondering how all this works with NTLM, the older challenge-response protocol used in Windows NT 4 and still used today in some circumstances, we see a similar picture. The only difference is that the client doesn't transit the trust path. The client and server perform a three-leg challenge-response handshake; then the server takes the results and hands them up to its domain controller (the resource domain). This domain passes the request through to the client's domain, and group expansion occurs on the return trip in the same fashion: Global and universal groups are first expanded by the client's domain controller and sent back to the server's domain, where domain local groups are then expanded. The server's domain controller sends this entire list of domain groups back down to the server machine, which then expands local groups and privileges. Same deal, just a different mechanism.

Latency and Authenticity

One thing you may have noticed is that because groups are stored in Kerberos tickets (Item 59), and those tickets are typically cached in the client's logon session (Item 17) for the entire workday, a server that receives a ticket from a client will necessarily get stale domain group membership information. This wasn't a problem with NTLM, where the server always contacted the domain controller with each client authentication. Kerberos tickets in Windows are thus a double-edged sword: The caching they provide improves scalability (domain controllers aren't as flooded with authentication requests), but it also increases latency for authorization attributes like group SIDs, which are communicated via cached tickets. By default, tickets must be renewed every ten hours, which allows the domain to inject fresh groups. However, you need to realize that a client who authenticated with a particular server earlier in the day will probably be using the same ticket to authenticate later in the day, and if her domain group membership has changed the change won't be reflected in her ticket unless she's purged her ticket cache and forced the operating system to retrieve a new ticket for her, which most naturally happens when she logs off the machine (destroying her logon session and all the tickets cached inside it) and logs back on before contacting that server.

Another thing you might consider is the potential for a client to modify her ticket and add privileged groups to it, like `Domain Admins`, which can directly affect her authorization level on just about any server with which she authenticates. Normal Kerberos tickets that clients use with server processes are encrypted using a key derived from the password for the server account. If the server account has a lousy password, the client won't have any trouble at all performing this attack. Well, my mother probably couldn't carry this out, but any respectable hacker certainly could, and it only takes one bored teenager to write up that exploit and publish it for anyone to use. So if you run your server under a custom daemon account (Item 28), **make absolutely sure your daemon account uses a very strong password**. There's no reason you shouldn't use 20 characters or more, randomly generated, for every daemon account. No human needs to remember those passwords, and, as I discuss in Item 59, poor server passwords in Kerberos can fall victim to brute force and dictionary attacks because an attacker can easily obtain ciphertext encrypted with the server's master key, which is derived from the server's password. Besides, you can get tools[5] that help you manage passwords. Find one you trust and use it to manage your passwords.

---

5. Password Minder is a tool I wrote for this purpose, and I use it every day. You can download it from the book's Web site.

■ 21 ■
What Is a Privilege?

I N OUR SOCIETY, policemen are granted privileges. Think of the light-bar on a squad car and how the world around the policeman changes when he turns it on. People get out of his way, and he can drive through red lights as long as he's cautious. But he doesn't drive around all day with his lightbar on, because he knows that it's safer to drive normally.

A privilege in Windows is a lot like that lightbar. The benefit isn't available to you unless you've been granted the privilege via security policy, as a person can be granted a position on the police force. We generally do our best to hire good people as police, because it's a position of trust that can be abused. A good policeman uses his privilege only when it's appropriate, and he's very careful when he does. Privileges in Windows are similar: Once you've been granted a privilege, it's listed in your token with a bit that says whether it's enabled or not, and you can enable it to make the operating system behave differently toward you, like turning on the lightbar.

Let's get practical now. When are you ever going to need a privilege? If you want to impersonate a user, you may need the new `SeImpersonatePrivilege`.[1] If you want to change the time or reboot the system, those are privileged operations (`SeSystemtimePrivilege`,

---

1. I say new because this was introduced in Windows Server 2003 and is being actively backported to older systems (it shipped with Windows 2000 SP4 , for example, and it's also slated for release in Windows XP SP2).

SeShutdownPrivilege). To see a full list of privileges, open up your local security policy as an administrator and drill down into "User Rights Assignment" (see Figure 21.1). A quick way to get to this console is to type **secpol.msc** from a command prompt running as an administrator.

As an exercise, use the whoami tool.[2] If you type **whoami /priv**, this program will look at its token and provide a pretty listing of the privileges found there, including whether each privilege is currently enabled or disabled. Try this experiment from a normal user's command prompt (Figure 21.2), then from an admin's command prompt (Figure 21.3). You should see a big difference between the two.

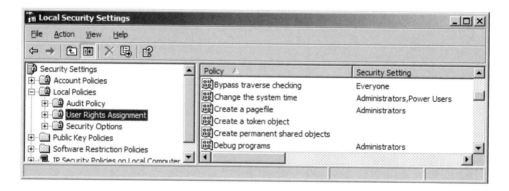

Figure 21.1 Privileges are assigned via security policy.

```
PRIVILEGES INFORMATION
----------------------


Privilege Name          State
====================== ========
SeChangeNotifyPrivilege Enabled
SeUndockPrivilege       Enabled
```

Figure 21.2 whoami /priv output for a normal user

---

2. This tool shipped with Windows Server 2003, but also comes with the Windows 2000 resource kit. Download it from *http://www.microsoft.com/windows2000/techinfo/reskit/tools/ existing/whoami-o.asp*, if necessary.

```
PRIVILEGES INFORMATION
----------------------

Privilege Name                         State
============================== ========
SeChangeNotifyPrivilege                Enabled
SeSecurityPrivilege                    Disabled
SeBackupPrivilege                      Disabled
SeRestorePrivilege                     Disabled
SeSystemtimePrivilege                  Disabled
SeShutdownPrivilege                    Disabled
SeRemoteShutdownPrivilege              Disabled
SeTakeOwnershipPrivilege               Disabled
SeDebugPrivilege                       Disabled
SeSystemEnvironmentPrivilege           Disabled
SeSystemProfilePrivilege               Disabled
SeProfileSingleProcessPrivilege        Disabled
SeIncreaseBasePriorityPrivilege        Disabled
SeLoadDriverPrivilege                  Disabled
SeCreatePagefilePrivilege              Disabled
SeIncreaseQuotaPrivilege               Disabled
SeUndockPrivilege                      Disabled
SeManageVolumePrivilege                Disabled
```

Figure 21.3 `whoami /priv` output for an admin

The normal pattern of usage for a privilege can be demonstrated by an example. Say you want to reboot the system. You know that this is a privileged operation, so you reach up into your process token and try to enable `SeShutdownPrivilege`. If you've been granted this privilege by policy, your token should have it, and so you'll be permitted to enable it. If you haven't been granted this privilege, your attempt to enable it will fail, at which point you'll need to deal with the fact that you're not allowed to reboot the system (in a desktop app, you could inform the user of her lack of privilege with a message box, for example). Assuming you've succeeded in enabling the privilege, you'll call the Win32 function `ExitWindowsEx` to request a reboot. Finally, you should disable the privilege. Notice the pattern here: enable, use, disable—just like the policeman with his lightbar.

Because you're rebooting the system, you might argue that disabling the privilege is a waste of time. But just as you should never get lazy and allocate memory without freeing it, you should never enable a privilege without disabling it as soon as you're done using it. You never know who will cut and paste your code in another project! Besides, how does the routine know that the reboot will actually happen and that your program will actually exit? Often users initiate a reboot only to cancel it when they realize they need to save some work first. It's tough to know all these things deep down in a routine that's responsible for actually implementing the reboot. Make sure each of your security primitives (like privilege usage) follows best practices. Don't take shortcuts.

Some privileges are meant to be enabled all the time if they're granted. `SeChangeNotifyPrivilege` (also known as "Bypass Traverse Checking"[3]) and `SeImpersonatePrivilege` are notable examples. These are like the policeman's handgun—he's granted the right to carry it on the street, and he's never on the job without it. If you're granted any of these privileges by policy, the operating system will enable them by default in that first token you get at login time, so you shouldn't need to worry about messing with them at runtime. Many Win32 functions (but not all) incorporate the enabling and disabling of privileges as a convenience. Furthermore, I expect that, as the .NET Framework continues to abstract more of the Win32 API, you'll have less and less need to worry about enabling privileges manually. But this is a technical detail. Security policy will still control who can and cannot perform privileged operations, so you should be aware of the privileges defined by Windows so that you know what requirements your programs will have with respect to security policy.

---

3. No, this is no typo. The programmatic name is very different from the friendly name, thus ensuring your job security as a Windows programmer.

■ 22 ■
How to Use a Privilege

REMEMBER THAT BEFORE you can use a privilege it must be in your token. The only way to get a privilege into your token is to have security policy grant it to you, and then to establish a fresh logon. The resulting token will have the new privilege, and it will be available for your use (in other words, don't forget to **log off and log back on** if you want a recent change to your groups or privileges to affect the programs you want to run).

Most functions don't require any special privileges, but if the documentation for a particular function indicates that a privilege is required, pay special attention to whether that function automatically enables the privilege or not. Some Win32 functions that use privileges can be called with the privilege enabled or disabled, and their behavior changes if you have a privilege enabled. Other functions always require a privilege and therefore will attempt to enable it for you as a convenience (since you always need to enable it to call the function successfully anyway).

With a desktop application designed to be run by many different users, some with high privilege and some with low privilege, you should plan how you'll deal with failure in case the user running your app doesn't have the required privilege. With a server application, you'll normally run under an identity that has all the privileges you need, so this won't be so much of an issue.

Some privileges are very dangerous to grant to code that accepts input from untrusted sources. Especially if that input comes over from an untrusted network such as the Internet. For example, `SeDebugPrivilege` can be used to elevate privileges because it allows a program to open any other process (including sensitive operating system daemons) for full permissions. If your server application has this privilege and accidentally gives control to an attacker who has sent you some malformed input, the attacker can use the privilege to read and write memory in any process he likes. This is really bad.

So, if you need a program to be both highly privileged and highly exposed to attack, consider factoring it into two parts: Pull out the small bits that require high privilege and host that code in a COM+ server application that runs under an account that's granted those sensitive privileges but doesn't accept input from the network. Use COM+ roles (Item 56) to limit the callers so that only the account under which your main server application runs can call it. This factoring technique can significantly slow down an attack, giving detection and reaction countermeasures (Item 2) time to kick in.

If you need to manually enable or disable a privilege, you'll have to use the Win32 API because as of this writing the .NET Framework doesn't wrap this functionality, and it doesn't look like version 2.0 will provide it either. But fear not: I've provided some Managed C++ code that will do the trick. A sample is shown in Figure 22.1.

The key Win32 function here is `AdjustTokenPrivileges`, which is what enables or disables privileges in a token. Each privilege in a token is represented with a 64-bit "Locally Unique Identifier" (LUID), which is allowed to change across reboots of the machine. So, before enabling privileges in a token, you need to look up the LUID for each one you plan on enabling. This is what `LookupPrivilegeValue` is for. Given a string like `SeBackupPrivilege`, this function will look up the corresponding LUID.

The `AdjustTokenPrivileges` function can also return a data structure that indicates the previous state of the privileges you enabled. This makes it really easy to reset them after you're done using them, which is what my `ResetPrivileges` class is for. Because this class implements

```
ResetPrivileges* Token::EnablePrivileges(WindowsIdentity* ident,
  String* privs[], bool wantResetObject) {
  if (0 == ident) {
    throw new ArgumentException(S"Cannot be null", S"ident");
  }
  if (0 == privs) {
    throw new ArgumentException(S"Cannot be null", S"privs");
  }
  const int privCount = privs->Length;
  if (privCount < 1 || privCount > 50) {
    // sanity check on number of privileges
    // (only about 30 are even defined)
    throw new ArgumentOutOfRangeException(S"privs",
      S"Number of privileges in array is out of range");
  }

  TOKEN_PRIVILEGES tp_simple;
  TOKEN_PRIVILEGES* ptpNew;
  if (1 == privCount) {
    tp_simple.PrivilegeCount = 1;
    ptpNew = &tp_simple;
  }
  else {
    ptpNew = _allocTokenPrivileges(privCount);
  }

  ResetPrivileges* resetter = 0;
  try {
    int i = privCount;
    LUID_AND_ATTRIBUTES* j = ptpNew->Privileges + privCount;
    while (i--) {
      _setupEnabledLuidAndAttributes(privs[i], --j);
    }

    int cb = 0;
    if (wantResetObject) {
      resetter = new ResetPrivileges(ident, privCount, &cb);
    }

    HANDLE htok = ident->Token.ToPointer();
    DWORD dummy;
    if (!AdjustTokenPrivileges(htok, FALSE, ptpNew, (DWORD)cb,
                    resetter ? resetter->old : 0, &dummy)) {
      throwWin32Exception(S"AdjustTokenPrivileges failed");
    }
```

continues

Figure 22.1 Enabling a privilege from Managed C++

```
      if (ERROR_NOT_ALL_ASSIGNED == GetLastError()) {
        throw new ApplicationException(S"One or more privileges "
          + "could not be enabled: the most likely problem is "
          + "that the token being adjusted does not have one "
          + "or more of the requested privileges");
      }
    }
    __finally {
      if (privCount > 1) {
        LocalFree(ptpNew);
      }
    }
    return resetter;
}

static TOKEN_PRIVILEGES* _allocTokenPrivileges(int privCount,
                                               int* pcb) {
  const size_t cb = sizeof(TOKEN_PRIVILEGES) +
    ((privCount - 1) * sizeof(LUID_AND_ATTRIBUTES));
  void* p = LocalAlloc(LMEM_FIXED, cb);
  if (!p) {
    throw new OutOfMemoryException(S"LocalAlloc failed");
  }
  if (pcb) *pcb = cb;
  return (TOKEN_PRIVILEGES*)p;
}

static void _setupEnabledLuidAndAttributes(String* priv,
                                  LUID_AND_ATTRIBUTES* p) {
  const wchar_t __pin* internalPriv = PtrToStringChars(priv);
  if (!LookupPrivilegeValue(0, internalPriv, &p->Luid)) {
    throw new ArgumentException(S"Unrecognized privilege name",
                                priv);
  }
  p->Attributes = SE_PRIVILEGE_ENABLED;
}
```

Figure 22.1 Enabling a privilege from Managed C++   (*continued*)

IDisposable, C# programmers can rely on a using statement to disable a privilege when it's no longer needed. Here's some sample code that shows how this works. For the entire sample library, see the Web site for the book.

```
using (ResetPrivileges r =
        Token.EnablePrivilege(WindowsIdentity.GetCurrent(),
                              "SeShutdownPrivilege", true)) {

    // use the privilege...


} // privilege setting will be restored here
```

■ 23 ■

How to Grant or Revoke Privileges via Security Policy

THE LOCAL SECURITY AUTHORITY (LSA) on each machine ultimately decides what privileges will be granted to a user when she logs in. The most direct way of affecting that decision is to open the local security policy of the machine and edit the privilege grants there. You can get to the local security policy either by running `secpol.msc` from an administrative command prompt (Item 9) or by looking on the Start menu for an administrative tool called "Local Security Policy." From there, drill down into "Local Policies" and select "User Rights Assignment." I show a picture of this editor in Item 21, Figure 21.1.

In a domain environment it's also possible to set privileges (and all other local security policy) at the domain, site, or organizational unit (OU) levels, and the local machine will download those updates at each reboot (or more frequently if you configure periodic refreshes). Check out Item 74 for more details.

Because privilege assignments are always expanded at the local machine, you can grant them to individual users from any domain or any group known to that machine. This includes all four types of group (Item 20). Privileges are very flexible this way. Note, though, that if you use group policy to set privileges for a large number of machines, you'll have to be careful about the types of group you use: Use only those that will have meaning on all the machines to which your group policy will apply!

The group names you specify in group policy aren't checked for validity: They're only stored as strings. It's not until the policy is actually deployed to individual machines that these names are used to look up real groups, converted into SIDs (Item 13), and stored in the local policy of the machine.

Also note that, like groups, any changes you make to privilege assignments won't take effect for any given user until she establishes a fresh logon on the machine. I've seen many developers who, after granting themselves a privilege on their machine and then starting a new process, expect the privilege grant to take effect immediately. Don't forget the latency that's inherent in each security context (Item 15)! If you start another process, you're just going to get a copy of the parent process's token, which won't have the new privilege in it. Log off and back on to get a fresh token.

On a few occasions I'll cheat by using the Secondary Logon Service (Item 30). For example, Windows XP has the annoying restriction (I can't imagine that it's intentional; it's probably a bug) that prevents nonadministrators from changing their power-saving settings. This makes it a pain for me to run as a non-admin on my laptop. When I get on a plane, I usually want to change my power settings to "max battery," but because each user profile (Item 19) has its own settings, I can't simply run **powercfg.cpl** from an administrative command prompt. I need to put myself in the local Administrators group temporarily and make the change in my own user profile. To avoid having to log off and log back on, I simply run the following batch file from my admin command prompt:

```
REM ********************************************
REM powercfg.cmd - temporarily elevate privilege
REM and launch the power configuration editor
REM ********************************************
net localgroup administrators keith /add
runas /u:keith "cmd /c powercfg.cpl"
net localgroup administrators keith /delete
```

This works because the Secondary Logon Service always establishes a fresh logon before launching the new process.

You can also grant (and enumerate) privileges programmatically, via the Win32 LSA API, but note that, just as when running the local security policy tool interactively, you must be an administrator to read or write privilege settings in policy. Figure 23.1 shows a C# program that uses a helper class

```
using System;
using System.Security.AccessControl;
using KBC.WindowsSecurityUtilities;

class Test {
  static void Main() {
    WindowsSecurityUtilities.Initialize();

    string account = @"BUILTIN\Backup Operators";

    PrintUsersWithShutdownPrivilege();

    Console.WriteLine("Adding privilege...");
    PrivilegePolicy.AddPrivilege(account,
        Privileges.Shutdown);

PrintUsersWithShutdownPrivilege();

    Console.WriteLine("Removing privilege...");
    PrivilegePolicy.RemovePrivilege(account,
        Privileges.Shutdown);

    PrintUsersWithShutdownPrivilege();

    WindowsSecurityUtilities.Terminate();
  }
  static void PrintUsersWithShutdownPrivilege() {
    foreach (byte[] sid in PrivilegePolicy.GetPrivilegeGrants(
        Privileges.Shutdown)) {
      SecurityIdentifier sid =
        SecurityIdentifier.CreateFromBinaryForm(sid, 0);
      Console.WriteLine(@"{0}\{1}", sid.DomainName, sid.AccountName);
    }
  }
}
```

Figure 23.1 Enumerating, adding, and removing privileges programmatically

to manage privileges in policy (you can download the entire sample library from the Web site for this book). The `PrivilegePolicy` class is written in Managed C++ and simplifies the programmatic use of privileges. Note that this code also uses the `SecurityIdentifier` class that's new in version 2.0 of the .NET Framework, which makes it easy to translate between SIDs and account names (Item 13).

■ 24 ■
What Are WindowsIdentity and WindowsPrincipal?

T HESE CLASSES WORK TOGETHER to represent a Windows token (Item 16) and provide implementations of the abstract interfaces IIdentity and IPrincipal, which I discussed in Item 15. Here are the public members of these classes.

```
namespace System.Security.Principal {
  public class WindowsIdentity : IIdentity {
    // I've omitted some redundant constructor overloads
    public WindowsIdentity(IntPtr token,
      string authnType,
      WindowsAccountType accountType,
      bool isAuthenticated);
    public WindowsIdentity(string userPrincipalName,
      string authnType);
    public bool IsAnonymous { get; }
    public bool IsSystem { get; }
    public bool IsGuest { get; }
    public virtual IntPtr Token { get; }
    public virtual WindowsImpersonationContext
      Impersonate();

    public static WindowsIdentity GetAnonymous();
    public static WindowsIdentity GetCurrent();
    public static WindowsImpersonationContext
      Impersonate(IntPtr token);
```

```
      // IIdentity implementation
      public bool IsAuthenticated { get; }
      public string Name { get; }
      public string AuthenticationType { get; }
   }

   public class WindowsPrincipal : IPrincipal {
      public WindowsPrincipal(WindowsIdentity id);
      public virtual bool IsInRole(int rid);
      public virtual bool IsInRole(WindowsBuiltInRole
        wellKnownGroup);

      // IPrincipal implementation
      public virtual IIdentity Identity { get; }
      public virtual bool IsInRole(string roleName);
   }
}
```

As you can see, these concrete classes expose quite a bit more functionality than the abstract interfaces they implement. For example, you can use `IIdentity` to ask about the user's name, but you can get the user's raw token via `WindowsIdentity.Token`. This allows you to find out much more about the user's security context, including what privileges (Item 21) she has, although you'll have to do so using P/Invoke to call the appropriate Win32 function (`GetTokenInformation`). If you use this property to retrieve the underlying token handle, be aware that you're just getting a peek at it. It's not a duplicated token or even a duplicated handle, so don't close it! I've asked the documentation team to clarify this.

It's interesting that these classes are not sealed and they provide virtual functions that you can override. This could be helpful if you wanted to provide a custom principal class that exposed application-specific roles instead of Windows groups, as I sketched out in Item 15.

Looking at `WindowsPrincipal`, note that there are a couple of overloads for `IsInRole`. The second is interesting because I can look for well-known SIDs in the token, as the following code snippet shows:

```
void ProbeToken(IPrincipal p) {
  WindowsPrincipal wp = p as WindowsPrincipal;
  if (null != wp) {
    if (wp.IsInRole(WindowsBuiltInRole.Administrator)) {
      Console.WriteLine("This is an administrator!");
    }
```

```
    if (wp.IsInRole(WindowsBuiltInRole.Guest)) {
      Console.WriteLine("This is a guest!");
    }
  }
  else Console.WriteLine("No token to probe! " +
    "This is not a WindowsPrincipal.");
}
```

What's unfortunate is that the `WindowsBuiltInRole` enumeration is quite limited. I couldn't care less if the user is a member of the antiquated `Account Operators` group. What I do care about is whether the `Authenticated Users` group is in the token, but unfortunately the `WindowsBuiltInRole` enumeration doesn't include this one. And the other overload that allows you to pass a relative ID (the least significant part of a SID, as I discussed in Item 13) only works for a very limited set of RIDs—namely, those represented by the `WindowsBuiltInRole` enumeration. Bah!

As for `WindowsIdentity`, under the covers it consists of a handle to a token and a couple of fields. One field is a Boolean and backs the `IsAuthenticated` property; the other tracks the "account type." This comes from the `WindowsAccountType` enumeration.

```
namespace System.Security.Principal {
  public enum WindowsAccountType : Int32 {
    Normal,
    Guest,
    System,
    Anonymous
  }
}
```

What's funny is that by looking at a token you can normally determine whether it's a `Guest`, `System`, or `Anonymous` logon just by the SIDs in it. But the `WindowsIdentity.IsSystem` property doesn't look at the token to decide, for example, whether it's a token for `SYSTEM`. Rather, it looks at the private account type field. So if you ever construct a `WindowsIdentity` from a token, you'll need to do these checks yourself and set the account type manually. The same goes for the `IsAuthenticated` property. I show how to do this in Item 25. The various properties on `WindowsIdentity` that start with `Is` are implemented by simply checking these two fields, which must be set up correctly when the `WindowsIdentity` is first constructed.

`WindowsIdentity.GetCurrent` is quite useful. It constructs a `WindowsIdentity` to wrap your process token, unless the thread that makes the call is impersonating (Item 31), in which case the thread token is used. I use this method all the time when diagnosing security problems. For example, if you're writing to a server and suddenly you find that you're being denied access to a file you're normally allowed to read, your first instinct should be to ask, "Gee, I wonder what security context I was in when I tried to open the file?" A quick call to `GetCurrent` will answer that question!

`WindowsIdentity.GetAnonymous` is odd, as I describe in Item 37. You would expect that, on a class dedicated specifically to dealing with Windows tokens, this would be implemented with a null session token (Item 35). Sadly it's not. Instead, it returns a `WindowsIdentity` whose token is set to `IntPtr.Zero` and can't be impersonated. This really restricts its utility! I show a better way to represent an anonymous user in Item 37.

The `AuthenticationType` property on `WindowsIdentity` is almost always hardcoded to be "NTLM", even though the token may have been generated via the Kerberos package, so don't put too much stock in this property.

To learn how to use the `Impersonate` method, check out Item 32.

One very useful feature of `WindowsIdentity` is that it tremendously simplifies group lookup for domain users in Windows Server 2003 and eases the use of a new feature on that platform called "protocol transition." Briefly, this feature allows a trusted server to obtain network credentials for a user without knowing that user's password. You can read more about the ideas behind this feature and how it works in Item 63. All this magic is worked through the deceptively simple constructor for `WindowsIdentity` that takes a single string as input. See Item 26 for details on how to use this constructor.

■ 25 ■
How to Create a WindowsPrincipal Given a Token

I F YOU'VE GOT A handle to a Windows token for a user, you'll likely want to wrap it in a `WindowsPrincipal` object. This will simplify basic tasks like group lookup, where you can just call `Windows-Principal.IsInRole`. It will also allow you to hang the token from the `Thread.CurrentPrincipal` property, which can be quite convenient (Item 33). At first glance it seems trivial to wrap a token, given the constructor on `WindowsIdentity` that takes a token handle.

```
// this approach is naïve!
WindowsPrincipal NaiveWrapToken(IntPtr token) {
  WindowsIdentity id = new WindowsIdentity(token);
  WindowsPrincipal p = new WindowsPrincipal(id);
  return p;
}
```

Unfortunately, as I discussed in Item 24, the resulting `Windows-Identity` won't behave like you might expect it to. For example, even if the token represents an authenticated user, if you look at the `Windows-Identity.IsAnonymous` property, you'll find that it returns false. The other properties that start with `Is` won't function properly, and the `AuthenticationType` property will be hardcoded to NTLM.

To solve this problem, you should call the more complicated constructor.

```
namespace System.Security.Principal {
  public class WindowsIdentity : IIdentity {
    public WindowsIdentity(
      IntPtr token,
      string authnType,
      WindowsAccountType accountType,
      bool isAuthenticated);

    // ...
  }
}
```

With this constructor, you can say what the IsAuthenticated property, as well as IsSystem and friends, should return, but because some tokens represent unauthenticated users (Item 35), you should first look inside the token for the NT Authority\Authenticated Users SID and make your decision based on its presence or absence. Because you're starting with a raw token, however, this means calling native Win32 functions, so I've provided a helper function that will wrap tokens for you. The function is shown in Figure 25.1, and is available in the downloadable library.

```
WindowsIdentity* Token::CreateWindowsIdentity(IntPtr token) {
    HANDLE htok = token.ToPointer();

    // one annoying failure mode we need to watch for
    // is that CheckTokenMembership insists on being
    // passed an impersonation token. IMHO this is broken.
    HANDLE dup = _dupTokenIfPrimary(htok);
    CloseHandleIfNonZero closeThis(dup);
    if (dup) {
        htok = dup;
    }

    // check for NT Authority\Authenticated Users
    BOOL isAuthenticated;
    if (!CheckTokenMembership(htok,
            &WellKnownSIDs::AuthenticatedUsers,
            &isAuthenticated)) {
        throwWin32Exception(S"CheckTokenMembership");
    }
```

continues

```
    // check for NT Authority\SYSTEM
    BOOL isSystem;
    if (!CheckTokenMembership(0,
            &WellKnownSIDs::LocalSystem,
            &isSystem)) {
        throwWin32Exception(S"CheckTokenMembership");
    }
    WindowsAccountType accountType;
    if (isSystem) {
        accountType = WindowsAccountType::System;
    }
    else {
        // check for BUILTIN\Guests
        BOOL isGuest;
        if (!CheckTokenMembership(0,
                &WellKnownSIDs::Guests,
                &isGuest)) {
            throwWin32Exception(S"CheckTokenMembership");
        }
        if (isGuest) {
            accountType = WindowsAccountType::Guest;
        }
        else if (!isAuthenticated) {
            accountType = WindowsAccountType::Anonymous;
        }
        else {
            accountType = WindowsAccountType::Normal;
        }
    }
    // ask the token where it came from and use that as the
    // authentication type
    TOKEN_SOURCE source;
    DWORD cb = sizeof source;
    int n = (int)htok;
    if (!GetTokenInformation(htok, TokenSource,
                            &source, cb, &cb)) {
        throwWin32Exception(S"GetTokenInformation");
    }

    // now we have enough information to create the wrapper
    return new WindowsIdentity(htok,
        new String(source.SourceName, 0,
                   sizeof(source.SourceName)),
        accountType, isAuthenticated ? true : false);
}
```

Figure 25.1 Wrapping a token intelligently in Managed C++

If the code in the figure seems more complicated than it needs to be, well, welcome to the world of programming security via Win32. No wonder my last book on the topic (Brown 2000b) was almost 600 pages long. Fortunately, as the .NET Framework matures we'll be seeing more and more high-level support for security programming, such as the ACL support slated for version 2.0. Let me clarify a few things about this code.

First of all, whenever you check for the presence of a group in a raw token, you should do so via the Win32 function `CheckTokenMembership`. This function is rather finicky. It only accepts what's known as an "impersonation" token. You see, impersonation tokens are designed to be used on a thread for impersonation (see Item 31) whereas the other type, the "primary" token, is designed to be put on a process. If you look at your process token by calling `WindowsIdentity.GetCurrent`, you'll be looking at a primary token. But given that there is a Win32 function for converting between these token types, the difference between them for all practical purposes is historical. It's not clear why `CheckTokenMembership` even cares, but it does—thus the call to the helper function `_dupTokenIfPrimary`, which basically calls `DuplicateTokenEx` to produce an impersonation token if necessary. It's this kind of esoterica that makes working with Windows security nightmarish (but ensures job security for the few folks that know how to do it). Of course, if we end up duplicating the token, we have an extra handle that needs closing, so I use the good old C++ destructor mechanism to ensure that it's closed before the function ends, by writing a little helper class called `CloseHandleIfNonZero` to do this cleanup when the function is done.

Next, I need to check for a couple of well-known SIDs (Item 13). A long time ago I got tired of having to look up the values for these SIDs and construct them manually every time I needed them. That's why you'll see my code referring to an unmanaged C++ class called `WellKnownSIDs`, another class I wrote as part of this helper library. I hope you find it useful. When you upgrade to version 2.0 of the .NET Framework, you'll find the `SecurityIdentifier` class and the `WellKnownSidType` enumeration helpful as well.

Finally, I determine the `AuthenticationType` by asking the token where it came from via a call to `GetTokenInformation`. This tends to be more accurate than simply hardcoding "NTLM" all the time!

Keep in mind that the `WindowsIdentity` constructors that accept a token handle as input will first duplicate the token. This means two things: Any changes (such as enabling privileges, as I discuss in Item 21) you make in one won't affect the other, and you'll be responsible for closing the token handle that you provided to the `WindowsIdentity` constructor. Because the code in Figure 25.1 ultimately calls one of these constructors, the same rules apply if you call my helper function to wrap a token.

■ 26 ■

How to Get a Token for a User

G ETTING A TOKEN (Item 16) for a user is tremendously easy if you
happen to be running on a Windows Server 2003 machine in a native
Windows Server 2003 domain. You can simply construct a new Windows-
Identity, passing in the user principal name (UPN) for the account, which
for ACME\Alice is typically something like alice@acme.com.[1] Here's an
example:

```
using System;
using System.Security.Principal;

class IsUserAnAdmin {
  static void Main(string[] args) {
    if (1 != args.Length) {
      Console.WriteLine("Usage: IsUserAnAdmin userPrincipalName");
      return;
    }
    string upn = args[0];
    // here's the magic constructor
    WindowsIdentity id = new WindowsIdentity(upn);
    WindowsPrincipal p = new WindowsPrincipal(id);
```

---

1. The UPN is typically an e-mail address, and it's stored as part of the user's account in
    Active Directory. Look on the Account tab for the user account in Active Directory
    Users and Computers, and it's the first thing you'll see: "User logon name." If you're
    logged in under a domain account, you can use **whoami /upn** to discover your own
    UPN as well.

```
    if (p.IsInRole(WindowsBuiltInRole.Administrator)) {
      Console.WriteLine("{0} IS an admin of this box", upn);
    }
    else {
      Console.WriteLine("{0} is NOT an admin of this box", upn);
    }
  }
}
```

This feature is new to Windows Server 2003. It only works with domain accounts and has some restrictions that I talk about in Item 63.

Calling LogonUser

If you're trying to do the same thing with a local account, or a domain account on a Windows 2000 or Windows XP box, you'll need the user's password to get a token for it. Where are you going to get the user's password, though? If you need to do this sort of thing, prompt the user for a password (Item 71). If the user won't be present, then you'll need to store the password someplace where the machine can read it. This is really bad news because, even if you do this as carefully as possible (Item 70), root compromise of the machine eventually leads to compromise of these secrets, and you can't prevent this. This should be a major consideration in your threat model (Item 3)!

Now that I've warned you adequately, there is a Win32 API that you can call to authenticate a name and password: LogonUser. This API takes the user's name, authority (domain name for a domain account or machine name for a local account), and password; verifies this information with the authority; and establishes a logon session (Item 17). It returns a token that references the new session which you can use to impersonate the user, find out what groups she's in, and so on.

But there's a flaw in the Windows 2000 implementation of LogonUser. This function is implemented in terms of a lower-level (and much more powerful) function called LsaLogonUser, which takes about a hundred thousand parameters (I exaggerate, but only just a little). Anyway, this lower-level function is so powerful that only users with SeTcbPrivilege are allowed to use it, which basically means you need to run as SYSTEM to call it. Why? Because you're allowed to inject arbitrary SIDs into the resulting token. Want to pretend that a user is really an administrator of the machine? This function allows you to inject the BUILTIN\Administrators SID into the resulting token, so clearly we don't want nonprivileged users calling it! But here's the thing: Because the very useful LogonUser function calls LsaLogonUser, it also requires this same privilege, even though it doesn't allow you to pass in those extra SIDs. Programs that need to call this function on Windows 2000 often end up being configured to run as SYSTEM, even though they might not normally need any special level of privilege. This is bad!

This flaw has been remedied in modern versions of Windows such as Windows XP and Windows Server 2003, so let's proceed for the moment assuming that we can simply call LogonUser to get a token for a user without having any special privileges. Later in this item I'll show a workaround for those of you running Windows 2000. In Figure 26.1 I provide a C# program that calls LogonUser via P/Invoke.

```
using System;
using System.Security.Principal;
using System.Runtime.InteropServices;
using KBC.WindowsSecurityUtilities;

class LogonAlice {
  static void Main() {
    WindowsSecurityUtilities.Initialize();
    // from our helper library
    string pwd = PasswordPrompt.GetPasswordFromCmdLine();
    IntPtr token;
    bool result = LogonUser(
        "Alice", "ACME", // "ACME\Alice"
        pwd,
        LogonTypes.Batch,
        LogonProviders.Default,
        out token);
    if (result) {
      // from our helper library
      WindowsIdentity id = Token.CreateWindowsIdentity(token);
      CloseHandle(token);
      WindowsPrincipal p = new WindowsPrincipal(id);

                                              continues
```

Figure 26.1 Calling **LogonUser** from C#

```
      // use IPrincipal/IIdentity to query the token
      Console.WriteLine("{0} is a User: {1}", id.Name,
        p.IsInRole(WindowsBuiltInRole.User));
      Console.WriteLine("{0} is an Admin: {1}", id.Name,
        p.IsInRole(WindowsBuiltInRole.Administrator));
    }
    else {
      Console.WriteLine("LogonUser failed: {0}",
        Marshal.GetLastWin32Error());
    }
    WindowsSecurityUtilities.Terminate();
  }
  [DllImport("advapi32.dll", SetLastError=true)]
  static extern bool LogonUser(
    string principal,
    string authority,
    string password,
    LogonTypes logonType,
    LogonProviders logonProvider,
    out IntPtr token);
  [DllImport("kernel32.dll", SetLastError=true)]
  static extern bool CloseHandle(IntPtr handle);
  enum LogonTypes : uint {
    Interactive = 2,
    Network,
    Batch,
    Service,
    NetworkCleartext = 8,
    NewCredentials
  }
  enum LogonProviders : uint {
    Default = 0, // default for platform (use this!)
    WinNT35,       // sends smoke signals to authority
    WinNT40,       // uses NTLM
    WinNT50        // negotiates Kerb or NTLM
  }
}
```

Figure 26.1 Calling `LogonUser` from C#   *(continued)*

When calling `LogonUser`, you must choose the type of logon you want the user to establish. There are four types, and each requires the user being logged on to hold a corresponding user right. You may recognize some of these user logon rights from poking around in security policy under "User Rights Assignment," the same place where privileges are granted (Item 21).

- Interactive logon: "Log on locally"
- Network logon: "Access this computer from the network"
- Batch logon: "Log on as a batch job"
- Service logon: "Log on as a service"

The easiest by far to establish is the network logon. Everyone is granted this right by default everywhere on the network. Denying it to someone is tantamount to saying, "I will not accept your credentials on this machine: get lost!" I would recommend sticking to a network logon if at all possible. It's also much faster than establishing an interactive logon when working with domain accounts. The other nice thing about the network logon is that you get to choose whether the resulting logon session will cache the client's master key (Item 59) so that you can contact remote servers while impersonating the user (Item 31). If you need network credentials for the user, choose the `LogonTypes.NetworkCleartext` logon option. Otherwise, by all means choose the `LogonTypes.Network` option so that the client's key will not be cached. This is an example of applying the principal of least privilege (Item 4).

The interactive logon is what **winlogon.exe** uses when you log on to a machine interactively. The only time you want to use it is when you want to run an interactive process as the user, but there's a much easier way of doing that than calling `LogonUser`. See Item 30 for more details. Finally, batch and service logons are used by COM servers and Windows services, respectively. Unless you're writing very specialized code for launching background processes, you should avoid these as well. The network logon is your friend!

The SSPI Workaround

Remember that flaw in `LogonUser` that essentially requires you to run as `SYSTEM` to call it on Windows 2000? Well, there's a workaround that's come in handy for a number of people I've helped, but it's limited in that the resulting logon session will not have network credentials for the user. Nevertheless, it might just get you out of a jam, so here we go.

The trick is to perform an SSPI handshake (Item 65) with yourself, playing the role of both client and server. And the cool thing is, with version 2.0

of the .NET Framework it's trivial to implement. I show how to use the
NegotiateStream class in Item 66 to build a client and server that authenticate
across the network. Well, to authenticate a user given her name and
password, you just do the same thing but without the network. Attach two
instances of NegotiateStream together, one for the client and one for the
server, and perform both sides of the handshake. The code is shown in
Figure 26.2.

```csharp
using System;
using System.Net;
using System.IO;

class LogonUserViaSSPI {
  static WindowsIdentity Logon(string principal,
                              string authority,
                              string password) {
    MemoryStream couple = new MemoryStream();
    using (NegotiateStream clientStream =
           new NegotiateStream(couple))
    using (NegotiateStream serverStream =
           new NegotiateStream(couple)) {
      // we're the server, so the SPN is easy to calculate
      string spn = WindowsIdentity.GetCurrent().Name;
      NetworkCredential cred = new NetworkCredential(
        principal, password, authority);

      // here's the handshake
      clientStream.ClientAuthenticate(cred, spn,
        ImpersonationLevel.Impersonation,
        SecurityLevel.None, true);
      serverStream.ServerAuthenticate(
        CredentialCache.DefaultCredentials,
        SecurityLevel.None);

      return serverStream.IsAuthenticated ?
        (WindowsIdentity)serverStream.RemoteIdentity :
        null;
    }
  }
}
```

Figure 26.2 Using SSPI to establish a network logon

The service principal name (SPN, introduced in Item 60) is easy to calculate. Because my process is acting as the server, I can just query my token
to find out which user is running the program (and thus acting as the
server). This is the reason I call `WindowsIdentity.GetCurrent`. I use this
name as the SPN.

Because you don't need to establish a secure channel (note that both
instances of `NegotiateStream` are discarded as soon as the handshake is
complete), choose a security level of `SecurityLevel.None`. This way the
only thing that SSPI will do is authenticate and get us a logon session and
a token for the user.

On success, you'll end up with a network logon for the user with no
network credentials. Thus you can use the resulting token on the local
machine, but don't try to impersonate using this token in order to authenticate with remote servers: It won't work. You'll end up establishing a null
session with the remote server instead (Item 35). If you need those network
credentials, you'll have to call `LogonUser` as shown above.

■ 27 ■
What Is a Daemon?

I N UNIX, A PROGRAM that runs in the background (not attached to a terminal) is called a "daemon." It's something you can't see, but it's alive and well doing work behind the scenes. In Windows, lots of programs run in this fashion, and they come in different forms, such as NT services, IIS worker processes, COM servers, and scheduled processes. As a programmer, it's important to know that, even though the plumbing for these daemons is different (compare an NT service with an instance of the IIS worker process, for example), there are lots of similarities among them. And it's important to know these similarities to help simplify your view of server code. Let's talk briefly about some characteristics of daemons on Windows.

Think about what happens when you, the interactive user, launch a new process, either via Explorer or via a command shell. The new process is bestowed with a copy of your token, which puts it in your interactive logon session (Item 17). It's also naturally placed in the interactive window station (Item 18), so you'll be able to see any windows it displays and interact with them. When you log off, that program will be closed.

Now think of what happens when you start a daemon. Say you start a service by typing **net start myservice**. In this case, **net.exe** talks to a daemon called the Service Control Manager (SCM), which was automatically started at boot time in the highly privileged SYSTEM logon session. The SCM's job is to launch the service process into a logon session and window station that allows it to run in the background, disassociated from your interactive logon. If you log out, that daemon can continue to run. The SCM looks at a configuration database in the registry to figure out what credentials to use for the new process (Item 28). If you've specified that the service run under an account that you've defined, the SCM will create a brand-new logon session using those credentials.

Now think about starting an IIS 6 worker process, which you can do by right-clicking an application pool and choosing Start. Instead of the SCM, some IIS plumbing is responsible for the launch. Instead of the registry, there's the metabase where identity is configured via application pool settings. Still, the procedure is very similar, and the result is a daemon process that continues to run even after you log off. COM is similar: It has an SCM and a configuration database of its own. A COM server can be configured to always run as a daemon simply by choosing any identity configuration option other than "Run as interactive user" or "Run as launching user."

Now think about what happens when a daemon process creates another process programmatically, say via `System.Diagnostics.Process.Start`. The new process inherits the creator's token, logon session, and window station. The new process is a daemon. Heck, the simplest way to write a program that runs as a daemon is to write a console application and launch it via the ages-old **at** command: **at 7:30pm mydaemon.exe**. This just adds an entry to the scheduler service's database, and the scheduler daemon will start the process. The major drawback here is that the **at** command will always start the scheduled process running as SYSTEM, which is a bad idea (see Item 4). This problem was solved as of Windows XP with the new **schtasks** command, with which you can choose an arbitrary identity for the scheduled process.

Daemons run in noninteractive window stations (Item 18), so don't ever do something silly like put up a modal dialog box from code that could run as a daemon (Item 29).

Daemons don't always have a user profile loaded (Item 19). Why should they? They only run under a single identity; they don't need a way to store per-user preferences. No daemon I've ever written has needed a `Favorites` folder! It turns out that the NT SCM does in fact load the user profile, most likely for historical reasons. If you configure an NT service to run as `Bob`, that service can use HKEY_CURRENT_USER, which will be mapped onto a registry hive in Bob's profile. However, the COM SCM doesn't load the user profile—apparently, the COM team decided this was a waste of time for a daemon. So, if a COM server configured to run as Bob tries to access HKEY_CURRENT_USER, it will end up getting mapped onto a default hive that's reserved for use by SYSTEM, where it likely will have only read permissions. The moral of the story is to avoid relying on user profile settings in daemon code. A couple of examples include secrets stored with DPAPI (Item 70) and certificate stores. Most Win32 APIs that both rely on user profiles and are typically used by daemons have a flag that usually contains the text LOCAL_MACHINE. These flags allow you to indicate that you're a daemon and you want to use a machine store, not a per-user, profile-based store.

Programming your daemon to use machine stores tremendously simplifies administration. You don't ever want the administrator to have to log in using your daemon's credentials; in fact, your daemon's user account probably should not even have the user right called "Log on locally" (Item 26). But if your daemon code relies on a user profile store, say for decrypting a DPAPI secret, and if the administrator is the one who is supposed to encrypt this secret in the first place, she'll need to be logged on using the daemon's user account in order to do this. And daemon accounts normally use long, random passwords that are very difficult for humans to type. This just makes no sense. So stick to machine stores in long-running daemon code!

■ 28 ■
How to Choose an Identity for a Daemon

WHEN CONFIGURING A daemon's identity (Item 27), you'll need to either use one of the built-in logon sessions (Item 17) or create a custom account. I've summarized the differences between the built-in logons in Figure 28.1.

SYSTEM is like root on UNIX. It's all powerful and is considered to be part of the trusted computing base (TCB). You should configure as little code as possible (preferably none) to run under this logon, as compromise of it immediately compromises the entire machine. (When you're part of the TCB, you're trusted to enforce security policy as opposed to being subject to it!) The other two accounts have low privilege, just like a normal user account, although they're granted SeAuditPrivilege and SeAssignPrimaryTokenPrivilege, allowing them to generate security audits and start processes in alternate logon sessions.

The two logons with network credentials can be authenticated on the network using the computer's domain account. So, for example, code running as Network Service on a machine named MAC26 in a domain called FOO is seen as FOO\MAC26 when making authenticated requests to other machines on the network, whereas Local Service is unable to authenticate and therefore is represented by a null session (just like J. Random Hacker) on remote machines (see Item 35 for more on null sessions). An important point: If the machine isn't in a domain or is in a legacy

Name	Privilege Level	Network Credentials
SYSTEM	High	Yes
Network Service	Low	Yes
Local Service	Low	No

Figure 28.1 Choosing a built-in logon for a daemon

Windows NT 4 domain, then **none** of these built-in logons will have network credentials.

Here's how to decide on an identity for your server process. If you need to be part of the TCB—that is to say, if you call functions that require the "Act as part of the operating system" privilege, as `LogonUser` used to require in Windows 2000—then run as `SYSTEM` or, even better, consider factoring your program into two parts, as I sketch out later. If you don't need high privilege, shoot for running as `Local Service` unless you need network credentials, in which case you should choose `Network Service`. Any privilege or network credential that you have but don't really need is one you're giving for free to any attacker that successfully compromises your process. Just say no!

If you find that you need a bit more privilege than what the low-privilege logons provide, don't break down and run as `SYSTEM`! And don't go changing security policy to elevate the privileges of the built-in logons either. Instead, create a custom account and assign to it exactly the privileges your daemon needs and nothing more. If you need network credentials, use a domain account. If you don't need network credentials, use a local account. Creating a custom account means more work at deployment time, but it's so much safer than running with too much privilege or raising the privilege level of a built-in logon used by many operating system services. Be sure to give your custom account a very long (20 characters at least) and randomly generated password. A human doesn't need to type in this password every morning to log on, so there's no reason not to do this! And change the password from time to time just as you would with a normal user account. (I postulated a couple of possible attacks against weak server passwords at the end of Item 20.) There are loads of tools to help manage passwords (including Password Minder, a tool I maintain that you can download for free from this book's Web site). Find one from an author you trust and use it!

If you use a custom account to run a daemon, make sure that it's granted the appropriate logon right. COM servers and IIS 6 worker processes use batch logon sessions and thus require the "Log on as a batch job" right, but services use service logon sessions and require the "Log on as a service" right. I remember the first time I tried to run an ASP.NET application pool under a custom account and was frustrated by the "Service Unavailable" error in my browser after I made the change. The problem was that the account I was using didn't have the batch logon right. Your best bet with IIS 6 is to simply add the account to the `IIS_WPG` group, which has the rights and permissions necessary to run most Web applications. If you run into this problem yourself, be sure to restart your application pool (just right-click it and choose Start) after fixing the problem.

Even when you do need high privilege, chances are that most of your process doesn't need high privilege, so consider factoring out the high-privileged code into another process. Figure 28.2 shows what this might look like. Use a secure form of interprocess communication (COM is a good choice here) and lock down the interface to the highly trusted code so not

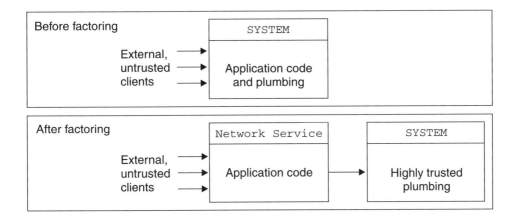

Figure 28.2 Factoring out high-privileged code

just anybody can call it, using role-based security (Item 56). Preferably only your low-privileged server process should be able to use the interface.

If you ever try to type in the name of one of these built-in logon sessions and the system acts as if it's not a valid name, try using the fully qualified name, including the authority (case doesn't matter):

- `NT AUTHORITY\SYSTEM`
- `NT AUTHORITY\Local Service`
- `NT AUTHORITY\Network Service`

Configuring the process identity for SQL Server 2000 is an example of where you'll need to type in the fully qualified name for `Network Service`. And if you're prompted for a password, just leave it blank for these guys.

■ 29 ■

How to Display a User Interface from a Daemon

D AEMONS (ITEM 27) NORMALLY run in noninteractive window
stations (Item 18). So, if you want to display a user interface from
daemon code, you've got a couple of options. Option one is to get yourself
into the interactive window station, and option two is to have a process
already in the interactive window station display a UI for you.

Let me describe a couple of ways to achieve the first option. An easy
way to put a daemon in the interactive window station (WinSta0) so it can
have its own user interface is to package it as a service that runs as SYSTEM
and check the box that says, "Allow service to interact with the desktop."
This tells the SCM to launch your service process in the SYSTEM logon session (Item 17) and to attach your process to WinSta0 instead of the noninteractive window station in which SYSTEM daemons normally run,
Service-0x0-0x3e7$. Another way is to dynamically migrate your
process from a noninteractive window station into WinSta0 by calling
SetProcessWindowStation, but ACLs (Item 43) on WinSta0 allow only
processes running as SYSTEM to do this sort of thing.

I'm not going to go into great detail on how to accomplish option one;
instead, I will implore you to avoid it. **Avoid putting daemons in WinSta0**,
especially if they run as SYSTEM. There's an inherent vulnerability to which
you expose yourself by putting daemon processes in the same windowing
environment as the interactive user: the threat of window message attacks

that are even nastier than the luring attack I described in Item 7. In the past there were successful attacks against interactive services, attacks that allowed the interactive user to inject and run arbitrary code in an interactive service's process. The most popular attack was named "shatter"[1] and basically involved sending a WM_COPYDATA message, copying exploit code into the address space of a highly privileged interactive service process followed by a WM_TIMER message, causing the service process to execute the exploit code. This elevation-of-privilege attack could have been carried out either by a user who had physical access to the machine or by a remote user logged in via Terminal Services. Microsoft issued a patch to change the way WM_TIMER worked to inhibit this particular flavor of attack, but that doesn't mean another avenue won't be found. Avoid doing this. Don't build interactive services. Having highly privileged code in the same sandbox as a restricted interactive user is just plain silly.[2]

What you should consider instead is option two: Use two processes instead of just one. One process must be launched in the interactive user's logon session and WinSta0. It should contain all the user interface elements you need, and it can connect to your daemon process using any secure form of interprocess communication you're comfortable with, such as COM.[3] Just don't try to use window messages to communicate; it won't work, as you'll see shortly. You should realize that, unless your daemon is running as SYSTEM, it's not likely to have enough privilege to start the GUI program directly. If you use COM, you can configure the GUI program to run as the Interactive User (Item 57), and the COM SCM does this tricky work for you. (The SCM runs as SYSTEM and therefore is allowed to do sensitive things like injecting code into someone else's logon session.) The best choice is to simply have the user start the GUI program manually whenever it's needed or, if it's always to be running, have it auto-start when the user logs on. This can be as simple as dropping a shortcut to the program in the user's Startup folder the first time the user launches your program.

---

1. Google for "shatter attack windows security" for more details.

2. I've heard rumors that Microsoft may eventually stop supporting interactive services entirely as a feature. This would be a good move, in my opinion.

3. You could also use .NET Remoting if you can secure it (Item 67). What you need is authentication support so you can limit who can use your interface.

If your GUI simply consists of a message you need to send to the inter-active user, you don't even need to write a second program. There's already infrastructure in Windows that pops up a message box on behalf of a daemon; it's built in to the client-server subsystem **csrss.exe** (which runs in WinSta0) and is exposed via MessageBox in the .NET Framework. Here's an example of some C# code from a daemon that asks **csrss.exe** to show a message box.

```
DialogResult AskQuestionFromDaemon(string text) {
   return MessageBox.Show(text, "Keith's Daemon",
                MessageBoxButtons.YesNoCancel,
                MessageBoxIcon.Question,
                MessageBoxDefaultButton.Button2,
                MessageBoxOptions.ServiceNotification);
}
```

Note the use of MessageBoxOptions.ServiceNotification. This tells **user32.dll** not to display the dialog box directly but have **csrss.exe** dis-play it instead. And you don't need any special privileges to do this. There are two things to note about this technique. First, the dialog will be dis-played even if no user is logged in at the console. This means that your dialog might show up on top of the logon prompt! If you don't want this to happen, use the MessageBoxOptions.DefaultDesktopOnly option instead. Second, you should know that **csrss.exe** queues up requests like these and executes them one at a time. So, if two threads (possibly from two different processes) make this call at the same time, only one message box shows up. The second message appears immediately after the user dis-misses the first message. Also note that MessageBox.Show won't return until your message box has been dismissed by the user. Don't be surprised by this.

You might wonder why you can't inject an arbitrary dialog into the interactive user's window station using a similar technique. Apparently Microsoft considered a simple message box to be a fairly benign beast. A daemon can't use it to ask the user for information (the classic attack here is to ask the user for his password—users fall for this one so easily). Remember, the idea behind window stations is to have a clean separation between daemons and interactive users. We want to prevent both daemons and the interactive user from elevating privileges by leaching off one other, especially highly privileged daemons or interactive users. Allowing even a message box blurs this boundary—I can imagine a daemon using a simple message to lure the user into taking an action that the daemon isn't authorized to perform. Remember that the weakest link in a secure system is usually that warm body sitting behind the console, the "wetware."

■ 30 ■

How to Run a Program as Another User

T HERE ARE THREE WAYS of doing this: via Explorer, via a command-line tool, and programmatically. Using Explorer, right-click the program you want to run and choose the "Run As" option. You'll see the dialog shown in Figure 30.1. If the "Run As" menu option doesn't show up in the context menu when you right-click, try holding down the Shift key on your keyboard while right-clicking. That should do the trick.

In case you've ever wondered what the other option in this dialog is for, the one that says, "Protect my computer and data from unauthorized program activity," it's designed specifically for people who normally run as administrators but want to run an application without administrative privileges. What this does is duplicate the caller's token into a restricted token that sets a special flag on the BUILTIN\Administrators group so that it becomes a "deny only" group. This means that, even though this SID will be in your token, it will never be used to grant access, but can only be used for permission denials (such as someone explicitly denying access to Administrators[1]). In other words, it allows you to continue running with the same user profile (Item 19) but demotes you to a normal user. If you find

---

1. If you think about it, this is a pointless thing to do because an administrator can change any DACL in the system by taking ownership of the object if necessary (Item 41).

Figure 30.1 The Run As dialog

yourself doing this a lot, maybe you should consider running as a non-admin (Item 8) on a regular basis!

To use the command-line option, there's the **runas** utility (you'll be prompted to type in a password, of course):

```
runas /u:xyzzy\alice "cmd /K title ALICE"
```

This command establishes a fresh interactive logon for `Alice` and executes **cmd.exe** with a command line of **/K title ALICE**, which sets the command prompt's window title to "ALICE." By default, her user profile will be loaded (Item 19), but if you're running a program that doesn't make use of the user profile, you can speed up the launch significantly by using the /noprofile switch.

Here's another rather trippy thing you can do with this command:

```
runas /u:SalesDomain\Bob /netonly "cmd /K title NetBob"
```

This runs the command prompt as you but with the network credentials of `SalesDomain\Bob`, which is really convenient if you are running on a computer that's not part of a domain but you need to use your domain credentials to access network resources. I used these tricks in Item 9 to set up a privileged command prompt for use when developing code as a normal user.

Finally, you can invoke this feature programmatically via a Win32 API called `CreateProcessWithLogonW`. Be careful about using this function, though, because it requires a password, and where are you going to get that? Don't be hardcoding passwords into your code, now! If you need to do this sort of thing, prompt the user for a password (Item 71) or, if you must store the password on the machine, do it as carefully as possible (Item 70). I show an example of calling this function in Figure 30.2 and use helper code developed in Item 71 to prompt the user for a password.

```
using System;
using System.Runtime.InteropServices;
using System.IO;
using KBC.WindowsSecurityUtilities;

class RunCommandShellAsAlice {
  static void Main() {
    StartupInfo si = new StartupInfo();
    si.cb = Marshal.SizeOf(typeof(StartupInfo));
    si.title = "Alice's command prompt";

    ProcessInfo pi = new ProcessInfo();
    string app = Path.Combine(Environment.SystemDirectory,
                              "cmd.exe");

    Console.WriteLine("Please enter Alice's password:");

    if (CreateProcessWithLogonW(
        "alice", // user name
        ".",     // domain name, or "." for a local account
        PasswordPrompt.GetPasswordFromCmdLine(),
        LogonFlags.LOGON_WITH_PROFILE,
        app, null,
        0, IntPtr.Zero, null,
        ref si, out pi)) {
        CloseHandle(pi.hProcess);
        CloseHandle(pi.hThread);
    }
    else Console.WriteLine("CPWL failed with error code: {0}",
      Marshal.GetLastWin32Error());
  }
```

continues

Figure 30.2 Programmatically starting a program as another user

```
[Flags]
enum LogonFlags {
  LOGON_WITH_PROFILE         = 0x00000001,
  LOGON_NETCREDENTIALS_ONLY  = 0x00000002
}

[Flags]
enum CreationFlags {
  CREATE_SUSPENDED            = 0x00000004,
  CREATE_NEW_CONSOLE          = 0x00000010,
  CREATE_NEW_PROCESS_GROUP    = 0x00000200,
  CREATE_UNICODE_ENVIRONMENT  = 0x00000400,
  CREATE_SEPARATE_WOW_VDM     = 0x00000800,
  CREATE_DEFAULT_ERROR_MODE   = 0x04000000,
}

[StructLayout(LayoutKind.Sequential)]
struct ProcessInfo {
  public IntPtr hProcess;
  public IntPtr hThread;
  public uint dwProcessId;
  public uint dwThreadId;
}

[StructLayout(LayoutKind.Sequential,
              CharSet=CharSet.Unicode)]
struct StartupInfo {
  public int     cb;
  public string  reserved1;
  public string  desktop;
  public string  title;
  public uint    dwX;
  public uint    dwY;
  public uint    dwXSize;
  public uint    dwYSize;
  public uint    dwXCountChars;
  public uint    dwYCountChars;
  public uint    dwFillAttribute;
  public uint    dwFlags;
  public ushort  wShowWindow;
  public short   reserved2;
  public int     reserved3;
  public IntPtr  hStdInput;
  public IntPtr  hStdOutput;
  public IntPtr  hStdError;
}
```

continues

Figure 30.2 Programmatically starting a program as another user (*continued*)

```
    [DllImport("advapi32.dll", CharSet=CharSet.Unicode,
            ExactSpelling=true, SetLastError=true)]
    static extern bool CreateProcessWithLogonW(
       string principal,
    string authority,
    string password,
    LogonFlags logonFlags,
    string appName,
    string cmdLine,
    CreationFlags creationFlags,
    IntPtr environmentBlock,
    string currentDirectory,
    ref StartupInfo startupInfo,
    out ProcessInfo processInfo);

  [DllImport("kernel32.dll")]
  static extern bool CloseHandle(IntPtr h);
}
```

Figure 30.2 Programmatically starting a program as another user (*continued*)

■ 31 ■
What Is Impersonation?

I MPERSONATION IS ONE OF the most useful mechanisms in Windows security. It's also fragile and easy to misuse. Careful use of impersonation can lead to a secure, easy-to-administer application. Misuse can open gaping security holes.

After an application authenticates a user, the application can take on that user's identity through impersonation. Impersonation happens on a thread-by-thread basis to allow for concurrency, which is important for multithreaded servers as each thread might be servicing a different client. In Figure 31.1, the server process is configured to run as Bob. It contains five threads, two of which are impersonating in order to do work on behalf of authenticated clients.

In this scenario, if one of the three normal threads tries to open a file (or any other secure kernel object), the operating system makes its access-checking and auditing decisions by looking at the process token. If Bob has the requisite access, the call will succeed and any audits will show that Bob opened the file. On the other hand, if the thread impersonating Alice tries to open the same file, the operating system makes its access-check decision based on Alice's token, not Bob's, so Alice, not Bob needs to be granted access to the file in this case. As for auditing, the operating system cares about both identities and will record that Bob was impersonating Alice when the file was opened. Of course, auditing must be enabled for any audits to be generated at all (Item 10)!

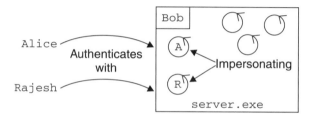

Figure 31.1 Impersonation basics

It may seem surprising that Bob can impersonate his client and actually become more privileged than before. This (and the reverse) is true. Bob might have very little privilege and have access to very few resources on his own, but think about the benefits of this model. If the server process is somehow hijacked by a bad guy, perhaps via a buffer overflow (Item 1), the bad guy won't immediately obtain access to lots of valuable resources. Instead, he'll immediately be able to use only the few piddly resources that Bob can access. Either he'll have to exploit another hole in the system to elevate privileges or he'll have to wait around until a client connects and use the client's credentials to access those resources (via impersonation!). And unless the client is highly privileged, the bad guy won't immediately have access to all the resources but rather only to the ones that that client can access. This can slow down an attack, giving your detection counter-measures (Item 2) time to kick in and allowing you to react and cut off the attack.

Imagine the opposite scenario, where the server runs as SYSTEM and impersonates incoming clients. If the server process is hijacked, it's pretty much over as far as any local resources go. And you should be aware that impersonating a low-privileged account, even the null session (Item 35), won't stop an attacker from simply removing the impersonation token by calling the Win32 function RevertToSelf before doing his evil deeds. This call requires no special privileges and no arguments. It simply removes the impersonation token from the thread, reverting the thread back to the process's identity.

You see, in the first scenario there's a trust boundary between the server process and the resources it's accessing. The resources won't accept Bob's credentials but rather want proof that an authorized client has connected.

There's also a trust boundary between the server process and the operating system. There's none in the second scenario! These trust boundaries become even more important when impersonation turns into delegation (Item 62).

None of this is perfect. Even when Bob is untrusted, he can still do bad things. He can collect client tokens (Item 16), which never time out and so effectively elevate the overall privilege level of his process over time. When Alice connects and asks to read resource A, Bob can instead choose to misuse her credentials and write to resource B. But don't let that dissuade you from running your servers with least privilege (Item 4). Security is a balancing act, and least privilege usually gives the defender an advantage.

Pitfalls to Watch For

As you've seen, impersonation can be a very useful tool in the hands of an architect. Implemention pitfalls abound, however, so read on to make sure you don't fall into one. First of all, impersonation puts your thread into a somewhat wacky state. You've got two identities, controlled by your process token and your thread token. In some cases, this can cause surprising behavior. For example, almost all my students are surprised when I tell them how process creation works. Say the thread impersonating Alice in Figure 31.1 creates a new process, perhaps by calling Process.Start. Alice will need to have execute permissions on the EXE being launched, but the new process will run with a copy of Bob's token. That's right—even when impersonating, new processes are naturally launched with a copy of their parent's **process** token. A special function, CreateProcessAsUser, allows you to specify a different token, but it's very tricky to use (Brown 2000a), and you can often accomplish the same thing more easily with the Secondary Logon Service (Item 30).

Here's another gotcha. When making an outgoing DCOM call, unless a rather esoteric feature called "cloaking" is enabled, COM ignores the impersonation token and uses your process's credentials to make the call. Thus a COM server sees Bob making the call instead of Alice in our example. Now in many important cases, cloaking is enabled by default, such as in any COM+ server process (**DLLHOST.EXE**) or in an IIS worker process (**W3WP.EXE**). But if you write a service, for example, and you don't call `CoInitializeSecurity` yourself (Item 52), cloaking won't be on by default.

Here's a nasty one. Imagine you're running a trusted server such as in our second example, which ran as `SYSTEM`. Say you're impersonating some low-privileged account and you make some call that happens to either create a new thread or switch threads to implement the call, perhaps via an asynchronous delegate (`BeginInvoke`). As of this writing, the operating system makes no effort to propagate the impersonation token to the secondary thread. Let me give you a classic example that lots of people have run into in ASP Web applications and that's still present today in ASP.NET. A trusted ASP.NET application is configured to run as `SYSTEM`. It's also configured for impersonation so that it impersonates each client as it performs its work. If part of that work is to call to an in-process COM component that's thread unaware (like all those VB6 components out there), there will be a hidden thread switch during the call and the component will run on a COM worker thread instead of on the caller's thread.[1] That VB6 component is now running as `SYSTEM`, and that's probably not what you intended!

Here's a rather esoteric gotcha in ASP.NET. If you write an asynchronous handler by implementing `IHttpAsyncHandler`, realize that if you want to handle the request on a worker thread, you need to propagate any impersonation token manually. This is the case if, for example, you set up your **web.config** file to enable impersonation for your application.

```
<configuration>
  <system.web>
    <identity impersonate='true'/>
  </system.web>
</configuration>
```

Manually propagating the token won't be that hard. Just call `WindowsIdentity.GetCurrent()` to get a `WindowsIdentity` that wraps the impersonation token (Item 24) in your `BeginProcessRequest` code, and communicate it to your worker thread. Before your worker thread executes the request, it should call `WindowsIdentity.Impersonate` and then `Undo`

---

1. If you know anything about the COM apartment model, here are the details: The .NET Framework runs in the multithreaded apartment by default, but VB6 components run in single-threaded apartments, which causes the often unexpected thread switch.

the impersonation after the work is finished. Assume that each request comes from a different user. Be absolutely certain that each request executes using the correct impersonation token. Don't get those tokens crossed!

On a final note, be careful to close kernel handles aggressively when impersonating. You see, handles to objects are like preauthorized sessions. Once a handle is open to a file, registry key, mutex, and the like, the system performs no further access checks when it is used. The handle itself is tracked by the operating system based on which permissions were granted when it was opened, so the system can ensure that a handle opened for reading isn't subsequently used for writing. But if our thread in Figure 31.1 impersonating `Alice` decides to open a file that only `Alice` has access to, nothing but careful programming prevents any other threads in that process from using that handle as well. If the handle isn't closed when `Alice` disconnects, it might "leak" and be used by the server accidentally when the next user connects. In a nutshell, handles are insensitive to security context changes. Start impersonating, stop impersonating, impersonate someone else—no matter: The handles you've already opened don't care (even with auditing enabled, the only time an event is normally recorded is when a handle is first opened). Oh, and you're not exempt if you're using the .NET Framework library to open files and other objects. Each `FileStream` holds a file handle under the covers, so call `Dispose` on those `FileStream` objects aggressively!

32

How to Impersonate a User Given Her Token

I F YOU HAVE A token for a user, it will be represented in the .NET Framework as a `WindowsPrincipal` (Item 24). You can impersonate that user by telling Windows to attach the token to your thread (Item 31). Here's an example from an ASP.NET Web application.

```
<%@page language='c#'%>
<%@import namespace='System.Security.Principal'%>

<script runat='server'>
void Page_Load(object sender, EventArgs args) {

  IPrincipal p = this.User;
  WindowsIdentity id = (WindowsIdentity)p.Identity;

  Response.Output.Write("<h2>Process running as {0}</h2>",
    WindowsIdentity.GetCurrent().Name);

  // impersonate temporarily
  WindowsImpersonationContext wic = id.Impersonate();
  try {
    // do some work while impersonating the client
    Response.Output.Write("<h2>Now impersonating {0}</h2>",
      WindowsIdentity.GetCurrent().Name);
  }
  finally {
    // restore our old security context
    wic.Undo();
```

```
  }
  Response.Output.Write("<h2>Once again running as {0}</h2>",
    WindowsIdentity.GetCurrent().Name);
}
</script>
```

To make this page work, drop it in a virtual directory that uses integrated Windows authentication and use the following **web.config** file to force authentication:

```
<configuration>
  <system.web>
    <authentication mode='Windows'/>
    <authorization>
      <deny users='?'/>
    </authorization>
  </system.web>
</configuration>
```

Let's analyze what's going on in the page's `Load` event. First of all, I ask ASP.NET for the client's token, represented by an `IPrincipal`. I then ask the principal object for its corresponding identity, which I need to impersonate the user. Note that this code assumes I've got a Windows token for the user because I'm casting to `WindowsIdentity` and this cast will throw an exception at runtime if I end up with some other type of identity (such as the `GenericIdentity` used by Forms Authentication). So this code is making some assumptions about its environment. It assumes that the Web server has been configured to allow Windows authentication to occur, typically using Kerberos (Item 59).

Before impersonating, I print out the current security context (Item 15) and, since I'm not impersonating yet, this should be the process identity (`Network Service` by default on Windows Server 2003 or `ASPNET` on older platforms). Next I call the `WindowsIdentity.Impersonate` method to ask the operating system to put the client's token (held inside the `WindowsIdentity` object) on my current thread. This method returns a `WindowsImpersonationContext` that allows me to `Undo` the impersonation later. I then enter a `try` block. This is critical! Changing security contexts is a dangerous business, and I need to ensure that my code doesn't accidentally leave the function without reverting back to my normal security context. In the corresponding `finally` block, I `Undo` the impersonation using the only interesting method on `WindowsImpersonationContext`. The output from the Web page looks like this on my Windows XP box:

```
Process running as XYZZY\ASPNET
Now impersonating XYZZY\Keith
Once again running as XYZZY\ASPNET
```

The reason the .NET Framework uses this class to revert impersonation is so that it can preserve the previous security context for the thread. For example, look at the following code snippet.

```
void foo(WindowsIdentity alice, WindowsIdentity bob) {
  WindowsImpersonationContext wic = alice.Impersonate();
  try {
    Console.WriteLine(WindowsIdentity.GetCurrent().Name);
    bar(bob);
    Console.WriteLine(WindowsIdentity.GetCurrent().Name);
  }
  finally {
    wic.Undo();
  }
}

void bar(WindowsIdentity bob) {
  WindowsImpersonationContext wic = bob.Impersonate();
  try {
    Console.WriteLine(WindowsIdentity.GetCurrent().Name);
  }
  finally {
    wic.Undo();
  }
}
```

This program should print out something like the following (assuming `Alice` and `Bob` have accounts in a domain called QUUX).

```
QUUX\Alice
QUUX\Bob
QUUX\Alice
```

But let's get real. You'll rarely want to write programs that use nested impersonation like this. Trust me. Impersonation is tricky (as I tried to point out in Item 31), and you should limit your use of it: Keep it as simple as possible wherever you do decide to use it.

My example used ASP.NET, but if you were implementing some other type of server that used Windows authentication, the procedure for impersonating would be the same. Get the `WindowsIdentity` for the user, and call the `Impersonate` method, being very careful to `Undo` when you're done. See Item 25 if you've got a raw token instead of a `WindowsPrincipal`; it's easy to convert back and forth between the two.

Impersonation in ASP.NET

ASP.NET provides a configuration option that causes all threads servicing Web requests in an application to impersonate by default. Here's the first way this can be done:

```
<configuration>
  <system.web>
    ...
    <identity impersonate='true'/>
  </system.web>
</configuration>
```

What this says is that the ASP.NET thread calling into your application should impersonate the same account that IIS normally impersonates in a classic ASP or ISAPI application: the `IUSR_MACHINE` account for anonymous requests or the client's account for authenticated requests.

A second way to use this element is to impersonate a fixed account, which can be useful if you're stuck using IIS 5, where all ASP.NET applications are forced to share a single worker process (IIS 6 has a much more robust process model). Here's how to impersonate a fixed identity.

```
<configuration>
  <system.web>
    ...
    <identity impersonate='true' userName='...' password='...'/>
  </system.web>
</configuration>
```

You should use the **aspnet_setreg** tool to set the user name and password attributes, as I describe in Item 70.

Regardless of which mechanism you choose, you'll eventually find the need to stop impersonating temporarily. For example, if there's a file that your ASPX page needs to read regardless of who your client is, you shouldn't be impersonating when you open it. This is one particular place where `WindowsImpersonationContext.Undo` can come in really handy (see Figure 32.1).

```
WindowsImpersonationContext wic =
  WindowsIdentity.Impersonate(IntPtr.Zero); // revert to self
try {
  // do some stuff while not impersonating
}
finally {
  wic.Undo(); // resume impersonating
}
```

Figure 32.1 Temporarily reverting impersonation

■ 33 ■
What Is
Thread.CurrentPrincipal?

T HIS HUMBLE STATIC PROPERTY of the Thread class is central to the way role-based security works in the .NET Framework, as I show in Item 34. It's used as a simple channel for communicating client identity and authorization information from plumbing to application developers. (Authentication is tricky, so we let frameworks like ASP.NET do this heavy lifting for us, and then we look for the results via this property.) Think of Thread.CurrentPrincipal as simply a hook that each thread exposes on which we can hang a user identity. It's just extra context information that the runtime helps us track.

I gave a security talk at Tech Ed 2003 in Dallas, and while I was there, a training company asked me to post some code in their booth as a quiz for developers walking by. So I posted the following code, which compiles just fine, and asked folks to enumerate what must be true about the system in order for the code to run without exceptions on Windows Server 2003. Here's the code.

```
// this process is running as Bob
Thread.CurrentPrincipal = new WindowsPrincipal(
  new WindowsIdentity(@"DomainA\Alice"));
new FileStream(@"c:\hello.txt", FileMode.Open,
          FileAccess.Read, FileShare.Read).Close();
```

It was interesting to see how many people thought that `Alice`, as opposed to `Bob`, had to have permissions to the file merely because I was setting `Thread.CurrentPrincipal`. It turns out that this property of a managed thread has no effect on how the Windows operating system perceives your code. This is not the same as impersonation (Item 31). `Thread.CurrentPrincipal` is simply a helpful property for keeping track of a principal, and is primarily used in server applications to track client identity. But the operating system knows nothing about it. So in my code `Thread.CurrentPrincipal` was a red herring—it's `Bob` who needs to be granted permissions to the file via an ACL.

One interesting property of `Thread.CurrentPrincipal` is that it propagates during asynchronous activities (well, usually it does, as you'll see shortly). Say you're doing work on thread 101 for `Alice` and so `Thread.CurrentPrincipal` holds an `IPrincipal` that represents her. Now you make an asynchronous call through a delegate, using `Begin-Invoke`. The worker thread that eventually calls through the delegate only does so after setting `Thread.CurrentPrincipal` for you. Thus role-based security continues to work even when you switch threads in this case. The same thing happens if you create a new thread: The CLR copies the `Thread.CurrentPrincipal` reference to the new thread for you. This is all based on the principle of least surprise, and it's a good thing. Contrast this to the way impersonation works in the underlying operating system, where thread switches don't propagate the impersonation token (Item 31).

As of this writing (version 1.1 of the .NET Framework), `System.Threading.Timer` is an asynchronous vehicle that doesn't propagate `Thread.CurrentPrincipal`. The same is true with `ThreadPool.QueueUserWorkItem`. So, if you use these low-level mechanisms, be sure to propagate `Thread.CurrentPrincipal` manually if you're using role-based security.

As an aside, the evidence-based security architecture in the CLR considers setting `Thread.CurrentPrincipal` to be a privileged operation.[1] Partially trusted code likely will not be allowed to change this property. This makes sense, as plumbing like ASP.NET will always be fully trusted while application code such as ASPX pages may run under partial trust.

---

1. The permission required is part of SecurityPermission. See the documentation for `SecurityPermissionFlag.ControlPrincipal`.

■ 34 ■
How to Track Client Identity Using Thread.CurrentPrincipal

T HERE'S A SIMPLE PATTERN for using this property. Plumbing sets it, and application code reads it. The most common example of this is the ASP.NET plumbing that sets `Thread.CurrentPrincipal`.[1] The page (application code) can then read the value any time it needs to make an authorization check against its client. Here's the basic idea.

```
// plumbing provided by a framework like ASP.NET
class Plumbing {
  ApplicationCode appCode;

  public void DoHeavyLiftingThenCallAppCode() {
    // plumbing...
    Thread.CurrentPrincipal = _authenticateUserSomehow();
    // more plumbing...

    appCode.RunBusinessLogic();
  }
}
```

---

1. The heavy lifting is done by various modules, such as `WindowsAuthentication-Module` and friends, during the `AuthenticateRequest` event; then the `Default-AuthenticationModule` sets up this property during the undocumented `Default-Authentication` event that immediately follows.

```
// application code provided by developer (e.g., ASPX page)
class ApplicationCode {
  public void RunBusinessLogic() {
    _methodOne();
    if (Thread.CurrentPrincipal.IsInRole("Staff")) {
      _methodTwo();
    }
    _methodThree();
    _methodFour();
  }
  void _methodOne() {}
  void _methodTwo() {}

  [PrincipalPermission(SecurityAction.Demand, Authenticated=true)]
  void _methodThree() {}

  [PrincipalPermission(SecurityAction.Demand, Role="Managers")]
  void _methodFour() {}
}
```

Note that `Thread.CurrentPrincipal` can be tested two ways: imperatively and declaratively. The application apparently doesn't care about the client's identity when calling `_methodOne`, but in this particular case it wants to restrict the call to `_methodTwo` so that it's only called if the client principal is in a role called Staff. Contrast this to `_methodThree`, which is always protected by a declarative attribute. This is logically the same as writing the following code at the beginning of `_methodThree`.

```
if (!Thread.CurrentPrincipal.Identity.IsAuthenticated) {
  throw new SecurityException();
}
```

In our case the CLR handles this check automatically because of the attribute on the method.

Finally `_methodFour`, which is also declarative, tests for the presence of a particular role. Keep in mind that if you're using a `WindowsPrincipal`, the roles are based on fully qualified group names, which include either domain names (for domain groups) or machine names (for local groups). You really don't want to be hardcoding machine or domain names into an application. But remember what this turns into.

```
if (!Thread.CurrentPrincipal.IsInRole("Managers")) {
  throw new SecurityException();
}
```

Nothing stops you from providing a custom implementation of `IsInRole` by simply implementing `IPrincipal` yourself. I discussed this idea in Item 15. If you're using Forms Authentication in ASP.NET, you're already using a different implementation called `GenericPrincipal`, and you can configure the roles however you like. In fact, version 2.0 of the .NET Framework provides an entire role management infrastructure for Forms Authentication (Brown 2004) and yet another implementation of `IPrincipal`.

Note that you can also place `PrincipalPermissionAttribute` on classes, which means that the restriction applies to all methods of the class, as shown in Figure 34.1. Be careful about using this attribute at the class level. If the class to which you apply it happens to have a static constructor (or, even worse, if it may get one in the future), realize that this attribute applies to the static constructor as well! Why is this a problem? Well, if a static constructor throws an exception, the class is latched into a mode where each future attempt to call the static constructor leads to the previous exception being rethrown (Brumme, 2003). So, if the first caller to use the class doesn't satisfy the permission demand, no future callers in the entire AppDomain will be able to use that class!

Figure 34.1 also demonstrates another gotcha: When you stack up multiple instances of `PrincipalPermissionAttribute` on a method (or even a class), the effect is an "OR," not an "AND." So the `Contractors-OrEmployees` method can be called by anyone in the Contractors role or in the Employees role. **You don't have to be in both roles to call this method**.

```
[PrincipalPermission(SecurityAction.Demand, Authenticated=true)]
public class AuthenticatedUsersOnlyClass {

  [PrincipalPermission(SecurityAction.Demand, Role="Managers")]
  public void ManagersOnly() {}

  [PrincipalPermission(SecurityAction.Demand, Role="Contractors")]
  [PrincipalPermission(SecurityAction.Demand, Role="Employees")]
  public void ContractorsOrEmployees() {}
}
```

Figure 34.1 More sophisticated uses of **`PrincipalPermissionAttribute`**

Watch out for this, because a misunderstanding here could lead to a security hole!

It's not rocket science, but this is what the .NET Framework calls role-based security. There's not a whole lot to it, as you can see. But the hooks are there to build some very interesting plumbing on top of what the CLR provides.

■ 35 ■
What Is a Null Session?

A NULL SESSION IS HOW Windows represents an anonymous user. To understand how it is used, imagine the sort of code you have to write in a server to deal with authenticated clients. After authenticating a client using Kerberos (Item 59), say, your server receives a token for that client that contains group SIDs, and you can use that token to perform access checks against ACL'd resources (Item 39). For instance, given the client's token it's quite easy to check whether that client should be granted write access to a file. We can simply impersonate the client (Item 31) and try to open the file for writing. The operating system will compare the DACL on the file with the client's token (that we're impersonating) to make this determination. The administrator can control access to files by editing their ACLs. But what if you also service anonymous requests—that is, those for which you won't get any token for the client at all? It's impossible to impersonate a client for whom you don't have a token.

This is where the null session comes in. It's a logon session that represents anonymous users, and here's how you use it. In your code that services anonymous requests, grab a token to represent the anonymous logon by calling the Win32 API `ImpersonateAnonymousToken` (see Item 37 for sample code). This is a null session token, and it has a user SID of ANONYMOUS LOGON and a single group SID, Everyone.[1] One group SID

---

1. In some cases the token will also contain the NETWORK SID as well.

conspicuously not present is `Authenticated Users` (all tokens other than null sessions or guest logons have this special SID, in case you were wondering). This is the key to using the null session. By granting access to `Everyone`, you're granting access to all users, both authenticated and anonymous. By granting access only to `Authenticated Users`, you're implicitly denying anonymous users. This simple model allows an administrator to use ACLs to control access to all users, both authenticated and anonymous.

Sometimes you'll find yourself using a null session when you don't necessarily mean to. For example, say `Alice` (a remote client) authenticates with you and you impersonate her (Item 31). If you attempt to authenticate with another machine while impersonating `Alice`, you'll very likely find that you've established a null session on that machine instead of establishing a logon for `Alice`. This is because `Alice` was happy to prove her identity to you but she didn't send along any credentials that you could use to prove to another server that you are `Alice` (note that this protects `Alice` from your misusing her credentials on the network). For more information on this topic, see Item 62.

Null sessions are quite useful when used properly, but historically Windows has granted way too much access to them. For example, many older Windows systems are configured to allow an anonymous remote user connected via a null session to enumerate user account names. Heck, once I know the names of all the local accounts on a machine, I can mount a brute force or dictionary attack against their passwords. If you read books like *Hacking Exposed* (McClure et al. 2001), you find that hackers often use null sessions to attack machines running Windows. So over the years more and more constraints have been placed on them. For example, there's a security option in the local security policy of Windows XP called "Network access: Let `Everyone` permissions apply to anonymous users." If this option is disabled (and it's disabled by default) null session tokens on the machine omit the `Everyone` SID. In this case, granting access to `Everyone` doesn't grant access to null sessions because they don't have that SID. Weird, don't you think? To grant access to a null session in this case, you need to explicitly grant access to `ANONYMOUS LOGON`.

The file server in Windows has some built-in limitations on null sessions. If you look in the registry under `HKLM/SYSTEM/Current-`

ControlSet/Services/lanmanserver/parameters, you'll find a couple of named values: NullSessionShares and NullSessionPipes. By default, null sessions can't access any shares or named pipes unless they're listed here.

Oddly enough, regardless of a COM server's required authentication level, null sessions are allowed in. The only way to block them from using a COM server is via the server's access control policy. For this reason, you should avoid adding the Everyone group to a role in a COM+ application, unless you really do want to include anonymous users. If you're not sure, stick with Authenticated Users instead, as I suggested earlier.

IIS has a unique way of dealing with anonymous users. Instead of relying on the null session, when installed it creates a special account on the machine called IUSR_MACHINE, where MACHINE is replaced by the machine's name. IIS keeps a logon session for this account lying around and uses it to represent any anonymous requests. This is very similar in spirit to the null session, and you've got to wonder why the IIS team isn't simply using the null session instead. The main drawback to the IIS approach is that the resulting token for IUSR_MACHINE contains the Authenticated Users SID, which pretty much breaks the whole idea of what Authenticated Users is supposed to represent. So much for consistency!

Here's a good practice you should learn. Get out of the habit of using Everyone when working with ACLs, and start using Authenticated Users. Only when you're absolutely sure you want to allow anonymous users should you consider using the Everyone SID to grant access.

36

What Is a Guest Logon?

B ESIDES THE NULL SESSION (Item 35), the guest logon is another way to represent an anonymous user. However, a guest logon differs a bit from a null session. First of all, to enable any guest logons on a machine you must first enable the local Guest account. Then you must assign it either a real password or an empty password. If you assign a real password, clients attempting to connect must prove knowledge of that password before being allowed a guest logon. If you assign an empty password, this proof isn't required and any client password will do.

An example will best demonstrate how a guest logon occurs. Take a couple of machines that don't have any domain affiliation, and say one of them has a local account for a user named Alice. If Alice is logged in to the first machine and she tries to authenticate with the second machine (which doesn't have any such account), and if the guest account is enabled on the second machine, a challenge-response handshake will verify that Alice's password matches the Guest password. If this is true, Alice will be granted a logon on the second machine. If the Guest account on the second machine has an empty password, the handshake still occurs; however, Alice isn't required to have any particular password, so it's not much of a challenge! She'll always be allowed a guest logon in this case. But note that if the second machine did have an account named Alice, a guest logon wouldn't even be considered—you'd simply see a normal challenge-response handshake to validate Alice's password. Thus guest logons work only for account names that are unknown to the server (and any domains it trusts). It's a rather sketchy mechanism that should normally be disabled (by disabling the Guest account). The Guest account is disabled by default on all versions of Windows I've seen.

If you do allow guests on a system, here are the SIDs the resulting token will have:

- Guest (this is the user SID)
- Everyone
- Guests
- NETWORK

As was the case with the null session (Item 35), Authenticated Users doesn't show up here, so this can be used to gate access to both null sessions and guest logons. By granting access to Authenticated Users instead of Everyone, you're implicitly denying null sessions and guests.[1]

---

1. Last time I checked, which was around service pack 4, Windows NT 4 had this wrong: Guest logins there did have the Authenticated Users SID, but SYSTEM didn't! Windows 2000 fixed these flaws, but please tell me you're not still using Windows NT 4!

■ 37 ■
How to Deal with Unauthenticated Clients

IF YOU'RE WRITING a server application and you wish all of your clients to be authenticated, you should read Items 35 and 36 to learn how to limit access to anonymous clients. One important approach is to avoid ever granting access to Everyone, preferring Authenticated Users when you want to grant a permission to all your clients.

If you want to provide service to unauthenticated users, and you won't be bothering to authenticate any of your clients, then you won't be performing any authorization (since you don't know the identity of any of your clients) and therefore this item doesn't apply to you.

But if you want to service *both* authenticated *and* unauthenticated requests, then, if you're going to be using Windows security (accounts, ACLs, etc.), you'll want to use a null session token (Item 35) to represent anonymous users. To grant permissions to all authenticated users, use the Authenticated Users SID. To grant permissions to all users, including unauthenticated users, further grant access to ANONYMOUS LOGON. Avoid granting access to Everyone because this SID won't always be present in a null session, as I detailed in Item 35.

To get a null session token, you need to call a Win32 function called ImpersonateAnonymousToken. Figure 37.1 shows some sample code that uses this function to grab the anonymous token and wrap it in a WindowsIdentity. It's unfortunate that the only way to get this token is

```
WindowsIdentity* AnonymousWindowsIdentity::GetAnonymousIdentity()
{
  HANDLE curThread = GetCurrentThread();
  HANDLE originalThreadToken;
  if (!OpenThreadToken(curThread, TOKEN_IMPERSONATE, TRUE,
                       &originalThreadToken)) {
    DWORD err = GetLastError();
    // only expected and acceptable error here is when
    // the thread has no impersonation token to begin with
    if (ERROR_NO_TOKEN == err) {
      // there's no thread token that needs replacing
      originalThreadToken = 0;
    }
    else {
      throwWin32Exception(S"OpenThreadToken", err);
    }
  }

  // it's really annoying that this is the only documented way
  // to get a null session token. I'd prefer a function like
  // GetAnonymousToken, Microsoft, in case you're reading ;-)
  if (!ImpersonateAnonymousToken(curThread)) {
    throwWin32Exception(S"ImpersonateAnonymousToken");
  }

  // I open this for MAXIMUM_ALLOWED,
  // because I've no idea how you plan on using the token
  HANDLE nullSessionToken;
  if (!OpenThreadToken(curThread, MAXIMUM_ALLOWED, TRUE,
                       &nullSessionToken)) {
    DWORD err = GetLastError();
    SetThreadToken(0, 0); // be sure to revert!
    throwWin32Exception(S"OpenThreadToken", err);
  }

  WindowsIdentity* id = 0;
  __try {
    // replace the original thread token
    // if there was none, this will simply stop impersonating
    if (!SetThreadToken(0, originalThreadToken)) {
      throwWin32Exception(S"SetThreadToken");
    }
    id = new WindowsIdentity(nullSessionToken, S"Anonymous",
                             WindowsAccountType::Normal, false);
  }
  __finally {
    // WindowsIdentity.ctor dups the handle, so we need to
    // close nullSessionToken before we leave
    CloseHandle(nullSessionToken);
  }
  return id;
}
```

Figure 37.1 Creating a `WindowsIdentity` to wrap a null session token

to impersonate (Item 31), because if you're already impersonating, if you're not careful (as my sample is), you'll clobber your existing impersonation token with the null session token.

Now, you might be wondering why I didn't suggest that you simply call `WindowsIdentity.GetAnonymous`. Well, sadly, this doesn't really get a token for the null session. It creates a `WindowsIdentity` object that doesn't have any token at all behind it, and it's completely useless as far as the Windows operating system is concerned. Avoid it.

You might also wonder why, when I created the `WindowsIdentity` object, I specified `WindowsAccountType::Normal` instead of `Windows-AccountType::Anonymous`. This is because of some (in my opinion, broken) code in `WindowsIdentity` that I've shown in Figure 37.2. If you call `WindowsIdentity.Impersonate`, it throws an exception if the identity object is flagged with `WindowsAccountType::Anonymous`, complaining that you aren't allowed to impersonate an anonymous user. Apparently whoever wrote this code knew nothing about the null session!

The way my code is written, the resulting `WindowsIdentity` will return `false` from `IIdentity.IsAuthenticated`, (exactly what you want for an anonymous user). However, if you call `WindowsIdentity.IsAnonymous`, it will return `false` as well, but there's not much I can do about that.[1] In any case, as long as you stick to the normal role-based security mechanisms that `IPrincipal` and `IIdentity` expose, which include `Principal-Permission`, you'll be fine. Impersonation will work as well. This will give you pretty much everything you need to represent an anonymous user in a natural way for the operating system.

```
if (acctType == WindowsAccountType.Anonymous) {
  throw new InvalidOperationException(...);
}
```

Figure 37.2 Peering inside `WindowsIdentity.Impersonate`

---

1. Why does this property even exist, you must ask? You'd think that `IIdentity.Is-Authenticated` would be good enough!

Once you've gotten a `WindowsIdentity` for the anonymous user as I've detailed above, you can use it in several ways. You can wrap it in a `WindowsPrincipal`, then drop that on `Thread.CurrentPrincipal` and use the .NET Framework's role-based security infrastructure to do your own application-level access checks (Item 33), you can impersonate it (Item 31) and access operating system resources that are protected with ACLs (including remote resources that allow null session access), or you can use a combination of the two!

PART III
Access Control

■ 38 ■
What Is Role-Based Security?

ROLE-BASED SECURITY IS a form of user-level security where a server doesn't focus on the individual user's identity but rather on a logical role she is in. This can be implemented many ways. One way is to simply install some local groups on the server machine that represents roles. The server application can then look for these group SIDs (Item 20) and make security decisions based on the groups' presence or absence. For example, if special privileged access to the server is restricted to members of the Admins role, a local group called APP_NAME_Admins can be created to represent that role.

What's nice about this simple role-based architecture is that it simplifies life for both the developer and the administrator because both rely on well-understood and solid operating system mechanisms to implement security. The administrator uses the tools built in to Windows to add users (and possibly domain groups) to the application's roles (which are themselves simply local groups on the server machine), and the server program relies on the Windows operating system to provide authentication and authorization information via Kerberos (Item 59). The server program reads these details in the resulting token it gets for the client (Item 16). The easiest way to do this is by calling the IsInRole method on the WindowsPrincipal representing the user. This principal object can be obtained in many ways, but most well-written server-side plumbing such as ASP.NET make it visible via Thread.CurrentPrincipal (Item 33).

In a simple desktop application, don't bother with `Thread.Current-Principal`, which is really only necessary for server applications. In a desktop app, you can get a `WindowsPrincipal` for the user running your application with one line of code.

```
IPrincipal WhoIsRunningThisApplication() {
    return new WindowsPrincipal(WindowsIdentity.GetCurrent());
}
```

Some systems like COM+ (Item 56), Authorization Manager (Item 49), and even SQL Server provide their own role-based infrastructure, so it's not necessary to create groups. But the idea is the same.

One thing to notice about a role-based system is that it's not as granular as an ACL-based system (Item 39). Security in role-based systems is centered around the user, not around the particular object the user is trying to access. But this also means it's less complex (count how many items in this book relate to ACL-based security and how many relate to role-based security!). There's something to be said for simplicity in secure systems, but let me defer to Ferguson and Schneier (2003):

> There are no complex systems that are secure. Complexity is the worst enemy of security, and it almost always comes in the form of features or options.

39
What Is ACL-Based Security?

S ECURITY BASED ON ACCESS CONTROL LISTS (ACLs) focuses more
on objects than on users (as opposed to role-based security, discussed
in Item 38). The idea in an ACL-based system is that each object will have
its own access control policy represented by a list of permissions stored in
an ACL (Item 43). Whereas a role-based system might control whether a
user in a particular role may access a set of objects in a certain way, an ACL-
based approach allows each individual object to control which users can
touch it and in what ways. An object typically grants permissions to groups
(Item 20), and an ACL-based access check requires comparing the request-
ing user's groups to the permissions granted in the object's ACL.

This leads to more complexity than in a role-based system, but also
allows for finer-grained control. When there are millions of objects, each
with its own ACL, something needs to be done to simplify the management
of these ACLs. In Windows this comes in the form of ACL inheritance,
which I discuss in Item 45.

Windows uses a discretionary, ACL-based approach to securing objects,
such as files, registry keys, services, and kernel objects such as processes
and threads. What this means is that the discretionary ACL (DACL) for any
given object is controlled by whoever creates the object (this user becomes
the object's owner). Ownership is a very interesting property that not
enough developers are familiar with, so I recommend reading Item 41 to

get a better feel for what it means. To learn more about discretionary access control, check out Item 40.

In a simple desktop application, you don't have to write any code to take advantage of ACL-based security. The operating system performs access checks each time a program opens a secured object such as a file (for example, the `FileStream` constructor will throw an exception if this access check fails). This is because the operating system ensures that each process has a token (Item 16) representing the user on whose behalf the process is running, and this is visible to the operating system each time the process makes a system call.

In a server application, things are a bit different. ACL-based security is still in force, but you've got to remember that your server application will be assigned a token based on how it's configured. If you configure the server to run as `Bob`, you'll have a token for `Bob` and so all access checks for your process will be based on `Bob`'s permissions rather than on those of his client. If the server wants to use his client's credentials to access a secured resource such as a file, it should impersonate the client before opening the file. But impersonation is not something to be taken lightly, so read Item 31 to learn more about it.

Whereas role-based security is an optional feature that usually requires writing some code (as shown in Items 34 and 56), ACL-based security is always present and really quite transparent to most applications.

◾ 40 ◾
What Is Discretionary Access Control?

IN MILITARY AND OTHER high-security computer systems, a policy of mandatory access controls is used. The goal in these systems is to restrict the dissemination of information. Objects in these systems (such as files) are assigned security labels that restrict who is allowed to access them. A label contains the required clearance level, which often ranges from unclassified to classified, secret, top secret, and so forth.[1] Users of the system are assigned clearance levels. A user with a clearance level of classified may read documents that are classified or unclassified, but may not read documents more restricted, such as secret or top secret. This same user may actually create documents that are secret or top secret, which creates an interesting situation—a user can create documents she can't subsequently read.

As you can see, with mandatory access control the user doesn't have control over her own documents. The system mandates who can read and write everything. Once again, remember the goal: Limit the dissemination of information. Figure 40.1 shows how the information is organized from a security perspective. It's easy for information to flow inward, where access is more restricted, but information flow is tightly restricted the other

---

1. Labels also compartmentalize data, to limit access to resources based on "need to know."

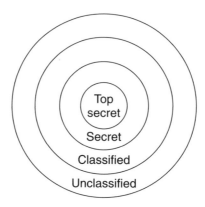

Figure 40.1 Mandatory access control puts perimeters around information.

way. To demote information from secret to classified, for example, requires special privilege.

Commercial operating systems like UNIX and Windows take a totally different approach, using discretionary access control. This puts control of an object into the hands of the person who creates it. For example, if `Alice` creates a file on a Windows server, she becomes the owner of that new file. The owner SID is tracked as part of the security descriptor that the file system (NTFS) maintains for the file (Item 42). The owner is implicitly granted permission to read the security descriptor and change the DACL for the file, as I detail in Item 41.

In layman's terms, discretionary access control means that each object has an owner and the owner of the object gets to choose its access control policy. There are loads of objects in Windows that use this security model, including printers, services, and file shares. All secure kernel objects also use this model, including processes, threads, memory sections, synchronization objects such as mutexes and events, and named pipes. Discretionary access control is so prevalent in Windows, understanding it is really important for anyone writing secure code for Windows. I encourage you to read Item 41 to learn how ownership works because, as a developer who likely runs as an administrator most of the time, you probably haven't had to deal with it much yourself.

■ 41 ■
What Is Ownership?

O NE OF THE MOST IMPORTANT components of ACL-based security in Windows is unfortunately also one of the most subtle and overlooked: ownership. Discretionary access control is all about ownership. If I create an object, I become its owner, and ownership conveys certain inalienable rights: the right to read and to change the object's access control policy. A car, for example, has a very simple access control policy: It's either locked or it's not. When the car is locked, it denies access to everyone, regardless of who they are. When the car is unlocked, it allows access to everyone. As the owner of the car, you hold the keys that allow you to change the car's access control policy. You're always allowed to do this. Of course, you can give your keys to someone else, but then you've given ownership away.

Windows carefully tracks who owns each kernel object, each file, each service, and so forth. Any object that implements discretionary access control in Windows has a security descriptor associated with it (Item 42), and two important parts of that descriptor are the owner SID and the DACL (Item 43). The owner and DACL are tightly related.

A funny thing about the owner SID is that it can be a user or a group. The latter is a special case that occurs only with the local `Administrators` group. Microsoft likes to simplify administration by removing as many barriers as possible from system administrators. In this spirit, the operating system has traditionally set the default owner SID for administrators to be the Administrators local group, which means that, if Alice is an administrator on her machine, when she creates objects the owner SID won't be Alice personally but rather the Administrators group. If the machine in question is used only by administrators, for example, it's highly unlikely that anyone ultimately will be denied access to anything because they all share ownership. It's as if they all have copies of those car keys I was talking about earlier. The owner SID won't be set to a group for a normal user though, and in modern versions of Windows workstation products, it may not even be set this way for an administrator.[1] Figure 41.1 shows an example of this special case behavior. One file was created by a normal user, the other by an administrator. Oh, and if you're not sure how to find these dialogs, just bring up the security properties for a file, press the Advanced button, and select the Owner tab.

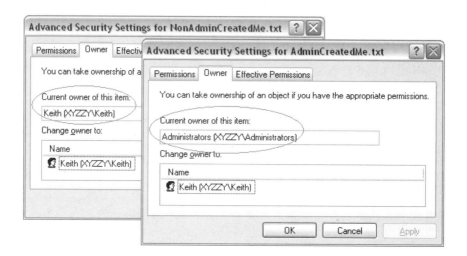

Figure 41.1 Who owns these files, anyway?

---

1. As of Windows XP, this behavior can be controlled via security policy (see the security option entitled "System objects: Default owner for objects created by members of the Administrators group"). On Windows XP, the default policy has changed: Administrators have personal ownership of objects they create, just as normal users do. On Windows Server 2003, the default policy is what it has always been: Administrators are treated specially, and they share ownership of objects by default.

Sadly, because most developers run as administrators (Item 8), they never have to deal with this notion of ownership and thus they never really learn about it. This is yet another reason to develop code as a non-admin (Item 9), because you'll start to see firsthand how Windows security works. Okay, I'll get off my soapbox now.

Technically, as the owner of an object, Windows implicitly grants you two permissions (Item 44):

- READ_CONTROL ("Read Permissions")
- WRITE_DAC ("Change Permissions")

So, if you're the owner of an object, you're always allowed to open it for one or both of these permissions, regardless of what the DACL says! It's like walking up to your car with its doors locked. The DACL on the car says everyone is denied access, but that doesn't keep you out. Using your keys, you can change that DACL to allow everyone in, then hop in the car. Once inside, you can change the access control policy again if that helps make you feel any safer.[2]

There's a very important permission that you should know about because it impacts ownership in a big way. Its friendly name is "Take Ownership," and the programmatic name for it is WRITE_OWNER. This is a permission that you can grant to anyone via an object's DACL, and it's specifically designed to be used to transfer ownership from one user to another. Here's a very typical example that shows how it works. The administrator of a system, say Alice, has created a file for some user, say Bob. She's gone to all the work of initializing the file and putting it in the right place, and now she wants to hand ownership off to Bob. So she edits the DACL on the file, granting Bob the "Take Ownership" permission. Bob can now bring up the security properties for the file, hit the Advanced button, select the Owner tab (as shown in Figure 41.1), and change the owner of the file by selecting his name from the "Change owner to" list box and pressing Apply. Now that he's the owner, he can change the DACL

---

2. Note that I'm conveniently ignoring the special case that anyone inside the vehicle can change its access control policy. Also note that there's a race here (a bad guy can jump in the car before you get the door locked again). It's not a perfect analogy, but I hope it helps.

however he likes. Note that the actual change of ownership was instigated by the new owner. I know of no way in Windows to assign ownership directly to someone other than by using `SeRestorePrivilege`, which allows you to set the owner to any user..

It may come as a surprise that when you grant someone "Full Control" over an object, you're also granting permission for a transfer of ownership! As a practical example, take a look at Figure 41.2 and note the subtle difference between the two permission grants I've given to `Alice`.

In the right screen, I granted `Alice` permission to read and modify the file, but I didn't grant "Full Control." What's so subtle about this is that, if you look in the "Advanced" dialog that enumerates the granted permissions (Figure 41.3), you'll see what "Full Control" really means. These dialogs show the permissions actually granted based on the settings in Figure 41.2. Granting "Full Control" is subtly different from just granting Read and Modify permissions: It also allows the user to change the DACL and take ownership of the object. So be wary about giving out "Full Control." It's bad enough to allow someone less trusted to change the DACL of your object, but taking it away from you permanently via an ownership transfer is even worse.

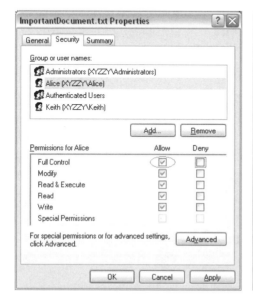 

Figure 41.2 Forfeiting ownership accidentally?

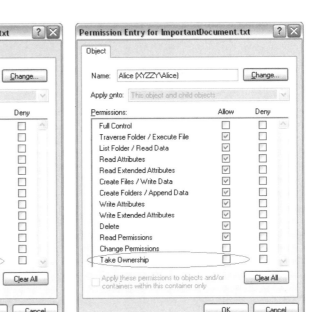

Figure 41.3 Subtle difference between Read and Modify and Full Control

There's one last thing to say about ownership. Windows has a privilege (Item 21) that allows its holder to wrest ownership away from someone without his or her knowledge or consent. It's called SeTakeOwnership-Privilege, and if it's been granted to you and you've enabled it (Item 22), you can open up any object in the system for WRITE_OWNER permission, which means that you can transfer ownership to yourself. Needless to say, this is a very useful tool in the hands of a trusted administrator but a terribly dangerous one in the hands of a bad guy. By default it's granted to the Administrators local group. See Item 46 to learn how to use this privilege.

■ 42 ■
What Is a Security Descriptor?

E ACH OBJECT PROTECTED BY THE Windows discretionary access control system must have some state associated with it to track its security settings. This little bundle of state is often referred to as a "security descriptor." Logically, here's what that state must contain:

- Owner SID (Item 41)
- Group SID
- DACL: Discretionary Access Control List (Item 43)
- SACL: System Access Control List (Item 43)
- Control flags

Windows doesn't document how this little bundle of state is physically stored for each type of object, but we do know that there's no global repository. So the security settings for a file, for example, will be stored as metadata somewhere in the file system (NTFS). The registry also must have some metadata for each key that can hold this state. These two examples you can't see because this metadata is hidden from view. But in other cases you can actually see some of these little bundles. For example, if you bring up the registry editor (run it as an administrator) and drill down into the service database to, say, `HKLM/SYSTEM/CurrentControlSet/Services/ClipSrv`, you'll see a subkey under the service's key called `Security` and a binary named value that contains this state, as shown in Figure 42.1.

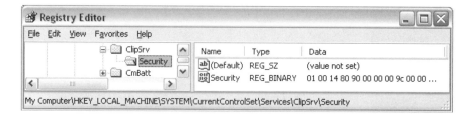

Figure 42.1 Security descriptor for the Clipbook service

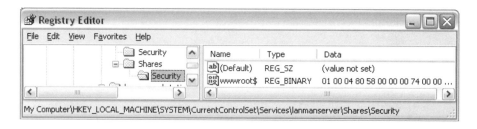

Figure 42.2 Security descriptor for the **wwwroot$** file share

What you're looking at is a serialized security descriptor that contains all the information I enumerated earlier (owner SID, DACL, etc.). The service control manager uses this information to figure out who should be allowed to start and stop the Clipbook service.[1] Similarly, if you poke around in the file server's section of the registry, you'll see that each share tracks its security settings in a similar way (Figure 42.2).

Here's what the components of an object's security descriptor mean. The owner SID is the user[2] that is always allowed to control the DACL of the object. In layman's terms, this means that the owner can control who is allowed to use the object and in what ways. See Item 41 for more about ownership.

The group SID, also known as the "primary group," isn't used at all by Win32 applications. It's actually there to support UNIX applications that run in the optional POSIX subsystem. If you're familiar with the UNIX file

1. Technically there are many other actions besides starting and stopping the service that are also controlled by the service's DACL: pause, resume, reconfigure, delete, etc.

2. The owner can be a group in one special case that I document in Item 41.

system (Stevens 1990), recall that each file has an owner and a group associated with it and that permissions can be granted to three entities: owner, group, and world. So the group SID is a way of tracking a group for each object, which allows support for UNIX-style permissions. As a Windows programmer, you can safely ignore this SID. If you want to write UNIX apps, pull out your Linux box, already.[3]

The discretionary access control list (DACL) contains a list of permissions granted or denied to various users and groups. The reason it's called "discretionary" is that the owner of the object is always allowed to control its contents. Contrast this to the system access control list (SACL), over which the owner has no special control. In fact, usually the owner of an object isn't even allowed to read it. The SACL is designed for use by security officers, and it specifies what actions will be audited by the system. I like to think of the SACL as the "Big Brother" bits. To learn more about how ACLs work, see Item 43.

Finally, there are two control flags that arguably should be part of the DACL and SACL headers but instead are specified as part of the security descriptor.

- `SE_DACL_PROTECTED`
- `SE_SACL_PROTECTED`

These flags control the flow of inherited Access Control Entries (ACEs) in a hierarchical system. Check out Item 45 to learn more about how this works. Note that there are several other control flags defined for a security descriptor; however, they aren't actually persisted with the object, and most are so historical in nature that you won't ever need to know about them. Consider yourself lucky.

As a .NET developer, you should also consider yourself lucky because version 2.0 brings a managed representation of security descriptors and ACLs to the party. The abstract base class that defines the basic functionality of a security descriptor is called `ObjectSecurity`, and two concrete derived classes represent security descriptors for simple objects or

---

3. Apparently some devs at Microsoft do some UNIX work on the sly: Many of them have stickers on their laptop lids proclaiming, "My other machine is your Linux box!"

container nodes in a hierarchy of objects: `LeafObjectSecurity` and `ContainerObjectSecurity`, respectively. The former is the class you'll usually use if you need to program ACLs (Item 47) on simple objects such as files, file shares, services, or kernel objects like processes and threads. The container class deals with container nodes in a hierarchical system, including folders and registry keys, where ACL inheritance (Item 45) is more of an issue. As you'll see in Item 47, these classes really simplify programming security descriptors.

■ 43 ■
What Is an Access Control List?

Access Control Lists (ACL; rhymes with "cackle") are used in two ways in Windows security. One type of ACL is designed to gate access, and the other is designed to audit access. The structure is the same in both cases, but the semantics of how the ACL is used differs. I'll focus first on ACLs that gate access, and then discuss how ACLs used for auditing differ. If you've read my discussion of security descriptors in Item 42, you'll recognize where these two types of ACLs are found. The DACL in a security descriptor is used to gate access whereas the SACL is used for auditing.

The basic structure of an ACL is shown in Figure 43.1. Each record in it is called an Access Control Entry, or ACE, and includes the SID (Item 13) of a single user or group along with a 32-bit access mask that specifies the permissions being granted, denied, or audited. Each entry also includes a set of flags used to determine how it participates in ACL inheritance, if at all. Inheritance applies to hierarchical systems such as the file system, registry, and directory service, and I'll talk more about it in Item 45. Before you read about inheritance, however, make sure you understand the basics in this item first.

Imagine a DACL on a file. Let's give it an ACE that grants access to a group, say Engineers. This is a "positive" ACE—it grants permissions. Let's also add an ACE that denies access to some users, say Contractors. This is a "negative" ACE—it denies permissions. Assuming the Engineers

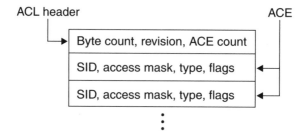

Figure 43.1 Logical structure of an Access Control List

group might include some contractors, this is an easy way to say, "All engineers except contractors are granted access." Figure 43.2 shows how this is represented in an ACL (I'm going to be omitting ACL headers in these diagrams for clarity).

Note the order of the ACL in Figure 43.2. Order is important because, when performing an access check, the kernel evaluates the ACL from top to bottom and stops as soon as access is either fully granted or even partially denied. Not all ACEs are necessarily evaluated. For example, if a user who is both an engineer and a contractor attempts to open this file for permissions 1 and 3, only the first ACE needs to be evaluated to discover that the user should be denied access. In this case the kernel stops evaluating the ACL and denies access immediately after evaluating the first ACE. If the ACL is ordered the other way, with the positive ACE first, the kernel evaluates the first ACE, sees that all permissions requested have been granted by that ACE, and stops evaluation, granting access immediately. So let me state the rule the kernel follows. **When performing access checks, ACEs are evaluated in order, from top to bottom, until either all requested permissions are granted or one or more requested permissions are denied.**

SID	Access mask	Type
Contractors	0x1FF	
Engineers	0x1FF	

Figure 43.2 All engineers except contractors are granted permissions 0x1FF.

As long as you use the built-in ACL editor in the Windows user interface, you're assured that deny ACEs will take precedence over grants because the editor puts them first in the ACL.[1] This means that you should use negative ACEs to surgically remove a subset of users from a grant, not the other way around. For example, it's easy to construct an ACL that says, "All authenticated users except Bob should be granted Read permission." Imagine what that ACL would look like: The first ACE would deny Read permission to Bob, and the second would grant read permission to Authenticated Users. Very natural. But just for kicks, consider the opposite policy: "All authenticated users except Bob should be denied read permission." In this case, we want to deny a large set of users and grant permissions to a small subset (well, Bob).

Let me say right up front that this scenario isn't supported by the built-in ACL editor. Technically the kernel supports this scenario if you're willing to manually construct an ACL in reverse order, so that the positive ACE comes before the negative one. Think about it for a minute and you'll see that this will work. If Bob requests Read permission, the kernel evaluates the first ACE, sees that he's been granted all the permissions he requested, and stops evaluating the ACL. For any authenticated user other than Bob, the kernel continues to the second ACE and denies access at that point. Once again, while the kernel supports this ordering, the user interface doesn't (the built-in ACL editor always puts negative entries at the top), so unless you're going to write your own ACL editor, I advise you to keep things simple by using negative entries to exclude smaller subsets from larger permission grants. In other words, use deny entries carefully, like you use salt when cooking.

An ACL with negative ACEs can be tricky to get right. Throw ACL inheritance (discussed in Item 45) into the mix and things can get confusing really fast. You should test these tricky scenarios to make sure you've actually achieved the semantics you want!

One last note on ACL order. Don't let the ACL editor's main page fool you—it's just a condensed summary of permissions in the DACL for an object (see Figure 43.3). First of all, it doesn't attempt to show the detailed

---

1. Inherited ACEs are always ordered last, so technically an inherited negative ACE can be overridden by a direct positive ACE. See Item 45 for the story.

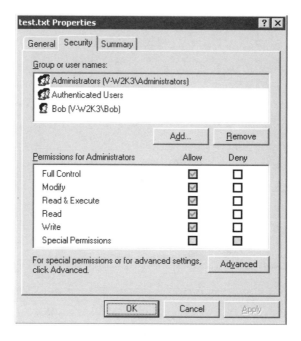

Figure 43.3 The "summary" view of a DACL

permissions being granted. Rather, it condenses permissions into generic categories like "Read," "Modify," "Full Control." Sometimes permissions don't fit nicely into these categories. I've even seen cases on older systems where an entry on the summary page didn't have any permissions checked at all! But what's often even more confusing is that the condensed entries are shown in alphabetical order. If you really want to see what the DACL looks like, you should press the Advanced button to get a more detailed dialog.

Figure 43.4 shows the "Advanced…" dialog from Windows Server 2003 (it looks a little different on Windows XP). This dialog provides access to the other properties of the security descriptor (Item 42) besides the DACL, and it provides a much more precise view of the DACL itself. Note that each ACE is shown, and you can see how the ACEs are actually ordered in the ACL (of course, if you press any of the sort buttons at the top of the list to sort by type, name, and so on, you'll have to close the window and reopen it to see the real, physical order again). Compare this with the summary page in Figure 43.3. When I really care about an ACL, I come to this page to look at it.

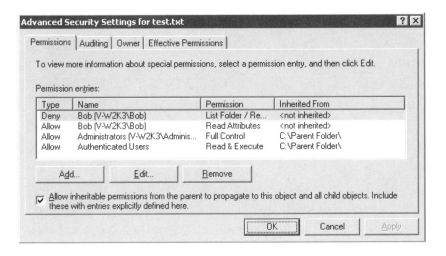

Figure 43.4 The "advanced" view of the same DACL

Each ACE contains a set of permissions. Permissions are represented as bits in a 32-bit binary mask, sometimes referred to as an "access mask." So, if an ACE contains a mask of 0x00000003, it's talking about permissions 1 and 2. Depending on the type of ACE, this may be a permission grant, deny, or audit. The layout of the permission mask is interesting enough to warrant its own separate topic, and you can read more about it in Item 44.

Note that the ACL editor does its best to provide a human-readable description of the access mask. For example, in Figure 43.4 the first positive entry grants Bob a single permission, "Read Attributes." This is easy to name. Similarly the next entry grants all permissions, or "Full Control." The last entry grants special permissions that are commonly granted as a set, "Read & Execute." These permissions are all you'll see on the summary page (Figure 43.3), which is another reason I recommend drilling into the "Advanced…" dialog when you want more than just a trivial view of a DACL. Sometimes you'll see the editor refer to "Special Permissions." There's really nothing special going on here; it's just that the editor doesn't have a stock way of representing a particular combination of permissions. This often happens in the summary page, which has very few named permission sets—typically "Full Control," "Read," "Write," and the like.

There are three different types of ACEs: permission grants, denials, and audits. DACLs contain only grants and denials, whereas SACLs contain only audits.[2] Because the most commonly used part of a security descriptor (Item 42) is the DACL, that's what is summarized on the main page of the built-in ACL editor. To see the owner and SACL, you'll need to head back to the "Advanced..." view, shown in Figure 43.4. Note the tabs for Owner and Auditing. In case you were wondering about the last tab, Effective Permissions, that's just a worksheet that lets you enter an account name. It then calculates the permissions someone with that SID would be granted.[3]

Let's take a look at the SACL now, which specifies the audit policy for an object. Each ACE in the SACL indicates a condition under which an audit should be generated. We'll use Figure 43.5 as an example. The first ACE says that if the kernel receives a request to open this object for one or more of the permissions included in the mask 0x1FF, and if the token used for the request has the Everyone SID, and the request is denied, then an audit should be generated in the security event log. Note that if the request is granted, this ACE is effectively ignored because it only audits failures. However, the second ACE audits both successes and failures. So if someone who is a member of Contractors tries to open the object for either of permissions 1 and 2, regardless of whether the request is granted or denied, an audit is generated. (If you're wondering what I mean by "permissions 1 and 2," check out Item 44.)

The SACL can be ordered however you like, because there are no "negative" ACEs in a SACL that can prevent an audit from being generated.

SID	Permissions	Audit success?	Audit failure?
Everyone	0x1FF	N	Y
Contractors	0x3	Y	Y

Figure 43.5 Peering into a SACL

2. Microsoft has discussed the possibility of adding new types of entries to the SACL, namely alarms, but don't expect to see them any time soon—it's been talked about since early versions of Windows NT.

3. Although this sheet seems to work reasonably well on Windows Server 2003, on Windows XP it doesn't consider permissions granted to the groups in which the user is a member, which is broken.

ACEs may be inherited, just as in the DACL, which eases the management of large hierarchical systems (Item 45). Also note that there's a switch you need to flip in security policy before the system even bothers looking at SACLs and generating audits. You must enable auditing of "object access" (Item 10). With this switch you must choose whether you want to generate success or failure audits, or both.

There's one other important thing you should know about the SACL. Only specially privileged users are allowed to even *see* it. Look at the difference between the acronyms DACL and SACL. The first is the "discretionary" access control list. The second is the "system" access control list. You see, the SACL is nondiscretionary (Item 40). Even the owner of an object (Item 41) has no special rights to it! The only principals allowed to read and write the SACL of any object are those who have been granted `SeSecurityPrivilege`, the idea being that security officers should be the only ones who control (or even know) what's being audited in a system. This privilege is granted to the `Administrators` local group by default, so in practice, unless you're running with admin privileges, you won't be allowed to modify or even look at the auditing settings for any objects in the system. Thus, if you bring up the "Advanced..." dialog and don't see the Auditing tab, don't worry that something is broken; you're probably just not running as an administrator. Good for you!

■ 44 ■

What Is a Permission?

THROUGHOUT MY DISCUSSIONS of access control and ACLs in this book, I often talk about permissions as numbers. For example, I might talk about 0x1FF as being a "set" of permissions, or granting "permissions 1 and 2" to someone. What I'm doing is being very generic and using literal access masks or numbered permissions. I'm not specifying what types of objects I'm talking about; I'm just talking about how access control works for all types of objects.

So let's make this concrete and look at examples of permissions for some real objects in Windows. Let's start with, oh, a registry key. Peeking at a Win32 header file called **winnt.h** shows us the following.[1]

```
// excerpt from winnt.h
#define KEY_QUERY_VALUE          (0x00000001)
#define KEY_SET_VALUE            (0x00000002)
#define KEY_CREATE_SUB_KEY       (0x00000004)
#define KEY_ENUMERATE_SUB_KEYS   (0x00000008)
#define KEY_NOTIFY               (0x00000010)
#define KEY_CREATE_LINK          (0x00000020)
```

Let's also look at the permission definitions for a thread.

```
// excerpt from winnt.h
#define THREAD_TERMINATE          (0x00000001)
#define THREAD_SUSPEND_RESUME     (0x00000002)
```

---

1. For brevity, I've omitted three permissions that are specific to 64-bit Windows.

```
#define THREAD_GET_CONTEXT              (0x00000008)
#define THREAD_SET_CONTEXT              (0x00000010)
#define THREAD_SET_INFORMATION          (0x00000020)
#define THREAD_QUERY_INFORMATION        (0x00000040)
#define THREAD_SET_THREAD_TOKEN         (0x00000080)
#define THREAD_IMPERSONATE             (0x00000100)
#define THREAD_DIRECT_IMPERSONATION    (0x00000200)
```

If you wanted to grant `Alice` permission to create a new registry key under some existing key, you'd edit the existing key's DACL and add an ACE (Item 43) that grants `Alice` the `KEY_CREATE_SUB_KEY` permission. Pretty simple. But look at those permissions again and tell me how you'd grant `Alice` the permission to delete the key she just created!

That's right, the registry subsystem doesn't bother defining a permission for deleting a key. That's because it's such a common permission (most secure objects can be deleted) that it's included as part of a standard set of permissions that are common across all types of objects. Here are the standard permissions that are allowed to be put in an ACL:

```
// excerpt from winnt.h
#define DELETE           (0x00010000L)
#define READ_CONTROL     (0x00020000L)
#define WRITE_DAC        (0x00040000L)
#define WRITE_OWNER      (0x00080000L)
#define SYNCHRONIZE      (0x00100000L)
```

Compare the numerical layout of the standard permissions to the specific permissions defined for registry keys. Note how the standard permissions all fall in the upper word of the 32-bit mask whereas the specific permissions are defined in the lower word. Notice that the same technique is used for the thread permissions. You see, each class of object is allowed to define up to 16 specific permissions, and they must all be in that lower word so they don't conflict with permissions Microsoft has already defined for all objects, such as the standard permissions shown above.

The standard permissions are quite straightforward. Let me briefly explain what they mean. `READ_CONTROL` ("Read Permissions") controls whether you can read the owner and DACL in the object's security descriptor. If you don't have this permission, you're not even allowed to see what permissions you do have! `WRITE_DAC` ("Write Permissions") and `WRITE_OWNER` ("Take Ownership") say whether you're allowed to change the object's DACL or take ownership of the object by changing the owner SID to be your own SID (for more detail, see Item 41). SYNCHRONIZE says whether you can wait on an object (this is most often used with synchronization objects such as a mutex or semaphore). By limiting SYNCHRONIZE access, you can prevent an untrusted user from grabbing a mutex that your program depends on and deadlocking you. And DELETE is pretty obvious.

Let's say you want to grant Alice permission to read a registry key. It would make sense to grant her a combination of the following:

- KEY_QUERY_VALUE
- KEY_ENUMERATE_SUB_KEYS
- KEY_NOTIFY
- READ_CONTROL

If you binary OR these values together, you'll end up with 0x00020019. This is the access mask you put into the ACE (Item 43) to grant Alice read access to the key. For an example of code that modifies an ACL programmatically, check out Item 47.

Look at the following access mask and try to figure out what it means: 0x00130000.[2] Now try to decode this one: 0x00000001. Surely this one is easier! Oh wait, I didn't tell you what type of object we're talking about. If it were a registry key, this would be KEY_QUERY_VALUE—a fairly benign permission to grant, at least compared to THREAD_TERMINATE! You see, given a random permission mask, you really can't tell what it means if you don't know the type of object to which it applies unless it simply consists of standard permissions, which are defined centrally for all objects.

With this in mind, think about a permission mask generic enough to grant read permission to any type of object in the system, including registry keys and threads. For a registry key, we want 0x00020019, as we calculated earlier for Alice. But for a thread we want 0x00020048. That's a very different mask. As you can see, because no two types of object can be expected to have the same sorts of permissions, at first glance it's impossible to treat objects polymorphically with respect to permissions. But if you

---

2. It means DELETE, READ_CONTROL, and SYNCHRONIZE.

look a bit further into **winnt.h**, you'll find the following rather interesting definitions:

```
// excerpt from winnt.h
#define GENERIC_READ      (0x80000000L)
#define GENERIC_WRITE     (0x40000000L)
#define GENERIC_EXECUTE   (0x20000000L)
#define GENERIC_ALL       (0x10000000L)
```

What do you think would happen if you added an ACE to a registry key's DACL that granted Alice GENERIC_READ? Think about it for a moment. If you guessed that the system would convert the access mask from 0x80000000 to 0x00020019 before storing the new DACL in the metadata for the registry key, you'd be correct. Each class of object in Windows defines a mapping from these four generic permissions onto standard and specific permissions. This allows us to make statements like, "By default, I'd like to grant full control to SYSTEM and myself for any object I create. Oh, and I'd also like Alice to have read access as well." Here's a text representation of just such a DACL:

```
grant SYSTEM 0x10000000
grant Keith  0x10000000
grant Alice  0x80000000
```

It turns out that Windows makes a statement like this for every process! Inside the token (Item 16) is a default owner and DACL that are used whenever you create new objects.[3] For example, if you were to create a thread, how would the system know what the DACL for that thread should look like? Well, it looks at this default DACL that's tucked away inside your token.

Here's what a default DACL would look like for me on my laptop:[4]

```
grant SYSTEM 0x10000000
grant Keith  0x10000000
```

---

3. By "objects" I mean any object that has a security descriptor (Item 42), such as a process, thread, or mutex.

4. If you want to do this experiment, you should download the Token Dump component from this book's Web site. I don't know of any built-in tool that shows this information.

So by default any new threads that I create, or semaphores, shared-memory sections, and so on, start life with DACLs that specifically grant my account and `SYSTEM` full control. Nobody else will be able to touch the objects I create, except highly privileged users such as administrators, who can ultimately control access to all objects using privileges like `SeTake-OwnershipPrilivege`. Note that hierarchical systems like the file system and registry prefer to use ACL inheritance to come up with a default DACL; this ensures that permissions remain consistent through the branches of the hierarchy. See Item 45 for more details.

The default DACL is one of the few mutable bits of data in a token. In most cases you shouldn't ever need to change it, as it's already about as tightly secured as it can be. If you ever find the need to adjust it, look at the Win32 function `SetTokenInformation`.

■ 45 ■
What Is ACL Inheritance?

W INDOWS USES SECURITY DESCRIPTORS (Item 42) with access control lists (Item 43) to track the security settings of sensitive objects in the operating system. Many of these ACLs are created and managed by the operating system automatically, such as those for kernel objects like processes, threads, shared memory sections, and so on. Although the programmer is allowed to specify these ACLs manually, it's rarely necessary. But an administrator usually needs to manage ACLs in places like the file system, directory service, and even sometimes the registry. Take the file system as an example. Have you ever counted the number of files on a file server? There can be hundreds of thousands, or even millions, of files, and every single one needs to be assigned an ACL. Windows uses a technique known as inheritance to simplify management of ACLs in large hierarchical systems like this.

One goal of ACL inheritance is to allow an administrator to focus on setting permissions for entire branches of the tree, instead of manually setting permissions one file at a time. Another goal is to avoid chaos.[1]

---

1. It wasn't until Windows 2000 that the chaos problem was addressed by tracking inherited ACEs in an ACL. Without this, the Windows NT 4 inheritance model wasn't as robust as it is now. See Brown (2000b) if you're curious how the Windows NT 4 inheritance model worked.

ACL inheritance occurs on an ACE-by-ACE basis, and the best way to learn how it works is to see it for yourself. If you're not in front of a computer, go find one. Bring up Explorer and create yourself a temporary directory on a local NTFS drive. Pop quiz: Who owns this new directory (Item 41)? If you're not sure, you'll find out soon enough. Bring up the property sheet for your new directory, click the Security tab, and press the Advanced button. Take a peek at the owner of the directory (it should be you personally, or possibly the Administrators group if you're an admin and running on a server version of Windows). Now flip back to the Permissions tab and uncheck the top checkbox in the dialog to block inheritance at this directory. You'll be prompted to either copy or remove inherited permissions; for now just click Remove. You should have a completely empty ACL at this point. Figure 45.1 shows what this looks like. Pop quiz: What permissions do you have to this directory? Would you be completely locked out if you pressed Apply at this point? If you're not sure, remember that you own this directory and review Item 41.

Press the Add button and provide your own account name when prompted. You're going to grant yourself full control to this directory for our experiments. Figure 45.2 shows the dialog you should be looking at now, after clicking the "Full Control" checkbox under the Allow column.[2] Note that I'm collapsing some of these dialogs so they don't take up so much space in the book. The real dialog will be bigger than mine.

Pay special attention to the combo box that I've highlighted in Figure 45.2. This is where you control inheritance for the ACE you're adding. Note that the default setting says this ACE should be inherited by all types of children, which helps ensure consistency as you add new files and folders. The entire tree below this directory (it's empty at the moment, but not for long) will automatically receive the ACE you just added; thus you'll inherit full control for all files and folders created in this branch of the file system. Now drop that combo box down so you can see all of the inheritance options (Figure 45.3).

---

2. If you're running Windows 2000 you won't have the "Full Control" checkbox, so you have to check the entire row of Allow checkboxes manually. Sorry.

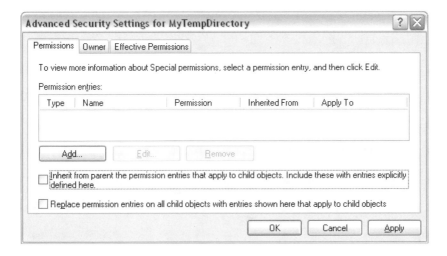

Figure 45.1 Starting with an empty ACL

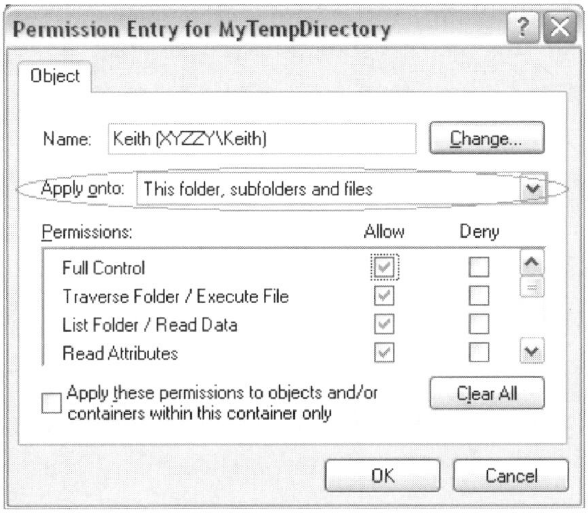

Figure 45.2 Adding an ACE

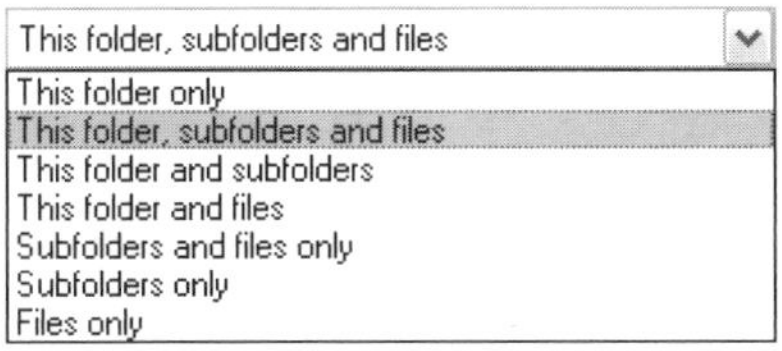

Figure 45.3 Inheritance options

This might look a bit daunting, but these options are simply the various combinations of the following three flags, defined in **winnt.h**:

```
// excerpt from winnt.h
#define OBJECT_INHERIT_ACE      (0x1)
#define CONTAINER_INHERIT_ACE   (0x2)
#define INHERIT_ONLY_ACE        (0x8)
```

If an ACE has neither of the first two flags, it won't be inherited by children—thus "This folder only" in Figure 45.3. You could call this a "non-inheritable" ACE because it will never propagate to child objects. On the other hand, if either one of those first two flags are set, we have an "inheritable" ACE. If both of the first two flags are set, we arrive at the default inheritance setting, "This folder, subfolders and files." If only CONTAINER_INHERIT_ACE is set, we get "This folder and subfolders," and so on. If you mix in INHERIT_ONLY_ACE, the ACE doesn't apply to this folder at all! It's just a placeholder to be inherited by children, which leads to the last three inheritance options shown in Figure 45.3.

Last but, well okay, least, is a fourth, rather esoteric flag, NO_PROPAGATE_INHERIT_ACE. If enabled for an inheritable ACE, it says that when the ACE is copied to any children, the child's copy should have all inheritance flags turned off, which prevents the ACE from flowing to grandchildren. This flag can be toggled via the checkbox at the bottom of the dialog shown in Figure 45.2.

Press OK to get back to the advanced ACL editor. You should now see a single ACE that looks something like Figure 45.4. Note that when you

Figure 45.4 A direct, inheritable ACE on a folder

select this ACE in the permission list all three buttons (Add, Edit, and Remove) are available. You could remove this ACE if you wanted to (not now, though).

Press OK to get back to the summary view of the ACL and note that there's no indication about ACE inheritance in the summary (that is, you can't tell which ACEs are inheritable and which aren't). This is yet another reason why you should go to the "Advanced…" dialog if you want to know what's really going on in an ACL. Press OK again to get back to your folder, and create a child folder there called A. Bring up A's permissions in the advanced ACL editor. Before you do anything else, note that the ACE you defined earlier on the parent directory has automatically propagated to this new child directory. Using the Advanced permission dialog, go ahead and add a second ACE to A that grants `Authenticated Users` the "List Folder / Read Data" permission. Accept the default inheritance setting for this ACE, and be sure to press Apply to commit the change. You should end up with something that looks like Figure 45.5.

If you click back and forth on the two ACEs, just selecting them in the list, you should notice something interesting. When you select the inherited ACE, the Remove button should be grayed out. You're not allowed to remove that one, but you are allowed to remove the ACE you just added. This brings us to one of the most important concepts of inheritance: When an ACE is inherited, it's marked with a special flag: `INHERITED_ACE`. So in Figure 45.5 the first ACE is "direct," that is, not inherited. But the second ACE has the `INHERITED_ACE` flag and is treated specially. In Windows

Figure 45.5 Direct versus inherited ACEs

2000, the only way you could tell the difference between direct and inherited ACEs was to look for a bright or grayed-out icon in the list box, but as of Windows XP the ACL editor uses some heuristics to show not only that an ACE was inherited but also from which folder it was inherited.[3] In figure 45.5 the editor is telling you that the "parent object" (the parent folder) was the one that defined this inherited ACE. Other times you'll see the full path to the directory where the inheritable ACE was originally defined—in other words, where in the tree this inherited ACE originated. My screenshots were taken on a Windows Server 2003 machine so yours may look a little different, but the idea is the same.

There are two reasons Windows keeps track of inherited ACEs. The first is to avoid chaos by keeping the flow of inherited ACEs consistent throughout the hierarchy. Although the user is allowed to add, modify, or remove any direct ACEs on an object, the inherited ACEs should always be managed by the operating system. Click back and forth on those two ACEs once again to see that the system is preventing you from removing the inherited ACE. You might wonder at this point why the editor seems to allow you to "edit" the inherited ACE, but if you click the Edit button, you'll see that the only thing you can do is add a deny ACE, which will be a new direct ACE. The original inherited ACE won't be modified. It can't be: That would break the model and lead to chaos. As long as the operating system ensures the consistency of inherited ACEs, we avoid chaos. Of course, there are low-level Win32 APIs that you can call that will allow you to create an ACL that completely violates these rules, and there are tools out there that use these gnarly old APIs, but I'll steer you clear of them!

To prove to yourself that the ACL editor does in fact keep inheritable ACEs consistent, back up to the parent folder (the temporary folder you created at the beginning of this item), bring up the advanced ACL editor, and edit the single ACE there. Remove the "Delete" permission from the access mask and press OK; then apply your change. Revisit the child folder A and take a close look at the inherited ACE. What you'll see is that the change you made to the parent has flowed down to the child. But

---

3. Take this information as a "best guess." It's inaccurate in some cases and there simply to help you find out how far up the directory hierarchy you need to go before you can edit the inheritable ACE that's been propagated down to you.

notice that your direct ACE that grants permission to Authenticated Users is still there. Because Windows tracks inherited ACEs with the INHERITED_ACE flag, it's very straightforward to keep the inherited ACEs consistent while leaving any direct ACEs alone. Here's how it works: Any time the ACL editor updates an ACL on a folder, Windows visits every child, deleting all of the old inherited ACEs and creating new ones based on the parent's new settings (note that this doesn't touch any direct ACEs on the child). If this results in a child's ACL changing, the same process continues down the tree recursively. Can this be expensive? Yes! Is it worth it? Absolutely. In large systems this helps an administrator cope with hundreds of thousands of objects. It helps avoid chaos by keeping the tree consistent, and consistency in security policy leads to better security!

Go back to the parent folder and edit the ACE again to grant yourself full control once more. Verify that this change has propagated to the child folder. Auto-propagation is a neat feature, don't you agree? It was introduced in Windows 2000, and you should know that it's not perfect. Here's the first problem with it: The Win32 API exposes two families of functions for submitting new ACLs. There are the "low-level" functions such as SetFileSecurity, and then there are the "high-level" functions called SetSecurityInfo and SetNamedSecurityInfo. If you ever need to programmatically update ACLs on folders, registry keys, or any other type of container object in a hierarchy, know this: **The low-level functions do NOT auto-propagate inheritable ACEs.** You should avoid them! If you use the managed classes being introduced in version 2.0 of the CLR to update ACLs, you'll be fine, because they do the right thing.

There's another tool commonly used to manage file system ACLs called **cacls.exe** (it ships with Windows). I'm sad to say that as of this writing it uses the low-level functions to update file system ACLs and so it doesn't auto-propagate inheritable ACEs as it should. This tool was written for Windows NT 4, and that's the only place you should use it until it's fixed.[4] Why do I mention it? Because it's an example of a program that runs on Windows but doesn't follow the modern inheritance paradigm. Using it can lead to chaos, as I'll show you here. I want you to see what happens

---

4. A newer version of this tool that comes with the resource kit is called xcacls.exe, but it suffers the same problem.

when you don't use the correct APIs to update ACLs in hierarchical systems like the file system and registry.

Bring up a command prompt and run the following command (substitute my path for the full path to your temporary directory):

```
cacls c:\MyTempDirectory /E /G Administrators:F
```

This command tells **cacls.exe** to edit the DACL on the specified directory and add a new positive ACE that grants Administrators full control.

After running the command, have a look at the permissions on your directory (use the advanced ACL editor, not the summary view). Note how the new ACE that's been added is inheritable, which seems reasonable. Press **Esc** a couple times to get out of the editor without accidentally making any changes. Then peek at the child folder's ACL. Note that the inheritable ACL from the parent didn't auto-propagate! So we've got part of the file system that's out of sync now. A scary thing is that any time the file system is in this state, it's a bit unstable. What I mean is that, if you were to make any change at all to the child folder's ACL via Explorer's ACL editor, suddenly the parent's inheritable ACE would auto-propagate, and you might not even notice it (and it would auto-propagate all the way down the tree). Leaving a user's file system in a state like this is a really bad thing.

Here's an even nastier example:

```
cacls c:\MyTempDirectory /T /E /G "Power Users:R"
```

The /T option tells **cacls** to recursively add the ACE to all children as well as the main folder. This uses the low-level API to add an inheritable ACE to the MyTempDirectory folder, and then it does the same thing to all the children, which means you end up with direct entries on all the children, not inherited ones! If you subsequently go into Explorer and remove the inheritable ACE for Power Users, it won't have any effect on the children because they each have direct ACEs granting Power Users read access. This is horrible. It may be hard to hear for some folks, but **cacls** is pure evil. It was written for Windows NT 4 and should have either stayed there or been fixed when Windows 2000 shipped. If anyone from Microsoft is reading, I would be happy to help work on a fix for the program if you send me the source code and corresponding unit tests.

One last note on auto-propagation. If at some folder in the tree you don't have WRITE_DAC permission (that is, you don't have the right to change the permissions on a folder), perhaps because someone else owns that folder, then clearly any permissions that *you* add upstream in the hierarchy won't flow to this folder. If this happens, you'll end up in the unstable state that I mentioned above while flogging **cacls.exe**. You see, if the owner of that folder logs in and happens to change its DACL, suddenly the permission that was blocked before will auto-propagate. To avoid this sort of unpredictability, you might consider blocking inheritance completely at any nodes in the hierarchy where ownership changes. I'll show how this can be done toward the end of this item.

So the first reason that Windows tracks inherited ACEs is to enable auto-propagation and avoid chaos, and I think I've pretty much beaten that horse to death. The second reason has to do with priority. Direct ACEs always take precedence over inherited ACEs, and this comes into play whenever you have negative (deny) ACEs. Let me show you with another experiment. But before you continue, clean things up a bit: Change the DACL on your temporary folder so that it grants full control to your account, and remove any other ACEs that might be there from our previous experiments. Visit the A folder and remove any direct ACEs on it as well. Folder A should now only have a single inherited ACE that grants you full control. Apply your changes.

Now for the experiment: Drill all the way down into your temporary directory tree and create a file called **alice.txt** in the A folder. Grant Alice read permissions to the new file. If you don't have an Alice account, create a temporary local account for her but give it a strong password in case you forget to delete it right away. Now surf back up to your temporary directory, the parent of the A folder. Add a negative ACE here that denies Alice all permissions to the folder, making sure that the ACE you add is fully inheritable ("This folder, subfolders and files"). You will be prompted with a dialog that provides a brief explanation of how negative ACEs work. Read it carefully and then press the Yes button to commit the change. Now answer the following question: Will Alice be allowed to open **alice.txt** for read access, or will she be denied? Try it yourself by compiling the following C# program and running it as Alice (bring up a command prompt for `Alice` using the technique I described in Item 30 and run the program from there).

```
using System;
using System.IO;

class ReadAliceFile {
  // TODO: edit this path for your system
  static string path = @"c:\MyTempDirectory\A\alice.txt";
  static void Main() {
    try {
      using (FileStream fs = new FileStream(path, FileMode.Open,
              FileAccess.Read, FileShare.Read))
      using (StreamReader r = new StreamReader(fs)) {
        Console.WriteLine("It worked! Here's the file:");
        Console.WriteLine(r.ReadToEnd());
      }
    }
    catch (Exception x) {
      Console.WriteLine("It failed! ({0})", x.Message);
    }
  }
}
```

Were you surprised by the results? Think about what the ACL must look like on **alice.txt**. It inherited some ACEs, one of which denies access to `Alice`. It also has a direct ACE that permits `Alice` to read the file. Don't negative ACEs take precedence over positive ones, as I described in Item 43? Generally this is true, but inheritance muddies the waters a bit. Here's the full story on DACL order. Negative ACEs do take precedence over positive ACEs, but, even more important, direct ACEs take precedence over inherited ACEs. Even within inherited ACEs, entries from parents are ordered before those from grandparents (Figure 45.6). So the closer in the directory structure you are to the object you're trying to control the more control you have, until you're at the object itself, where the owner of the object has ultimate control. It's all about discretionary access control, after all (Item 40).

Thus our direct positive ACE that grants `Alice` access is ordered before the negative inherited ACE from the parent (or grandparent) directory. This allows an administrator to set an overall security policy for a directory, but the object's owner ultimately can micromanage her own individual files without disrupting the flow of inherited permissions. Verify that the DACL

Direct ACEs	Negative ACEs
	Positive ACEs
ACEs inherited from parent object	Negative ACEs
	Positive ACEs
ACEs inherited from grandparent	Negative ACEs
	Positive ACEs

Figure 45.6 DACL order in the presence of inherited ACEs

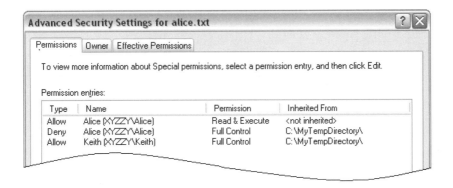

Figure 45.7 DACL order with inheritance

is ordered this way by looking at it in the advanced ACL editor (Figure 45.7 shows what mine looks like).

For a final demonstration, I created six temporary user accounts and used them to place both positive and negative ACEs through our little hierarchy of folders and files. As you can see, the resulting order is direct entries first, inherited entries from the parent second, and entries inherited from grandparents last. In each of those three categories, negative entries precede positive ones (Figure 45.8).

Even given the extreme flexibility of ACL inheritance, you might find a directory that really needs to diverge from the parent's access control policy. An example of this can be found in the operating system itself. If you look at the DACL on the `Documents and Settings` folder, you'll see that by default anyone in the local `Users` group is allowed to read from it.

Permission entries:

Type	Name	Permission	Inherited From
Deny	Child2 (XYZZY\Child2)	Full Control	<not inherited>
Allow	Child1 (XYZZY\Child1)	Full Control	<not inherited>
Deny	Parent2 (XYZZY\Parent2)	Full Control	C:\MyTempDirectory\A\
Allow	Parent1 (XYZZY\Parent1)	Full Control	C:\MyTempDirectory\A\
Deny	Grandparent2 (XYZZY\Grandparent2)	Full Control	C:\MyTempDirectory\
Allow	Grandparent1 (XYZZY\Grandparent1)	Full Control	C:\MyTempDirectory\

Figure 45.8 When parents and grandparents contribute

But underneath that folder lie home directories, also known as profiles (Item 19), and the contents of these subfolders must be protected more carefully. For example, the `Keith` subdirectory should grant `Keith` and perhaps `Administrators` full control. To ensure that this subfolder is protected from inadvertent changes to parent directory DACLs, a flag is set in the folder's security descriptor (Item 42). Two of these flags are defined, and when they're set in a security descriptor the system places a break in the flow of ACL inheritance at that point.

```
// excerpt from winnt.h
#define SE_DACL_PROTECTED    (0x1000)
#define SE_SACL_PROTECTED    (0x2000)
```

Look at the first checkbox in the "Advanced…" ACL editor (way back in Figure 45.1). Its wording has changed a bit between operating systems, but the idea has always been the same: The box is checked by default, and by unchecking it you're setting the `SE_DACL_PROTECTED` flag, thus blocking the flow of inherited ACEs into the DACL. At the very beginning of this item, I asked you to uncheck this box for the temporary directory you created. This was the only way to get rid of any inherited ACEs from the parent directory or drive. You may remember being prompted to either "Copy" or "Remove" the existing inherited ACEs. I asked you to remove them for our experiment, which left you with an empty DACL. But had you chosen to copy them instead, the ACL editor would have simply changed the inherited ACEs into direct ACEs and reordered the DACL appropriately.

After blocking the flow, realize that any ACL changes that occur upstream won't be seen at or below the point of the protected object. Just for kicks, imagine blocking the flow for every single directory on your file system. Oh the chaos that would ensue! You would have to manually apply access controls to every individual directory instead of letting the operating system flow permissions throughout branches of the file system automatically. Use this feature sparingly.

One last thing I should point out. Note the bottom checkbox in Figure 45.1. That's the sledgehammer checkbox. If you check it, when you commit your change you'll be warned to make sure you really want to swing the sledgehammer (Figure 45.9 shows an example where I checked this box for a directory called Y).

If it's not obvious from the wording of the warning, the sledgehammer walks to each child object, unblocking the flow (if it was blocked), removes any direct ACEs, and repropagates inheritable ACEs all the way down the tree, so that the only ACEs on child objects are those inherited from the node from which you swung the sledgehammer. This is really useful for synchronizing the access control policy of an entire branch of a tree, but it's really drastic and should be done only with the utmost care.

If you're going to use the sledge, realize that the recursive change you're applying silently fails for any folders that don't grant you the right to change their permissions. If you're the owner of the entire tree under that node, then this isn't a problem. So as an administrator, if you want this sledgehammer feature to be effective, you should seriously consider recursively taking ownership of that node before using the sledge. You can recursively take ownership via the Owner tab in the Advanced security settings dialog (for folders, there is a checkbox that allows you to make the change recursive).

Figure 45.9 You're about to clobber all child DACLs!

46

How to Take Ownership of an Object

TAKING OWNERSHIP of an object is easy when the operating system provides an interactive security editor. For example, to take ownership of a file all you need to do is bring up the security properties for it and press the Advanced button (as shown in Item 43). Then click the Owner tab and you'll see a property page that looks like Figure 46.1.

This user interface is pretty smart. Not only does it show you who currently owns the file, but, if you have permission to take ownership of the file either because you've been granted WRITE_OWNER permission to it or because you've been granted SeTakeOwnershipPrivilege on the machine (Item 41), this dialog tells you which accounts you may assign as the file's new owner. Note that we're talking about "taking" ownership here, not assigning it, so normally the only account in this list is the user account under which you're logged in. However, there's one special case: If you're a member of the Administrators local group, you'll see that account listed along with your user account. This is the only case where a group is allowed to act as an owner, as I discussed in Item 41. I was running under the built-in Administrator account when I took the screenshot in Figure 46.1, which is why you see those two accounts in the list box. If I wanted to take ownership at this point, I would just select one of the accounts in the list box and hit OK. Be careful not to do this accidentally if all you want to do is view the owner! If you're working with an object that

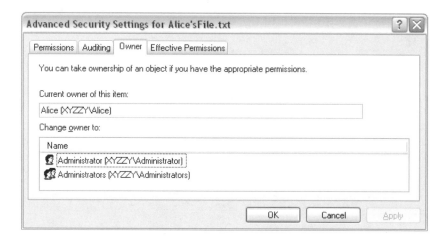

Figure 46.1 Getting ready to take ownership of a file

has children (like a folder or registry key), you'll also see a checkbox that allows a recursive change as well.

Although there are many different types of secure object, it turns out that very few of them sport an interactive security editor like the one shown in Figure 46.1. Think about a process, for example. It has an owner, a DACL, and a SACL, just like a file. But administrators don't normally bother modifying the security settings for individual processes because they're transient, so there's no built-in user interface for doing this. Windows services don't have a GUI for editing their security settings to control who is allowed to start and stop the service, or for auditing these actions. As of this writing, if you want to set the DACL on a service you need to either buy a third-party tool that does this or write some code to do it yourself.[1] Why am I talking about DACLs in an item that's dedicated to taking ownership? Because the only time you ever need to forcibly take ownership is when the DACL doesn't grant you WRITE_OWNER permission already. An extreme example is when you're completely locked out of an object—when its DACL doesn't grant you any permissions at all.

---

1. You could use group policy (Item 74) to make broad changes throughout a domain or organizational unit, but there's no built-in tool to do this locally on the machine where the service resides.

I remember back when I was first learning about Windows security, I accidentally locked myself out a Windows service. I had written some code to set its DACL programmatically so I could control who was allowed to start and stop it. But I accidentally set an empty DACL on the service, and because I wasn't the owner (SYSTEM owns all services) there was nothing I could do short of getting some code running as SYSTEM and granting myself access again. At this point, all I wanted to do was to delete the darned thing. As there wasn't a GUI to change the owner, I resorted to writing the code to do it programmatically. It was a good exercise in that it really drove home what ownership means. Here are the steps I had to take:

1. Enable `SeTakeOwnershipPrivilege` in my process token (Item 22).
2. Open the service object for `WRITE_OWNER` permission.
3. Change the owner SID to that of my user account.
4. Close and reopen the service for `WRITE_DAC` permission.[2]
5. Change the DACL to grant myself access (Item 47).
6. Close and reopen the service for `DELETE` permission.
7. Delete the service.

In version 2.0 of the .NET Framework, taking ownership of an object programmatically is almost trivial. Here's an example that takes ownership of a file:

```
using System;
using System.IO;
using System.Security.Principal;
using System.Security.AccessControl;

class TakeOwnershipOfFile {
  static void Main() {
    FileSecurity sd = File.GetAccessControl(@"c:\test.txt");

    Console.WriteLine("Current owner: {0}",
      sd.GetOwner(typeof(NTAccount)));
```

---

2. Remember, as the new owner of an object you're guaranteed only two permissions: READ_CONTROL and WRITE_DAC. See Item 44 if you're not sure what these permissions mean.

```
        sd.SetOwner(new SecurityIdentifier(
          WellKnownSidType.BuiltinAdministratorsSid, null));

        File.SetAccessControl(@"c:\test.txt", sd);

        Console.WriteLine("New owner: {0}",
          sd.GetOwner(typeof(NTAccount)));
    }
}
```

47

How to Program ACLs

N O BOOK ON WINDOWS security programming would be complete without showing you how to programmatically read, write, or modify an ACL. But frankly, before you run off and write lots of code to do this, consider whether it's really the right thing to do. Security policy is normally controlled by administrators, and programs usually can't make these decisions—even installation programs. Maybe what you really need is a graphical editor to allow an administrator to specify an ACL, and then you can simply persist that ACL somewhere until your program needs it. I like that idea a lot better than having people hardcode ACLs in their code!

To that end, I've uploaded some code to my Web site that I've been carrying around with me for a number of years. It uses the Win32 ACL UI interface (`ISecurityInformation`) to allow you to graphically construct any ACL you might need; then it spits out a stringified security descriptor (Item 42) that you can drop into a configuration file or even a registry key. It's called "EditSD," and you can download it from the Web site for this book. It's a reasonable starting place for an interactive ACL editor for a server application installation program, but you'll need to tweak it to customize the permission names and values, and integrate it into your installer. The language used to stringify the security descriptor is called the Security Descriptor Description Language (SDDL), and with one function call you can rehydrate that string into a security descriptor that can be applied to any object secured with a DACL (see Item 48 for more details).

Even with that tool, however, someone will still need to programmatically construct an ACL from time to time. For example, if you're writing code to automatically deploy a piece of software on a machine, you might need to set ACLs on files, directories, services, and so on. Before version 2.0 of the .NET Framework, you pretty much had to write this type of code in C++ because the Win32 API was full of nasty pointer arithmetic, scary-looking casts, and so on. But version 2.0 introduces a new namespace (System.Security.AccessControl) that brings access control programming to the managed world (I still recommend you avoid constructing ACLs in code if you can).

The sample code in Figure 47.1 reads an ACL from a file, prints it out, and then grants ACME\Bob permission to delete the file. If you've ever done ACL programming in C++, you'll seriously appreciate the simplicity of this code. The corresponding sample in C++ would require an order of magnitude more time and code.

```
using System;
using System.IO;
using System.Security.Principal;
using System.Security.AccessControl;

class ModifyFileDacl {
  const string path     = @"c:\work\test.txt";
  const string userName = @"ACME\Bob";

  static void Main() {
    FileSecurity sd = File.GetAccessControl(path);
    PrintOwerAndDACL(sd);

    Console.WriteLine("Granting DELETE to {0}", userName);
    ModifyDACL(sd);
    File.SetAccessControl(path, sd);

    PrintOwerAndDACL(sd);
  }

  static void PrintOwerAndDACL(FileSecurity sd) {
    Console.WriteLine("Owner: {0}", sd.GetOwner(typeof(NTAccount)));

    // rule represents an ACE
```

continues

```
    foreach (FileSystemAccessRule rule in
      sd.GetAccessRules(true, true, typeof(NTAccount))) {
      PrintACE(rule);
    }
  }

  static void PrintACE(FileSystemAccessRule rule) {
    Console.WriteLine("{0} {1} to {2} ({3})",
      AccessControlType.Allow == rule.AccessControlType ?
      "grant" : "deny",
      rule.FileSystemRights, // access permission mask
      rule.IdentityReference,
      rule.IsInherited ? "inherited" : "direct");
  }

  static void ModifyDACL(FileSecurity sd) {
    FileSystemAccessRule ace = new FileSystemAccessRule(
      new NTAccount(userName),
      FileSystemRights.Delete,
      AccessControlType.Allow);
    sd.AddAccessRule(ace);
  }
}
```

Figure 47.1 ACL programming in version 2.0 of the .NET Framework

The entire `AccessControl` namespace was redesigned from the ground up between the alpha (when I originally wrote this item) and beta 1 (that I'm looking at now as I make final edits). The beta 1 programming model, shown in Figure 47.1, is much cleaner than the alpha version, but doesn't cover as broad a range of objects. My original sample showed how to change the DACL for a service, but that's no longer possible in the beta. This doesn't discourage me in the least, because the new design is so much easier to use, and it only took me about 15 minutes or so to extend the object model to support my original example: setting the DACL for a service. Keep your eyes on my Security Briefs column in *MSDN Magazine,* as I'll surely be writing about this in the future as this namespace develops.

■ 48 ■

How to Persist a Security Descriptor

S OMETIMES IT'S NECESSARY to store security descriptors for later use. For example, when deploying software in an enterprise setting, it might be necessary to set ACLs on files, directories, or even other types of objects like services or registry keys from an installation program that may run on many different machines. While you could hardwire these ACL modifications into your code (I show an example of this in Item 47), it's usually best to provide a user interface that allows an administrator to construct the required ACLs graphically, using a familiar tool, and then simply persist these ACLs for later deployment.[1] To see an example of such a tool, download the "EditSD" sample from the book's Web site.

There are two ways to persist a Windows security descriptor: in binary form and in text form, the latter of which uses a language called Security Descriptor Description Language (SDDL). Version 2.0 of the .NET Framework provides support for round-tripping a security descriptor to and from

---

1. Keep group scope in mind (Item 20) if you decide to do this sort of thing. For example, you should discourage (or, better yet, prevent) the administrator from using custom local groups, which don't have any meaning when deployed to another machine. However, the built-in local groups (Administrators, Users, etc.) are the same everywhere and are safe to use. The same thing goes with domain local groups, which have meaning only in the domain where they're defined.

its text (SDDL) form. Here's some code that shows how to take SDDL as input and apply the security descriptor it represents to some different types of objects.

```
void ApplySDDLToFile(string sddl, string path) {
  FileSecurity sd = new FileSecurity();
  sd.SetSecurityDescriptorSddlForm(sddl);
  File.SetAccessControl(path, sd);
}


void ApplySDDLToRegistryKey(string sddl, RegistryKey key) {
  RegistrySecurity sd = new RegistrySecurity();
  sd.SetSecurityDescriptorSddlForm(sddl);
  key.SetAccessControl(sd);
}


void ApplySDDLToMutex(string sddl, Mutex mutex) {
  MutexSecurity sd = new MutexSecurity();
  sd.SetSecurityDescriptorSddlForm(sddl);
  mutex.SetAccessControl(sd);
}
```

Where can you store SDDL? In a text file, registry key, XML configuration file, and so on. Just make sure to consider attacks against these locations in your threat model (Item 3). Here's some code that shows how to stringify a security descriptor, after which you can persist the string to any appropriate media.

```
string GetSDDL(ObjectSecurity sd) {
  return sd.GetSecurityDescriptorSddlForm(
    AccessControlSections.Owner |
    AccessControlSections.Group |   // primary group
    AccessControlSections.Access); // DACL
}
```

■ 49 ■
What Is
Authorization Manager?

R OLE-BASED SECURITY has been evolving on the Windows platform since the first release of Windows NT. Using roles, the operating system can determine whether a process is privileged by checking
the security context for a group called BUILTIN\Administrators. The
operating system makes decisions based on this logical role (such as
whether to let you install services or device drivers). After installing the
operating system, you get to choose who will assume this role by adding
them to the Administrators group.

Microsoft Transaction Services (MTS) and COM+ tried to make role-
based security palatable for application developers, providing a simple
role-based authorization infrastructure for COM servers. The goal was to
enable a trusted subsystem model for multitier server applications, where
an application server is trusted by back-end resources to authorize requests. By performing authorization early, you avoid having to delegate
client credentials to back-end servers. Delegation wasn't such a viable
option before Windows Server 2003 because it could not be constrained in
space (see Item 62 for more details).

If you've been looking for a general-purpose authorization solution in
the middle tier, your search may very well be over.

Introducing Authorization Manager

Authorization Manager (commonly known as AzMan) is a general-purpose role-based security architecture for Windows. AzMan is not tied to COM+, so it can be used in any application that needs role-based authorization, including ASP.NET Web apps or Web Services, client-server systems based on .NET Remoting, and so on. As of this writing, Authorization Manager is available only on Windows Server 2003, service pack 4 for Windows 2000, and is slated to ship in a future service pack for Windows XP.

There are two parts to AzMan: a runtime and an administration UI. The runtime, provided by **AZROLES.DLL**, exposes a set of COM interfaces used by applications that employ role-based security. The administration UI is an MMC snap-in that you can try out by running **AZMAN.MSC** or by adding the Authorization Manager snap-in to your MMC console of choice. Note that you'll need to install the Windows Server 2003 Administration Tools Pack[1] in order to administer AzMan on older platforms such as Windows XP and Windows 2000.

The first thing you'll notice when you run the AzMan admin tool shown in Figure 49.1 is that it's much more complex than what COM+ offered. You no longer have only roles and role assignments. You now have low-level operations that can be assigned to tasks, which can then be assigned to roles. Tasks can include other tasks, and roles can include other roles. This hierarchical approach helps cap the seemingly unbounded set of roles needed in today's complex applications.

Here's how tasks and roles are created. The application designer defines the entire set of low-level operations that are considered security sensitive. The designer then defines a set of tasks that map onto those operations. Tasks were designed to be understandable by business analysts, so a given task is always composed of one or more low-level operations. If a user is granted permission to perform a task, he or she is granted permission to

---

1. Download from *http://www.microsoft.com/downloads/details.aspx?familyid= c16ae515-c8f4-47ef-a1e4-a8dcbacff8e3&displaylang=en*.

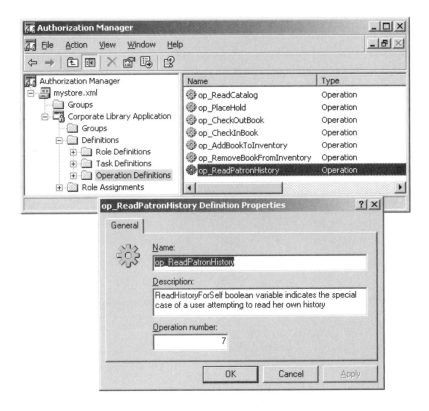

Figure 49.1 Authorization Manager

all operations in it. As an example, a task named "Submit purchase order" might consist of the following operations: "Acquire next PO number," "Enqueue PO," and "Send notification." Of course, you could always simply map each task to a single operation to keep things as simple as possible, but the flexibility of separating tasks and operations is available if you need it.

Once the tasks and operations are defined, you can start coding and include calls to the AzMan runtime any time a sensitive operation needs to be performed. This call is `IAzClientContext.AccessCheck`, and I'll show an example of its usage shortly.

At deployment time, the application setup program sets up an AzMan store either as part of Active Directory or in a simple XML file, and installs the basic low-level operations and tasks. The administrator uses the AzMan snap-in to see definitions and descriptions of the tasks for the application. She then defines roles that make sense for her organization. Just as a task is defined as a set of low-level operations, roles are usually defined as a set of tasks. The administrator can then assign users and groups to those roles. In fact, the administrator's main job in maintaining the application from here on out will be adding and removing users from roles as people join or leave the company or change job titles.

So far, I've focused on the application developer and the administrator, but there may actually be a third person helping with the deployment: the business logic scripter. Every task can have a script associated with it. The idea here is to find dynamic security decisions typically made through calls to `IsCallerInRole` and move them out of application code and into a place where an administrator can make changes to an application's security policy without having to modify and recompile code.

A Sample App: The Corporate Library

Let's look at an example. Imagine you're building a system to manage a company library. You need to be able to manage the book inventory, check books in and out, and so on. You use AzMan to implement role-based security.

First, you need to make a list of the sensitive operations that appear in your design:

- Read catalog
- Place hold (for self or another)
- Check out book
- Check in book
- Add book to inventory
- Remove book from inventory
- Read patron history (for self or another)

Note that a couple of operations are sensitive to information that you'll only have at runtime. For instance, when attempting to read a patron's history, the application must provide contextual information indicating whether the user is trying to access his own history or that of someone else. While prototyping, you can use the AzMan snap-in to add these operations to a simple XML store. Figure 49.1 shows what this looks like.

If you want to try following along on your own, run **AZMAN.MSC**, and make sure you're in developer mode via the Action | Options menu. Create a new store in an XML file, then create a new application in it. Next, add the operations one by one, giving them each a name and a unique integer that represents the operation number. This number is how the application developer identifies operations in calls to `AccessCheck`. Note that in naming operations I've encoded the names with the prefix "op." This is simply to avoid naming collisions later when creating tasks and roles, because these names all come from the same pool and must be unique.

The AzMan snap-in operates in two modes: developer and administrator. In administrator mode, you don't have the option of creating stores or applications and you aren't allowed to muck with the low-level operation definitions that the application code relies on. Frankly, nothing stops the system administrator from entering developer mode and doing these things, but the point is that in administrator mode the number of options in the UI is reduced to simplify the administrator's life and to help avoid mistakes. The next step is to define a set of tasks that map to these low-level operations so the administrator will have an easy job defining roles. Because you kept your list of operations simple, you can define a single task for each one. There's a good reason to keep things simple unless you absolutely need more complexity, and it has to do with business logic scripts—but more on that later. For now, let's define a list of tasks that are basically the same as the operations. Figure 49.2 shows what it looks like in AzMan when you edit a task definition.

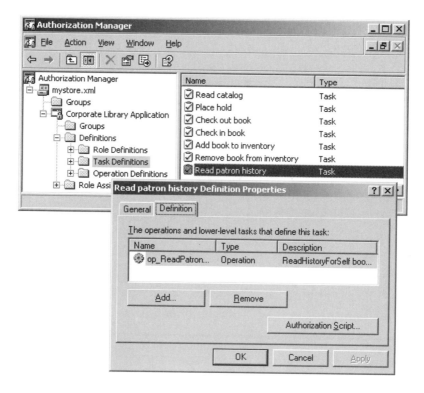

Figure 49.2 Task definitions

Authorization Store

It's time to switch hats and pretend that you're the administrator deploying the application. Switch to administrator mode under the Action | Options menu and note how the GUI changes: You're no longer allowed to edit the low-level operations for the application. Go ahead and add roles for the application as follows. Patrons should be allowed to browse the catalog, place holds, and review their history. Clerks should be able to do all that Patrons can do, with the addition of checking books in and out. Managers should be able to do all that Clerks can do, but also add and remove books from the inventory.

One way to simplify things here is by nesting roles. For example, Clerk can be defined in terms of the Patron role, with the addition of the "Check out book" and "Check in book" tasks, as I've shown in Figure 49.3. Try doing that in COM+! The last thing the administrator needs to do is make

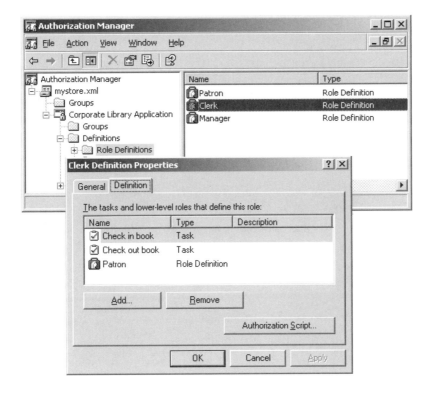

Figure 49.3 Nesting roles

these abstract roles concrete by adding real users to them. To do this, select the Role Assignments folder and choose the "Assign Roles" action. Note that a role doesn't actually become active in an application until it's been added to this folder. For example, the `IAzApplication.Roles` property only returns the collection of roles that has been added to the Role Assignments folder, as opposed to all roles that have been defined. Once a role has been assigned, right-click it to add either Windows users and groups or application groups that you previously defined in your AzMan store. I'll describe application groups later in this item.

The AzMan Runtime Interface

Once you have got some operations and tasks defined, you can start implementing access checks in code. The first thing you need to think about is authentication. If you can use some built-in Windows plumbing, like the

Web server's support for Kerberos authentication (Item 59), you can get a token for the client (Item 16). This is by far the most natural way to use AzMan because a token contains all the groups a user is in, making it fast to map that user onto a set of AzMan roles. If, on the other hand, you're using a form or X.509 certificate to authenticate the user, you won't have a token. Rather, you'll have only the user's name. This doesn't mean you can't use AzMan or even that you'll have to write more code. But it does mean that it'll be more expensive, since the AzMan runtime will have to look up the user's groups manually. This incurs round-trips to domain controllers.

The first things the app needs to do are initialize the AzMan runtime, point it to the store it plans to use, and drill down to the application where the authorization settings live. For now, let's use a simple XML-based store:

```
AzAuthorizationStore store = new AzAuthorizationStoreClass();
store.Initialize(0, @"msxml://c:\MyStore.xml", null);
IAzApplication app = store.OpenApplication(
    "Corporate Library Application", null);
```

To build this application, the project needs to reference the AzMan interop assembly, which can be found in `%WINDIR%\Microsoft.NET\Framework\AuthMan`.

Now that the application is bootstrapped, when a new client is authenticated you need to construct a representation of its security context. The context is a lot like a token in that it caches role mappings for a user.

```
IAzClientContext ctx =
    app.InitializeClientContextFromToken(htoken, null);
```

Where do you get the client's token? Well, that depends on what type of app you're writing. For example, here's some C# code from an ASP.NET page that obtains the token. In this case, web.config specifies the authentication mode as Windows, and IIS has been configured to require integrated Windows authentication.

```
WindowsIdentity id = (WindowsIdentity)User.Identity;
IntPtr htoken = id.Token;
```

If you only know the client's name and don't have access to its token, try to figure out if there's a token that you can get your hands on because it's the most authoritative way to discover groups for a client. It's also the fastest way, as I mentioned earlier. If you're sure that there's no token for the client available to you, then use this alternate method to initialize a context from an account name in the form `domain\user`. This call may incur round-trips to discover domain groups, so expect that it will take some time to execute.

```
IAzClientContext ctx =
  app.InitializeClientContextFromName(name, null);
```

Once you have a client context, you can run an access check. This call takes a number of arguments, but for now I'll keep things simple. Let's say you're implementing a function that adds a book to the inventory. I defined "Add book to inventory" as operation number five, so the code might look like what's shown in Figure 49.4.

The first argument, `nameOfBook`, is a string used if you've got runtime auditing turned on. It identifies the object on which you're performing the operation, so you should always provide some meaningful information

```
// always define constants or enums for your ops!
const int opAddBookToInventory = 5;
const int NO_ERROR = 0;

// later in the code...
object[] operations = { opAddBookToInventory };
object[] scopes = { "" };

object[] results = (object[])
  ctx.AccessCheck(nameOfBook,
                  scopes, operations,
                  null, null, null, null, null);
int result = (int)result[0];
if (NO_ERROR == result) {
  // access is granted
}
else {
  // access was denied, result holds error code
}
```

Figure 49.4 Performing an access check

here. I've used the default value for the second argument, scopes, which I'll explain a bit later. The third argument is where you list one or more operations that you want to test. The result is an array that's always the same size as the operations array, with an integer status code for each operation that indicates whether access is granted or denied. Zero indicates that the access check succeeded, and the client identified by the context is allowed to perform the specified operation. Any other value indicates failure (generally what you'll see is number five, which is ERROR_ACCESS_DENIED).

The AzMan runtime interface isn't strongly typed. It uses VARIANTs for most of its arguments. This allows classic ASP programmers who use scripting languages to use AzMan, but it means that programmers who use strongly typed languages like C# and Visual Basic .NET may make some mistakes when calling AccessCheck that won't be caught until runtime. For example, the operations array must be of type object[], not int[], but the compiler won't complain if you pass an int[] because the actual type of the argument is object. This bit me when I was first learning this API, and it took me a while to figure out exactly how to write the code to avoid getting runtime errors due to parameter type mismatches. I've heard rumors that eventually there will be a managed interface to AzMan, but until that happens, you might want to write a strongly typed wrapper around AccessCheck to avoid getting bitten. The following code shows an example that also simplifies the most common way you'll call the function.

```
public class AzManWrapper {
  public static int AccessCheck(
          IClientContext ctx,
          string objectName,
          int op) {
    object[] results = (object[])ctx.AccessCheck(
        objectName, new object []{""}, new object []{op}
        null, null, null, null, null);
    return (int)results[0];
  }
}
```

With a wrapper, you can provide your own overloads of AccessCheck to handle more sophisticated situations where other optional arguments are necessary. Using a wrapper for this function in particular should save you a lot of grief and will reduce clutter in your application code. You could even use this wrapper to convert `AccessCheck` failures into exceptions instead of returning a status code, along the lines of `IPermission.Demand`. Don't go crazy and wrap the whole suite of interfaces, though, since this function is really the only one that's tricky to call.

One thing you might be wondering at this point is whether you can use AzMan without Windows accounts to represent users. The runtime was designed with this in mind, although you need to define custom security identifiers (SIDs) for each user, which isn't terribly difficult, and you must call an alternate method to initialize a client security context—namely, `InitializeClientContextFromStringSid`. The biggest hurdle is that you won't be able to use the AzMan snap-in to manage your stores, which are pretty tightly coupled to Windows users and groups. For more details on how to approach this, see McPherson.

Stores, Applications, and Scopes

I want to back up for a moment and discuss the structure of the authorization store a bit. First of all, you have two choices for storing your authorization settings: You can drop the entire store into an XML file, or you can host it in Active Directory. I would strongly recommend using Active Directory for production apps, as it provides a lot more functionality and often better performance than a simple XML file.

If you have a test domain in a lab that you can play with, try bringing up the AzMan snap-in and creating a new store in Active Directory with a distinguished name like this: "CN=MyStore, CN=Program Data, DC=MyDomain, DC=com," replacing "MyDomain" with your own. To see what objects AzMan created in Active Directory, use a tool like **adsiedit.exe**, an MMC snap-in that you can install from your Windows Server 2003 CD by running **SUPPORT\TOOLS\SUPTOOLS.MSI**. Create an application in the store and bring up the new application's property page. You'll notice that there are Security and Auditing tabs that aren't present when you're using a simple XML file.

In Active Directory stores, you can delegate responsibility for administering individual applications within a store, and you can audit changes to the store at a very detailed level. With an XML file, you're limited to securing the file itself with NTFS permissions and auditing. Currently, run-time auditing is only supported if the store is housed in the directory, and auditing is tremendously important to most applications. If Active Directory is available, I strongly urge you to house your AzMan stores in it because it's the best place for hosting security policy on Windows.

A single store can house multiple applications. Each application has its own namespace for operations, tasks, and roles. Be aware of concurrency issues if you share a store among multiple applications, because stores don't yet support concurrent editing. If you think there's a chance two administrators might be editing a single store at the same time, you need to provide some external locking to serialize access to the store; otherwise, it might become corrupted. The AzMan snap-in doesn't provide this, and until it does you'll be better off limiting the contents of each store to avoid concurrent editing. The simplest solution is to limit each store to housing a single application.

Each application can also define multiple scopes, which is an advanced feature of Authorization Manager that I recommend only to people who have studied AzMan further and absolutely need this extra level of complexity. Scopes allow you to have different authorization settings for different parts of your application. For example, in a large Web application, roles might be assigned one way under a certain subdirectory; under a different subdirectory, they might be assigned differently or a totally different set of roles might be defined.

Scopes can be convenient in this case because they can share the low-level operation definitions and maybe even some tasks, roles, and application groups. Unfortunately, they can also be confusing and easy to misuse. For example, when you call AccessCheck the second argument is where you specify the scope you want to use for the check. If the user is providing the scope name, perhaps via the URL in the request, you'd better be sure that the name is canonicalized before you pass it to AccessCheck; otherwise, you may allow clever users to fool you into using a weaker scope by encoding the name in an unexpected way. If you're new to this type of attack, you should read the chapter on canonicalization in Howard and LeBlanc (2002). To learn more about advanced features like scopes, see McPherson.

Application Groups

There's a nifty feature in AzMan called application groups. In large organizations, it can be a real pain to get new groups added to the directory for your application to use. In fact, if only your application needs a particular group definition, you might be out of luck when an overworked domain administrator refuses to add yet another entry to his already barely manageable list of groups. In this case, application groups can save you. At the store, application, or scope level, you can define groups of users and assign a logical group name to them. You can then use these application groups in role assignments.

AzMan provides two types of application groups: basic and LDAP query. The basic groups are a lot like the groups in Active Directory but with a twist: You can define both included and excluded members. For example, you can define a group called `EveryoneButBob`, as I did in Figure 49.5. The benefits are increased functionality and convenience. The

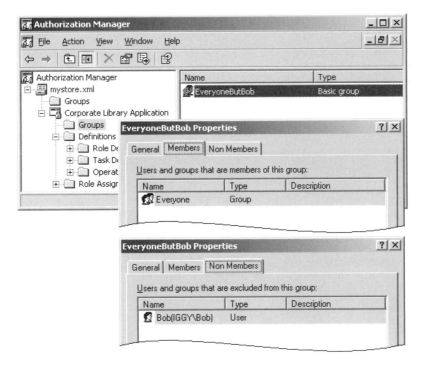

Figure 49.5 Allow everyone but Bob

drawbacks are the increased number of CPU cycles required to determine membership in the application group and the memory required to store the membership list in the application group, so use this feature with care. If you like the exclusion feature shown in Figure 49.5, you can still get it by using domain groups as members in your application groups, thus reducing the size of the membership list AzMan needs to keep in memory. LDAP query groups are an expensive but nifty feature of AzMan. Here you can use LDAP query syntax to define a group of users who are similar in some way. Here's how you might define the set of engineers who are at least 21 years old:

```
(&(age>=21)(memberOf= CN=eng,DC=foo,DC=com))
```

Regardless of the type, basic or LDAP query, the administrator can use application groups as alternative ways of assigning users to roles.

Scripts

For cases where static grants aren't enough, your application can provide extra context in the form of variables and object references to `AccessCheck`. This allows a script writer to add business logic using JScript or VBScript without having to change and recompile the application. For example, the "Read patron history" task defined earlier could be supplied with extra context, perhaps the set of roles in which the user is a member, and a Boolean indicating whether the client is accessing her own history or someone else's. This would enable you to write a script that permits Managers to review any Patron's history but restricts normal Patrons to reviewing only their own. A script such as the one shown in Figure 49.6 could be written for this task.

To associate the script shown with the "Read patron history" task, bring up the definition page for the task, browse to a file containing this script, specify the language as VBScript, and then press the "Reload Rule into Store" button.

```
' always start by being pessimistic
AzBizRuleContext.BusinessRuleResult = false
isManager = false
roles = AzBizRuleContext.GetParameter("roles")
for each role in roles
  if "Manager" = role then
    isManager = true
    exit for
  end if
next
if isManager then
  ' Managers are allowed to review
  ' any patron's history
  AzBizRuleContext.BusinessRuleResult = true
else
  ' anyone else is allowed to review
  ' their own history
  self = AzBizRuleContext.GetParameter("self")
  AzBizRuleContext.BusinessRuleResult = self
end if
```

Figure 49.6 Performing an access check

Supporting Authorization Scripts

To support the script shown in Figure 49.6, you'll need to pass a few more
arguments to any access check that involves the "Read patron history" task.
Because you've kept things simple and only defined one task per operation,
this means you can provide this context whenever you ask about the corresponding operation. Here's a snippet of code that shows how you would
provide these extra context variables for a script writer:

```
bool self = _userIsCheckingOwnHistory();
object[] operations = { opReviewPatronHistory };
object[] scopes      = { "" };
object[] varNames    = { "roles", "self" };
object[] varValues   = { ctx.GetRoles(""), self };

object[] results = (object[])
ctx.AccessCheck(nameOfPatronHistory,
                scopes, operations,
                varNames, varValues,
                null, null, null);
```

AzMan is a bit picky about the order of the varNames and varValues array. You must order varNames alphabetically, as I did. The varValues array must then provide the corresponding value for each named parameter in varNames, which is pretty obvious. If you want to get even fancier, you can use the last three arguments of AccessCheck to pass in named object references. This will expand the object model that the script writer sees beyond the default AzBizRuleContext object. I'll leave you to experiment on your own with that feature and address some of the challenges you'll run into if you decide to support scripting.

The first odd thing you'll probably notice about scripts is that they're defined at the task and role levels, not at the operation level. But application programmers perform access checks and provide context variables for individual operations, so how does the script writer know what variables will be available for a given task? Clearly it's up to the developer to document this carefully on a per-operation basis. One strategy is to keep things simple and always pass the same context variables no matter what operation is being performed. This certainly simplifies things for a script writer. In my library example, I was careful to define one task per operation so I could customize the context variables for each task. Remember, however, that administrators can define new tasks when running in admin mode. What would happen if the system administrator were to define a new task that incorporated two operations that each expected different context variables? Just try to keep things simple and document carefully how scripts should be written in order to avoid these nasty situations.

Another thing to watch out for when writing scripts is that the results of scripts are cached in the client context object for efficiency. Throw away the client context and you throw away the cache. This is good to know because some scripts might be dependent on external data that can change over time.

Be aware that scripts are designed to qualify the tasks or roles to which they're attached. Say, for example, that Alice is a member of roles R1 and R2. Role R1 is directly granted permission to perform operation X. Role R2 is granted the same permission, but this grant is qualified by a script. When Alice tries to perform operation X, AzMan doesn't even bother running the script in role R2 because operation X is already statically granted through role R1. Thus scripts cannot be used to deny permissions outright.

Scripts can only be used to decide whether a particular task or role should be considered in an access check. Just because a scripted task or role is omitted because its corresponding script evaluated to `false` doesn't mean there isn't an entirely different task or role that still grants the operation being tested. McPherson provides a very detailed description of how the runtime implements an access check. You'll find this in the Performance section. For anyone serious about using AzMan, I suggest you study this section carefully.

Auditing

Runtime auditing of access checks is an important feature that's available only if you're using an Authorization Manager store within Active Directory. If you want to enable this feature, right-click the application, choose Properties, and turn it on through the Auditing tab. At runtime, the account your server process runs under is important: It must be granted the `Generate Audits` privilege. The built-in logons `Local Service`, `Network Service`, and `SYSTEM` all have this privilege by default. Finally, note that the server machine must have auditing of object access turned on for these audits to be captured in the security event log.

What you'll see after enabling auditing is that each call to `AccessCheck` results in an audit entry, where the object name in the entry is whatever string you passed as the first argument to `AccessCheck`. The operation's friendly name is shown in the audit along with the client's name. If the check succeeded, a successful access is logged; otherwise, you see a failed access in the log. Whether you see both success and failure audits depends on what level of object access auditing you enabled via the Windows security policy.

Conclusion

Authorization Manager is an important tool for building secure systems on Windows. It expands the idea of role-based security popularized by MTS and COM+, but can be used by any server application, not just COM-based servers. Authorization Manager strives to help you centralize security logic into a concise security policy that can be stored in Active Directory, and it provides a simple API for performing access checks. Runtime auditing satisfies a longtime need as well.

Authorization Manager has loads of features, and part of your job when writing secure code is to figure out what subset of those features your application requires. Remember to keep things as simple as possible to avoid opening security holes.

PART IV

COM(+) and EnterpriseServices

■ 50 ■
What Is the COM(+) Authentication Level?

A UTHENTICATION IN WINDOWS is really about two things: helping the client and server develop trust in each other's identities (they're introduced to one another), and helping them exchange a cryptographic key (what we call the session key) to protect their communication channel. The COM authentication level for any given call controls whether authentication occurs at all and, if it does, how much protection you'll receive from that session key.

There are six levels, defined in order of increasing security.

1. RPC_C_AUTHN_LEVEL_NONE

2. RPC_C_AUTHN_LEVEL_CONNECT

3. RPC_C_AUTHN_LEVEL_CALL

4. RPC_C_AUTHN_LEVEL_PKT

5. RPC_C_AUTHN_LEVEL_PKT_INTEGRITY

6. RPC_C_AUTHN_LEVEL_PKT_PRIVACY

If a COM call goes out using the first level, no authentication occurs. The call appears to the server as anonymous, and the server is unable to determine the client's identity. The client has no idea who the server is, either. Zero protection. Avoid this.

The next level (CONNECT) says that the client and server authenticate only when the TCP connection[1] is first established. The client and server might as well throw the session key away, because it won't be used to provide any further security on the channel (Item 58). This is akin to the level of security you get with the file server by default.[2] It's really quite weak and should be avoided.

The next level (CALL) is not implemented (COM internally promotes this to the next, more secure level if you choose it). If it were implemented, the first fragment of each call would have its headers integrity-protected with a message authentication code (MAC). No other protections would be provided. Weak.

The next level (PKT) says that COM will MAC-protect the headers of each fragment of each call. Because only someone who knows the session key can form the MAC, this prevents an attacker from injecting new packets. It also turns on replay detection and detects message-reordering attacks. Security is getting better, but an attacker can still modify the payload of a message without being detected, so this level is still unacceptably weak.

The next level (INTEGRITY) says that COM MAC-protects the entire payload of each fragment of each call. This is the first level I would recommend even considering in any application that cares about security.

The last level (PRIVACY) provides all the protection of the previous level, and all payloads (not headers) are encrypted. Only someone who knows the session key (the client and server) is able to decrypt the messages. This is the level you should be using, unless you're debugging and need to see the payload in the clear, in which case you drop temporarily to the previous level. Be sure to use test data when debugging because everybody else on the network is seeing what you're seeing!

---

1. ... or the named pipes connection, SPX connection, or whatever connection-oriented protocol you happen to be using. Note that this level is internally promoted to the next more secure level if you're using a connectionless protocol like UDP, but COM uses connection-oriented protocols by default in Windows 2000 and beyond.

2. Unless you turn on a feature called SMB signing, which provides integrity checks. This feature can be enabled via security policy under Security Settings, Local Policies, Security Options. Look for two entries that start with the text, "Microsoft network server: Digitally sign communications . . ."

Level	Authenticate connection	MAC Protect		Encrypt
		Headers	Payload	Payload
None				
Connect	X			
Packet	X	X		
Packet Integrity	X	X	X	
Packet Privacy	X	X	X	X

Figure 50.1 COM authentication levels, summarized

Figure 50.1 sums it all up (I've omitted the level that's not implemented).

Now that you understand what the different levels mean, let me explain briefly how COM figures out which level to use for any given call. By default, when you unmarshal a proxy (Box 1998), the proxy starts life using a level that's negotiated between the client and server processes. You see, each process that makes or receives COM calls specifies its preferred authentication level, so the client and server are both specifying a level that they desire. COM sets the proxy to use the highest of these two levels by default. The server rejects any requests that come in with a lower level than what the server specified, but this should never be a problem with normal clients because the default level is negotiated up front, and should never be lower than what the server requires. An attacker might try to lower the level by calling `CoSetProxyBlanket`, but the COM server-side plumbing then will reject the call because it's below the level specified by the server.

If either the client or server specifies a level of "privacy," calls between that client and server are fully protected by default. This is goodness! Items 52 and 53 explain how to configure these settings for your process.

One important note: You might assume that if you configure a process to use an authentication level of "privacy" or, for that matter, anything other than "none," anonymous calls will be rejected. This is in fact what used to happen back in Windows NT 4 prior to service pack 4. However, for some odd reason some code was added to the NTLM security provider in that service pack that has been with us ever since. This code allows null sessions (Item 35) to go through the motions of authentication while really not proving anything. In other words, a COM client using a null session can connect to a server and make calls. The server sees a token for ANONYMOUS

LOGON, as expected, but what's dangerous is that if your process requires authentication you probably expect COM to reject these requests. Well, it doesn't. You must use access control to block null sessions to COM servers (and clients, which often expose COM objects to handle callbacks, events, and the like). So be very wary of granting access to Everyone. If you're about to do this, stop yourself and instead grant access to Authenticated Users. I talk more about this in Items 35 and 52. An odd bit of trivia is that if you've specified a level of "privacy" in your server (good for you!) and a null session is used to connect to you, the request *appears* to be encrypted on the wire. This is security theatre, though, not real security.[3]

---

3. This blew me away the first time I saw it. How can a null session possibly be encrypting data securely? With a null session, there's no cryptographic key exchanged between the client and server. Clearly some funny business is going on here. Perhaps a hardcoded key is being used. Whatever it is, it's *not giving you any real security!*

■ 51 ■
What Is the COM(+) Impersonation Level?

I F YOU READ Item 50, you learned that the COM authentication level is a setting that a client and server use to negotiate the protection of calls between them. The impersonation level is quite different, as it's designed purely as a protection for the client. You see, a secure server requires its clients to authenticate. And during authentication, if the server is trusted for delegation (Item 62), the underlying security plumbing normally sends the client's network credentials to the server via a Kerberos ticket (Item 59). The impersonation level is the client's control over whether this happens.

There are actually four levels, but only the last two of them are really meaningful in network scenarios:

1. RPC_C_IMP_LEVEL_ANONYMOUS
2. RPC_C_IMP_LEVEL_IDENTIFY
3. RPC_C_IMP_LEVEL_IMPERSONATE
4. RPC_C_IMP_LEVEL_DELEGATE

If you choose the last level (DELEGATE), you're telling COM you're happy to send your network credentials to the server if that server is trusted for delegation. This means the server can impersonate you (Item 31) and talk to other servers on the network on your behalf. Those other servers will think *you* are connecting directly! Clearly this implies a great deal of trust in the server. For more on delegation, see Item 62.

Any other level besides DELEGATE prevents the COM plumbing from sending your network credentials to any server, even one marked "trusted for delegation" in Active Directory. The difference between the other three levels isn't very important in a remoting scenario, as there isn't much difference in how much real protection is afforded the client, as I'll explain shortly. But you'll see that some of these levels might actually cause server code to fail, so here's a tip: When choosing an impersonation level for network scenarios, pick between the last two levels based on your delegation needs: IMPERSONATE or DELEGATE.

Let me show you what the first three levels mean so you can understand why I suggest the above policy. First of all, IMPERSONATE is the normal setting that says the server is allowed to impersonate you. IDENTIFY is a more restrictive setting that says the server is allowed to impersonate you but only for the purposes of making access control decisions. In other words, if the server impersonated you and then called the Win32 function Access-CheckAndAuditAlarm to decide whether you were allowed to do something (and perhaps generate an audit), this would work just fine. The server is allowed to identify you and check your groups, privileges, and so on. But while impersonating, a call to CreateFile would fail with a result of ERROR_ACCESS_DENIED because you didn't grant the server the right to open objects using your identity.

ANONYMOUS is weird. Take a remote case as an example. If the authentication level negotiated is something other than NONE, you authenticate with the server. But if the server attempts to get a handle to your token (the token produced as a result of authentication), this fails. The server process can't impersonate you or even identify you. But you've authenticated! You've sent a Kerberos ticket (Item 59) or answered an NTLM challenge! Clearly the server machine knows who you are, but the operating system conspires to keep the server process in the dark. Do you trust the server's operating system and its administrator with your identity? I guess what I'm trying to say is that if you don't want the server to know who you are, you shouldn't authenticate in the first place. Avoid using this setting. I doubt it's even received much testing, and it's likely to just break your code. This setting would make much more sense if used in conjunction with a server-to-client authentication protocol like SSL, but that's not terribly common under COM.

I hope you can see that ANONYMOUS and IDENTIFY really have no teeth in the remote case, because you ultimately have to trust the remote server's operating system to enforce these restrictions. This is why I suggest choosing a level of either IMPERSONATE or DELEGATE in network scenarios.

If you need to configure this setting for a base COM client, see Item 53. For a COM+ app, see Item 54. For an ASP.NET app, see Item 55.

■ 52 ■
What Is CoInitializeSecurity?

COM PROVIDES SEVERAL process-level security settings, and CoInitializeSecurity is the documented Win32 API for choosing them. Now, in many cases you won't need to call this function because other infrastructure takes care of this housekeeping for you. For example, in a COM+ application, you specify your process-wide security settings via the COM+ catalog, and the COM+ surrogate (**DLLHOST.EXE**) takes care of wiring up these settings. The same goes with an ASP.NET worker process. On Windows 2000, you can specify your COM security settings via **machine.config** (see the <processModel> section), and some plumbing in ASP.NET configures COM security on your behalf. But what about a Windows Forms app or a lowly console app?

You might not think that a client app needs to configure COM security settings. It's not like they're serving up COM objects and need an access control infrastructure, right? Well, hold on. If a Windows Forms application makes calls to remote COM servers, it very likely receives callbacks and therefore does indeed act as a server. So it absolutely does need to have COM security settings because a bad guy can use a DCOM call as a way to attack the client application. Even if the app never receives callbacks, it's still important to choose client-side security settings to protect the client and, in some cases, to simply get the client working! And because the .NET Framework doesn't provide any plumbing to automate COM security configuration for client apps, you've got to call CoInitialize-Security yourself, which can be a bit tricky, as I lay out in Item 53.

There are a couple of ways of using CoInitializeSecurity to specify your settings. If your application has registered an AppID for itself (this is a GUID under the registry key HKCR/AppID), you can use the Component Services MMC snap-in, which has a folder called DCOM Config (see Figure 52.1), to configure your settings. This tool shows a list of application names—these strings come from the default string value stored in the

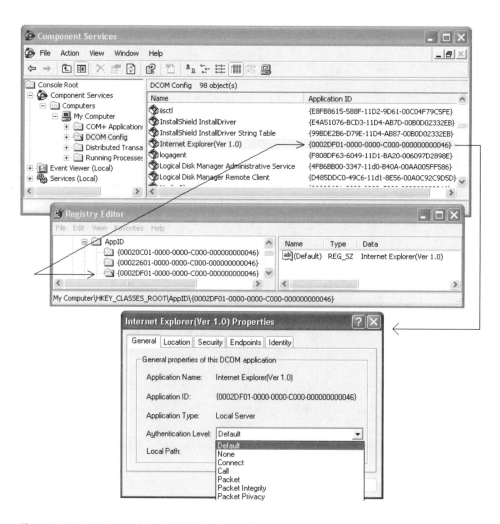

Figure 52.1 AppIDs and the DCOM Config tool

registry under the AppID.[1] And the way you tell COM what your AppID is (in other words, where to find your security settings) is to call `CoInitializeSecurity`. In fact, this is the easiest way to call this function because you only need to specify two things: a flag (`EOAC_APPID`) that says you're passing an AppID for the first argument of the function and the AppID itself. Here's some C++ code that does just that.

```
// the simplest way I know to declare a GUID in VC++ ;-)
struct __declspec(uuid("12341234-1234-1234-1234-123412341234"))
  MyAppID;

void main() {
  CoInitializeEx(0, COINIT_MULTITHREADED);
  CoInitializeSecurity(&__uuidof(MyAppID),
    0, 0, 0, 0, 0, 0, EOAC_APPID, 0);
  // app code goes here...
  CoUninitialize();
}
```

The benefits of using the method shown are twofold. First of all, it's incredibly simple to code. Second, Windows provides a tool for editing and persisting your security settings, and an administrator can use it to configure them. The drawbacks are twofold as well. First of all, you've got to create an AppID in the registry for your client program, and, because AppIDs for client apps aren't common, there isn't any infrastructure in the .NET Framework for doing this. So you'll have to have your setup application do it (it's not hard—you can use the registry classes in the `Microsoft.Win32` namespace, but it's a step you can't forget). The second drawback is that in using this technique you don't have quite as much control. The GUI doesn't allow you to configure every single COM security setting, and some of those settings you will want to control. You might prefer to manage these settings yourself and call `CoInitializeSecurity`, explicitly passing configuration parameters rather than simply referring to an AppID. I recommend this approach for new code.

---

1. If you're a COM veteran and you know about AppIDs, you may be surprised to know that even a COM client can have one. Often they should, to control their security preferences.

Here are the settings that the GUI allows you to control:

- Authentication level (Item 50)
- Impersonation level (Item 51)
- Access permissions

There are some other settings designed for base COM servers, including identity and launch permissions. But for client code that doesn't support activation, these aren't anything you need to worry about.

Here are some important additional settings that you can control if you call `CoInitializeSecurity` without using the `EOAC_APPID` hack I just described:

- Restrict the use of custom marshalers (`EOAC_NO_CUSTOM_MARSHAL`)
- Enable cloaking (`EOAC_DYNAMIC_CLOAKING`)
- Disable As Activator Activation (`EOAC_DISABLE_AAA`)

There are a few other things you can do as well, but they're so esoteric that I won't mention them here. See Brown (2000b) for more details if you care.

For the remainder of this item, I'll walk you through what these various settings mean. Because I've devoted Items 50 and 51 to the authentication and impersonation levels, I'll start with the access control setting.

The first argument to `CoInitializeSecurity` is a pointer to a security descriptor (Item 42). This is where you specify your access control policy. There are a lot of really annoying restrictions on how this thing has to be built, which is why I provided some helper code in the accompanying library (samples can be found in Item 53).[2] The only thing that really matters here is the DACL (Item 43), which is where you specify the users and groups allowed to call into your process. The helper code in the accompanying library defaults to using a DACL with a single ACE that grants access to `Authenticated Users`. Whatever you choose, make sure that `SYSTEM` ends up being granted access or COM won't work properly. Fortunately,

---

2. The descriptor must be in absolute format, and the owner and primary group must be set, which makes the function a lot harder to call than it should be.

as of Windows 2000 SYSTEM has the Authenticated Users SID, so this DACL makes COM quite happy.

For a COM client, a great place to start with this first argument is to simply limit access control to Authenticated Users. This blocks the null session (Item 35) and guest logons (Item 36), but allows the server to make callbacks to the client. Unfortunately, it also allows any other authenticated user to call your methods (fire events and the like), but it's a heck of a lot better than not specifying an access control policy and allowing all calls in. If you happen to know (or can find out) a list of users and groups that should be allowed to make calls to your code—for example, if you know the server account name that will be firing events to your client—by all means be more specific in your access control policy.

For a COM server, use groups to grant permissions to any users who need to make COM calls into the server process. If you can't do this, at least follow my earlier advice and grant access to Authenticated Users to block anonymous callers. If you do want to allow anonymous callers, pass a null pointer for this argument.

Restricting custom marshalers is a good idea, and you should use this feature. You see, a bad guy can send you a COM request that includes a custom marshaler CLSID that effectively tells COM to create an instance of that class in your process, and COM happily obliges. But if you turn on this restriction, the only CLSIDs that COM trusts to act as custom marshalers are classes built into the operating system or classes that have been marked with a special category, CATID_MARSHALER. Turn this feature on, please; otherwise, you're providing an attacker a very easy way to force you to load DLLs into your process that you don't need (but that help the attacker in some way). To turn this feature on, specify the EOAC_NO_CUSTOM_ MARSHAL flag in the penultimate argument to CoInitializeSecurity. My library turns this flag on by default for you (Item 53).

Cloaking is a feature that you should turn on as well. It's already turned on automatically in COM+ and ASP.NET worker processes. You probably won't ever actually use this feature in a COM client, but then again you may. It has to do with impersonation (Item 31). By default, COM ignores any impersonation token you might have on your thread when you make an outgoing COM call. So if your process is running as Bob and your thread is impersonating Alice, outgoing COM calls ignore the thread token and go out using Bob's credentials, which is probably not what you intended. Turning on cloaking fixes this so Alice's credentials are used instead. This is a good example of the "principal of least surprise." Specify the EOAC_DYNAMIC_CLOAKING flag in the penultimate argument to CoInitializeSecurity to enable this feature. My library turns this flag on by default for you (Item 53).

The last item, represented by yet another flag (EOAC_DISABLE_AAA), really doesn't make much sense for client code, but was designed for highly trusted COM servers, such as those that run as SYSTEM. If a highly trusted COM server made calls to an untrusted out-of-process COM server, it would be bad if that server were configured to run "as the launching user" because it would then be launched in the SYSTEM logon session, which is the most highly trusted logon on the machine! By default, then, you should turn this feature on for any COM servers that run with high privilege. It will prevent activation requests from being acknowledged by COM servers configured to run "as the launching user" or "As Activator."[3] For normal client code, you really don't want this feature because it breaks so many applications (most OLE automation apps like Microsoft Excel are configured to run as the launching user, which is quite natural). My library leaves this feature off by default.

Windows XP Service Pack 2

As this book is about to go to press, Windows XP service pack 2 is in beta. This service pack adds an additional layer of security for COM applications. There are two new machine-wide DACLs that can be edited via the computer property sheet accessible from the COM+ explorer. These control launch and access permissions for all COM servers on the machine, and any caller must pass these hurdles before COM even considers evaluating the individual server DACLs. As of this writing, it looks as though the default settings will prevent remote nonadministrators from launching COM servers on a Windows XP box. These settings won't place any further restrictions on calls into an already running process (callbacks into client

---

3. If you're wondering what the "AAA" stands for in the flag name, it's "As Activator Activation." Tell people this little tidbit at parties; it's a great way to get dates!

applications, for example) by any authenticated user, but will by default block all anonymous calls that don't originate on the local machine.

Another likely change in Windows XP service pack 2 is the addition of fine-grained permissions that distinguish between local and remote calls. Traditionally COM servers have used only a single execute permission, which indicates whether a request will be allowed. This is being split into two permissions—let's call them LOCAL_EXECUTE and REMOTE_ EXECUTE. You can grant these permissions individually to a user or group. For example, you can grant LOCAL_EXECUTE to Authenticated Users while granting REMOTE_EXECUTE to no one. This would allow a COM server to be used locally, but would prevent all remote access to that server.

Similarly, launch permissions are being split into local and remote flavors, and a new "activation" permission is being added. Whereas launch permissions dictate who can cause new COM server processes to start, activation permissions dictate who can create new COM objects (even in an already launched server). Activation permissions are also split into local and remote versions.[4]

---

4. For more information on the implications of service pack 2, see *http://msdn.microsoft.com/security/productinfo/xpsp2/default.aspx*.

■ 53 ■

How to Configure Security for a COM(+) Client

I
T'S A PITY THAT I even have to write this item or that it needs to be as complicated as this, but the COM interop team, although content to automate the call to `CoInitializeEx` for you, apparently doesn't feel the same about helping you with security. In fact, in a simple console or Windows Forms application, for example, nobody in the framework bothers to call `CoInitializeSecurity`. Didn't anyone on this team read Brown (2000b)? Arrrgh!

Here's the problem. If you're writing a COM client, especially one that communicates with remote COM servers, you need to have some control over your security settings, and if nobody in your process calls `CoInitializeSecurity`, well, COM does its best to figure out what settings your application needs. And the results are often not pretty. Some settings can be configured via the registry, but not all. And even if you do rely on registry settings and good old **DCOMCNFG.EXE** (or the MMC snap-in that has now replaced it), the link that ties your registry-based security settings to your application is fragile at best. It's a link in the registry that's based on your EXE name, and it breaks in many cases, such as when the name of the EXE is changed (well, duh!), and it can even break if you use a long file name in some cases. It's designed for **legacy** applications that didn't know how to call `CoInitializeSecurity`. You can do better. I've provided some code that makes calling this function pretty easy.

As a COM client, `CoInitializeSecurity` allows you to control your authentication and impersonation levels, which are really important, as I discussed in Items 50 and 51. Just as important is the ACL that says who is allowed to call into your client process (that's right, if you're a COM client, you very likely act as a COM server in some scenarios—think about callbacks and events). There are also some important security measures that you can control. For example, you can restrict custom marshaling so that an attacker can't load arbitrary DLLs into your process. In short, you really need to call this function if you're writing a COM client. But there's a catch. Because this function controls process-wide security settings, it can only be called once per process. And if you don't call it before doing something "interesting," like unmarshaling a proxy, COM will take matters into its own hands and effectively call it for you. So you need to call this function early.

Here's the fun part. Normally you should call `CoInitializeSecurity` when your program first starts up, right after your main thread calls `CoInitializeEx`. But the .NET Framework takes care of calling `CoInitializeEx` for you. It does it lazily the first time you make a COM interop call, but by the time you've made that call it's already too late to call `CoInitializeSecurity`! Bah!

Basically what you have to do is manually call three functions:

1. `CoInitializeEx`
2. `CoInitializeSecurity`
3. `CoUninitialize`

But you don't want to call that last function until your application is completely finished using COM. In other words, you want to perform steps 1 and 2 right at the beginning of `Main` and step 3 right at the end of `Main`, as shown here.

```
static void Main() {
    CoInitializeEx(...);
    CoInitializeSecurity(...);
    RunApplicationUntilItsTimeToQuit();
    CoUninitialize();
}
```

I've put together some code in the accompanying library[1] that makes this task pretty easy. This code configures COM for high security by default, ensuring that payloads are integrity protected and encrypted, locking down custom marshaling, and blocking anonymous callers using null sessions or guest logons. Here's how to use it from a Windows Forms application.

```
using System;
using KBC.WindowsSecurityUtilities;

[STAThread]
static void Main() {
    WindowsSecurityUtilities.Initialize();

    COM.InitializeCOM(false);       // choose STA threading model
    COM.InitializeCOMSecurity();  // use secure defaults

    Application.Run(new MainForm());

    COM.UninitializeCOM();

    WindowsSecurityUtilities.Terminate();
}
```

For those who need more control, I've provided overloaded versions of `InitializeCOMSecurity`, but be sure to read Item 52 so you know what the various settings mean.

---

1. You can download the library from the book's Web site.

■ 54 ■
How to Configure the Authentication and Impersonation Levels for a COM+ Application

F ROM THE COM+ EXPLORER, bring up the property sheet for the COM+ server application you want to configure. The authentication and impersonation levels can be selected via two dropdown lists at the bottom of the Security page, as shown in Figure 54.1.

If you're working with a library application, you've got much less control over your process-wide security settings. Figure 54.2 shows the controls from the COM+ explorer—note how different they are from those in Figure 54.1.

For library applications, you can't control the default impersonation level, nor can you control the default authentication level. These are process-level settings and are thus controlled by whoever called `CoInitializeSecurity` (Item 52) or, in the case of a COM+ process, by the server application in the process.

The one rather esoteric thing a library application can do is to create a "notch" in the host process's security policy to allow unauthenticated calls to the objects in the library application. You can do this by

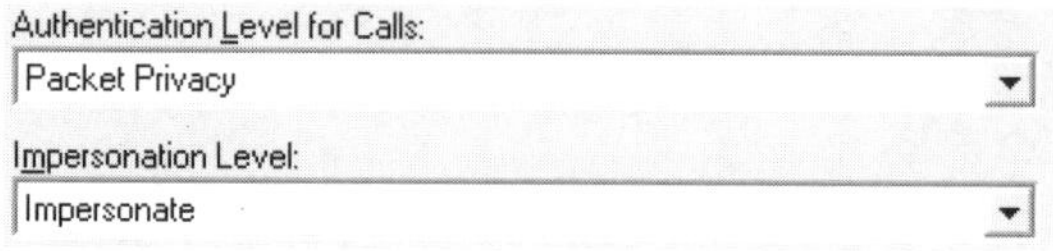

Figure 54.1 Server app authentication and impersonation levels

Authentication
☑ E_nable Authentication

Figure 54.2 You have less control with a library app.

unchecking the box entitled Enable Authentication. In Item 50 I described how the COM channel rejects incoming calls that are below the process's authentication level. Well, if you uncheck this box, you're allowing requests to enter at any authentication level. Leave this box checked.

■ 55 ■

How to Configure the Authentication and Impersonation Levels for an ASP.NET Application

YOU MIGHT BE WONDERING why you need to configure COM security settings in an ASP.NET application, but if your application makes or receives any out-of-process COM calls, you'll want to know how to control these settings. A lot of new ASP.NET applications rely on existing COM+ infrastructure. Even if your ASP.NET application acts only as a COM client, you still want these settings to be in your control.

If you're using IIS 5, it's quite easy to configure these settings for the ASP.NET worker process, **ASPNET_WP.EXE**. Just go into **machine.config**, find the <processModel> section, and edit the comAuthenticationLevel and comImpersonationLevel attributes. Here are the various settings they can take:

```
comAuthenticationLevel="Default|None|Connect|Call|
                        Pkt|PktIntegrity|PktPrivacy"
comImpersonationLevel="Default|Anonymous|
                       Identify|Impersonate|Delegate"
```

And here's how I suggest you configure these settings by default:

```
comAuthenticationLevel="PktPrivacy"
comImpersonationLevel="Impersonate"
```

In IIS 6, you can no longer use the `<processModel>` section to edit these settings. Instead, you must use some registry settings (for which I've found no documentation as of this writing[1]). When you configure the registry settings I'm about to show you, you're controlling the settings of all application pools; all IIS 6 worker processes use the same settings. Unfortunately, there's no way to configure them for individual application pools.

According to my sources inside Microsoft, by default each IIS 6 worker process calls `CoInitializeSecurity` with the following settings:

- Authentication level: default
- Impersonation level: impersonate
- Capabilities: dynamic cloaking

If you want to adjust these settings (in my opinion, you should), here's what you need to do. In the registry, find the key `HKLM\System\Current-ControlSet\Services\w3svc\Parameters` and create four named values of type `DWORD`. The first should be `CoInitializeSecurityParam`, and its value should be 1. This tells the worker process to pay attention to the next three settings: `AuthenticationLevel`, `ImpersonationLevel`, and `AuthenticationCapabilities`. If specified, each IIS 6 worker process will use these values when it calls `CoInitializeSecurity`. Figure 55.1 shows the settings I recommend, which ensure the following defaults for COM security in any IIS 6 worker process.

- All COM payloads will be integrity protected and encrypted (Item 50).
- Outgoing calls from the worker process will not forward credentials for delegation (Item 51).
- Rogue custom marshalers will be blocked (Item 52).
- COM will use the impersonation token (if present) for outgoing calls (Item 52).
- As Activator Activation will be disabled (Item 52).

If you're wondering where the numbers in Figure 55.1 came from, they're just the values that you pass to `CoInitializeSecurity`, and they're defined in the Win32 header files as shown in Figure 55.2.

---

1. But I'm sure that once someone from Microsoft reads this, a Knowledge Base article won't be far away!

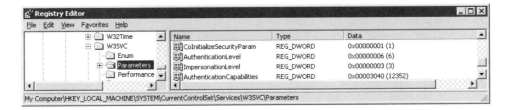

Figure 55.1 Configuring COM security in the IIS 6 worker process

```
// Authentication Levels
#define RPC_C_AUTHN_LEVEL_DEFAULT          0
#define RPC_C_AUTHN_LEVEL_NONE             1
#define RPC_C_AUTHN_LEVEL_CONNECT          2
#define RPC_C_AUTHN_LEVEL_CALL             3
#define RPC_C_AUTHN_LEVEL_PKT              4
#define RPC_C_AUTHN_LEVEL_PKT_INTEGRITY    5
#define RPC_C_AUTHN_LEVEL_PKT_PRIVACY      6

// Impersonation Levels
#define RPC_C_IMP_LEVEL_DEFAULT        0
#define RPC_C_IMP_LEVEL_ANONYMOUS      1
#define RPC_C_IMP_LEVEL_IDENTIFY       2
#define RPC_C_IMP_LEVEL_IMPERSONATE    3
#define RPC_C_IMP_LEVEL_DELEGATE       4

typedef enum tagEOLE_AUTHENTICATION_CAPABILITIES {
    EOAC_NONE                = 0x0,
    EOAC_MUTUAL_AUTH         = 0x1,
    EOAC_SECURE_REFS         = 0x2,
    EOAC_ACCESS_CONTROL      = 0x4,
    EOAC_APPID               = 0x8,
    EOAC_DYNAMIC             = 0x10,
    EOAC_STATIC_CLOAKING     = 0x20,
    EOAC_DYNAMIC_CLOAKING    = 0x40,
    EOAC_ANY_AUTHORITY       = 0x80,
    EOAC_MAKE_FULLSIC        = 0x100,
    EOAC_REQUIRE_FULLSIC     = 0x200,
    EOAC_AUTO_IMPERSONATE    = 0x400,
    EOAC_DEFAULT             = 0x800,
    EOAC_DISABLE_AAA         = 0x1000,
    EOAC_NO_CUSTOM_MARSHAL   = 0x2000
} EOLE_AUTHENTICATION_CAPABILITIES;
```

Figure 55.2 Definitions

■ 56 ■

How to Implement Role-Based Security for an Enterprise Services Application

I F YOU'RE WRITING a ServicedComponent and you want to secure it, there are several attributes in System.EnterpriseServices that you need to use. Let me walk you through a concrete example. Figure 56.1 shows a simple component that implements role-based security.

First of all, notice that the assembly has been given a public key: All managed COM+ components must be strongly named. Next, notice that I've given my application a name via ApplicationNameAttribute. I've also chosen a server app (as opposed to a library app) via Application-ActivationAttribute. This will ensure that my application gets its own process.

The next attribute, ApplicationAccessControlAttribute, is very important, as it controls several process-level security settings, including our old friends the authentication level (Item 50) and the impersonation level (Item 51). This also allows us to control two things with respect to role-based authorization: whether it's on at all and how granular it is. Note how I passed true as the first argument to the attribute. This turns on role-based checks for the application as a whole, which is a really important thing to

```
// PetStore.cs
using System;
using System.Reflection;
using System.EnterpriseServices;

[assembly: AssemblyDelaySign(true)]
[assembly: AssemblyKeyFile(@"..\..\pubkey")]
[assembly: ApplicationName("Pet Store")]
[assembly: ApplicationActivation(ActivationOption.Server)]
[assembly: ApplicationAccessControl(true,
  Authentication       = AuthenticationOption.Privacy,
  ImpersonationLevel = ImpersonationLevelOption.Identify,
  AccessChecksLevel  = AccessChecksLevelOption.ApplicationComponent)]

[ComponentAccessControl(true)]
[SecureMethod]
public class PetStore : ServicedComponent, IPetStore {
    [SecurityRole("Customers")] public void PetAnimal()  {}
    [SecurityRole("Customers")] public void BuyAnimal()  {}
    [SecurityRole("Staff")]     public void FeedAnimal() {}
    [SecurityRole("Owners")]    public void GiveRaise()  {}
}

public interface IPetStore {
    void PetAnimal();
    void BuyAnimal();
    void FeedAnimal();
    void GiveRaise();
}
```

Figure 56.1 A simple, secured managed COM+ component in C#

do! Then `AccessChecksLevelAttribute` allows me to specify the granularity of the checks. There are two granularity options:

- `AccessChecksLevelOption.Application`
- `AccessChecksLevelOption.ApplicationComponent`

The names might seem a bit confusing at first, but here's how they work. The first option tells COM+ to perform access checks only at the process level. These are checks 1 and 2 in Figure 56.2. The second option, which is the setting you should always stick with, adds access checks at the appli-

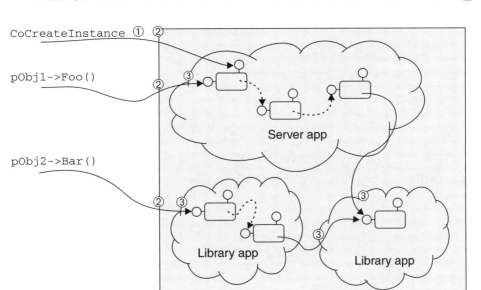

`CoCreateInstance`

`pObj1->Foo()`

`pObj2->Bar()`

Figure 56.2 The three different COM+ access checks

cation level (3) and turns on the "security call context," which allows you to programmatically ask questions about the caller at runtime, such as "Is my caller in the Managers role?"

Let me explain Figure 56.2 a bit. You see, COM+ access checks are performed only when a call crosses either a process boundary (1 and 2) or an application boundary (3). Access check 1 is the launch permission check, which is performed only if the server process hasn't yet been launched, and the SCM needs to determine whether the caller has permissions to launch it with her activation request. Access check 2 is the process-level access permission check, which is performed for each and every COM method call that comes in from outside the process. Both of these process-level checks are implemented in COM+ by simply checking to see if the caller is in at least one role for the server application in the process. If the caller isn't in any roles at all, he's denied the right to launch and denied the right to make any COM calls into the process.

The third access check (3) occurs whenever a normal COM method call crosses an application boundary. By normal, I mean a method call to an object that's already been created, and I'm not talking about methods like

`QueryInterface` or `Release`.[1] COM implements this third "component-level" access check by checking to see if the caller is in a role that grants access to the method (or the interface or class; any of these is sufficient to grant access).

Let's get back to the code in Figure 56.1. Note that I've placed a `ComponentAccessControlAttribute` on my class, passing `true` for its only argument. Don't forget this step because all classes without this feature turned on will have component-level access checks disabled for them. In other words, access check 3 in Figure 56.2 won't be implemented for those classes.

`SecureMethodAttribute` really needs better documentation. First of all, you need to realize that when you make a call from a managed COM+ client to a managed COM+ server, say `IPetStore.GiveRaise`, the `EnterpriseServices` infrastructure may elect not to use the `IPetStore` interface to dispatch the call. You see, there's an undocumented interface that's sometimes used to implement calls from managed clients to managed servers, and it's called `IRemoteDispatch`. If this little shortcut is used instead of the real interface, method-level role-based access checks aren't enforced for that call. By putting `SecureMethodAttribute` on a class, you're telling the `EnterpriseServices` guys, "Hey, I've got method-level access checks on this class. Don't use the `IRemoteDispatch` shortcut because I need those checks to be honored!" Until Microsoft deigns to tell us exactly why `IRemoteDispatch` is useful, as a rule make sure you put this attribute on all of your classes.[2]

Finally, note that I've placed a `SecurityRoleAttribute` on each method. This does two things: When you deploy this component in the COM+ catalog (via **regsvcs.exe**), it ensures there's a role with that name created for the application, which allows an administrator to add users to the role. Second, it assigns that particular role to the method so that anyone in the role will be allowed to call the method. You can also place this

---

1. These are low-level COM methods that are mainly called by plumbing and by anyone unfortunate enough to still be writing COM code in a language like C++.

2. As a security guy, I think this is totally backward. I'd rather see an attribute that allows use of `IRemoteDispatch` as an exception to the rule rather than the other way around. Prefer secure defaults!

attribute on interfaces or classes if you want to grant broader permissions. Remember that a caller only has to be a member of a role on the method, interface, or class. Any one of these is sufficient to allow the call to proceed.

One thing you'll notice when you deploy this component with **regsvcs.exe** is that a magical role called "Marshalers"[3] will be created in your application as well. You need to put everyone in this role who is allowed to use your application (either specify Authenticated Users or, if you can narrow it down further, use your own custom groups to restrict access to the overall application).

If declarative security on methods, interfaces, and classes isn't granular enough, you can add explicit role checks by calling ContextUtil.Is-CallerInRole. Note that this isn't available unless you've configured your application for the correct access control level (AccessChecksLevel-Option.ApplicationComponent), as I mentioned earlier. This additional logic allows you to take into consideration the parameters being passed to your method and other state that might change the outcome of the permission check. But please note that ContextUtil.IsCallerInRole always returns true if access checks are disabled. By disabling access checks, you're turning off not only any declarative security but also any explicit role checks you have programmed directly via ContextUtil.IsCallerInRole. Here's a simplified example of how you can use this method.

```
void Bank::WithdrawMoney(int accountNumber, int amount) {
  if (amount > 10000) {
    // for this much money, need to be a manager
    if (!ContextUtil.IsCallerInRole("Managers")) {
      throw new ApplicationException("Access Denied");
    }
  }
  //...
}
```

One important thing to note is that COM+ role-based security is a separate feature from the newer .NET role-based security exposed via

---

3. There is very little documentation on this role, and what little there is can be tough to find, since the spelling of "Marshaler" is often varied. The best I've seen so far is an article by Shannon Pahl in the MSDN library. You can find this article by searching for the following: "marshaller EnterpriseServices".

`IPrincipal`, `Thread.CurrentPrincipal`, and friends (Item 33). To check COM+ roles, you must use the `ContextUtil` class as I've shown.

If you're worried about an administrator turning off role-based checks, you might be tempted to use `ContextUtil.IsSecurityEnabled`, which will tell you if role-based access checks have been disabled. In fact, I've seen a lot of people write code that looks like this:

```
if (ContextUtil.IsSecurityEnabled &&
    ContextUtil.IsCallerInRole("Managers")) {
    // do some privileged operation
}
```

This is fine, but you need to realize that it's only protecting against someone accidentally disabling security for your application. If a rogue administrator really wants to disable role-based checks, all he needs to do is add the `Everyone` group to each role and he's effectively achieved the same thing. Checking `IsSecurityEnabled` won't detect this sort of fraud. This is just another reminder that the administrator owns the machine and ultimately must be trusted. How to hire trustworthy people is a topic beyond the scope of this book!

▪ 57 ▪

How to Configure Process Identity for a COM(+) Server Application

THIS IS AN EXTENSION of Item 28, which discussed some general strategies for picking server process identities. COM+ server apps have a large number of options for identity, as you can see from Figure 57.1.

The only choice that's really unique to a COM(+) server is the ability to run the server in the interactive user's logon session. The reason this feature exists is for debugging. Remember how window stations work (Item 18). Daemons normally run in noninteractive window stations, which aren't bound to hardware. If a daemon pops up a modal dialog box (perhaps because of an ASSERT statement in a debug build), it's catastrophic because nobody can see it, and the daemon's thread will hang waiting for someone to dismiss this invisible dialog, so sometimes it makes sense to run in the interactive window station while debugging. In a production environment, the drawbacks to running as the interactive user are clear enough: If nobody happens to be logged in to the server console interactively, all activation requests to the COM(+) server will fail. Conversely, if someone does happen to be logged on and the COM(+) server starts up, when that person logs off the COM(+) server will be terminated along with all the other processes in the interactive logon session. So use this setting for debugging in the lab, and if possible have someone log in to the server box

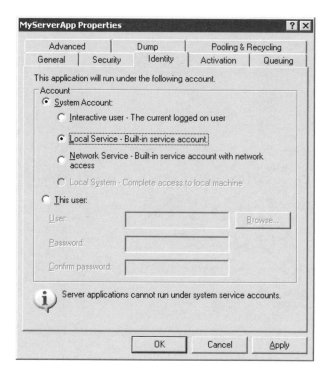

Figure 57.1 COM+ server identity in Windows Server 2003

interactively using the daemon account under which the COM+ server normally runs. Of course, if you normally run the server under one of the built-in logins such as Network Service, Local Service, or SYSTEM,[1] this won't be possible. If you need to debug your service and have it run interactively, the best you can do is log in with a temporary user account that has the same privileges and permissions as the built-in logon you'll be using during production. Of course, if your COM+ server is configured as a service running as SYSTEM, you can force it into the interactive window station by configuring the service to "interact with the desktop," but make

---

1.   Note that to run as SYSTEM you'll need to configure the COM+ server application to be an NT service, which can be done in Windows Server 2003 by checking a box on the Activation tab. And, of course, if you do decide to run a COM+ app as SYSTEM keep it very small, review its design and implementation carefully, and restrict who can call it. Your best bet is to allow only trusted callers from the local machine: It's terribly dangerous to allow untrusted input to be sent to a process running as SYSTEM!

sure to turn this off when you deploy the production system to avoid luring attacks (Items 7 and 29).

If you're configuring a base COM server, you have one other option: You can run the server as "The launching user" (Figure 57.2). This is also known as "As Activator Activation." Many interactive programs, like Microsoft Excel, are designed with OLE automation interfaces, which makes them COM servers. These apps weren't designed to serve multiple clients in a distributed system as COM+ servers normally do. They were designed to service the interactive user running a script or macro from another process (perhaps from Windows Scripting Host or another COM-enabled application like Microsoft Word). Ironically, these applications should never be configured to run as "The interactive user"! Instead, they should be configured using the default identity for base COM servers, which is to activate as "the launching user." Why? Well, in the normal usage scenario the interactive user will be the one launching the server, so there's really no difference. But in an attack scenario, imagine a bad guy who wishes to use a scriptable app like Microsoft Excel to attack the interactive user on some machine on the network. If Excel were configured to run as the interactive user, and if the attacker were able to launch it (this would require getting

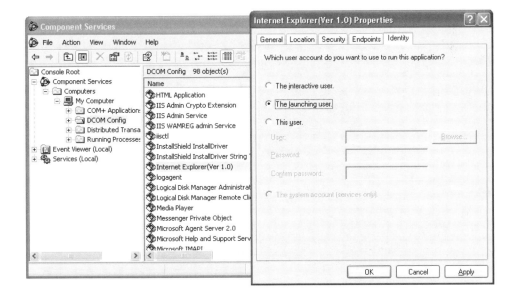

Figure 57.2 Base COM identity options

past COM launch and access permissions), he'd be running code in the interactive user's logon session immediately and could use Excel to do whatever he wanted with the interactive user's credentials. This would be a horrible situation. By configuring these OLE automation servers to run as "the launching user," we avoid this. If the attacker is able to launch Excel on some unwitting person's machine, Excel will run with whatever credentials the attacker happens to be using. If the attacker can't be authenticated, the activation request will fail. The moral of the story here is to run those OLE automation servers as "the launching user."

For COM servers that service many different clients in a distributed system, running as "the launching user" doesn't work very well. For one thing, you'll end up launching a distinct process for each unique authenticated user, which won't scale well at all (you'll be lucky if you can service over 50 clients this way). Second, you won't be able to service anonymous clients, which you may want to do in some cases. Finally, your process won't have any network credentials because you'll be running in a network logon for a remote client. It just doesn't make sense to configure a distributed server this way, which is why the COM+ identity GUI doesn't even offer this option.

To conclude, run macro-driven local OLE automation servers as "the launching user," which is the default for all base COM servers. Run debug builds of your COM+ server as "the interactive user" in the lab if you want to see any errant dialogs that might pop up, and in production pick a least-privilege daemon account (Item 28) for your server and run it noninteractively.

PART V
Network Security

■ 58 ■
What Is CIA?

I N SECURITY CIRCLES, we often talk about an acronym called CIA, which normally taken to mean confidentiality, integrity, and availability. But when talking about securing application communications on a network, I prefer to think of the "*A*" as "authentication" because not enough people understand how important it is. For example, when was the last time you paid attention to your browser when purchasing something online? Did you check to make sure you were running over SSL? I find it interesting that when I hover my mouse over the lock in Internet Explorer, I'm told that it's using "128-bit encryption." Sadly, that information is of little use. What I really need to know is **who is on the other end of the pipe, anyway**? I can use the strongest encryption known to man, but if the guy on the other end of the wire is my enemy, what's the point? I can double-click that little lock icon to view the server's certificate and find out the name of the server that my browser just authenticated using SSL, but it would sure be nice if my browser would put more emphasis on the identity of the server as opposed to the length of the encryption key.

We place way too much emphasis on the "*C*" in CIA. Sure, encryption is important, but aren't integrity protection and authentication even more important? For example, if an attacker is able to modify packets from an authenticated user or, worse yet, inject his own packets and make us think they come from an authenticated user, isn't that more ominous? In most threat models, this is a much more dangerous attack. Given the choice between the two evils, I'd guess that your bank would much prefer an attacker to be able to eavesdrop on your money transfers than to be able to change the account numbers on the wire. Oh, and let me dispel the common myth that if you're encrypting data, you're automatically integrity-protecting it. Not so. Depending on the cipher and the way it's used (the "mode"), an attacker may be able to easily make predictable modifications to the plaintext by modifying the ciphertext. And these changes won't be detected by the decryption algorithm. In many cases, the attacker can flip individual bits in the ciphertext, and the corresponding bits in the plaintext stream will be flipped. This can be used to change account numbers or amounts in a banking transaction, for example!

Let's talk about the "I" in CIA for a moment. We need to be able to integrity-protect each packet. What this means is that we want to ensure that it's not modified in transit or fabricated out of thin air by an attacker. Looking at the overall network conversation, we don't want packets being reordered, reflected back to their source, or otherwise replayed without our being able to detect it. We also prefer not to have packets deleted, although if our networking peer is utterly silent it may be tough to know whether this is because of a denial-of-service attack or because she stepped out for a coffee.

Message Authentication Codes

A key technique used for ensuring packet integrity is called a message authentication code, or MAC for short. There are lots of ways of constructing a MAC, but the idea is always the same. We want Alice and Bob (our network peers) to be able to compute a secure checksum of the message that nobody else can compute. Take a cryptographic hash, such as SHA1. Alone, it can't be used as a MAC because anyone can compute it. Alice can hash her message and send the message and the resulting hash code to Bob, and Bob can hash the message he receives and compare it with the hash value he received on the wire. If the hash values match, what does he know? Pretty much nothing because anyone can compute the hash of a set of bits. An attacker could have modified Alice's message and recomputed the hash, or simply sent his own message with a hash. No secret is required for this computation.

On the other hand, we could have `Alice` run a block encryption algorithm over the message. Block ciphers operate on small chunks of plaintext (16 bytes per block in most modern ciphers), so nontrivial plaintext messages are first broken up into blocks; then each block is encrypted individually. This is known as Electronic Codebook mode (ECB). Each block of ciphertext is calculated independently of the others. But other, more interesting modes exist. For example, in Cipher Block Chaining mode (CBC), before encrypting a block of plaintext we XOR the previous block of ciphertext into it, thus creating something like a feedback loop. For our purposes (constructing a MAC), we really don't care about any of the ciphertext except for the last block, which ends up being a unique residue[1] formed from all the bits of the message plus the encryption key (that we assume the attacker doesn't know). So the last block of ciphertext, typically 16 bytes, becomes the MAC that can be sent with the message (see Figure 58.1). If we assume that `Alice` and `Bob` share the secret key used to form the MAC,

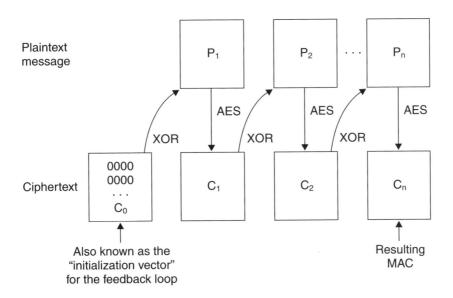

Figure 58.1 CBC-MAC using AES encryption

---

1. Whereas collisions are technically possible, they're highly unlikely (and computationally infeasible to force) if the block size of the algorithm is large enough.

when Bob receives the plaintext message and the MAC he can perform the same operation Alice did, using the message he received and the key he already knows. He can then compare the MAC that he computed with the MAC that arrived with the message. This technique is known as CBC-MAC. You see, an attacker who doesn't know the key can't compute the MAC, so if she modifies a packet or tries to inject her own, she won't be able to compute a MAC that's acceptable to Bob because she doesn't know the key. And with a 16-byte block size (128 bits), it would take the attacker an enormous number of guesses to find the correct MAC.[2]

A totally different approach to forming a MAC is to use a hash algorithm instead of an encryption algorithm. This is known as an HMAC. In a nutshell, Alice hashes a secret key concatenated with the message she wants to send to Bob. She then concatenates her key with the resulting hash and hashes again to avoid what is known as a length extension attack (Ferguson and Schneier 2003). Figure 58.2 illustrates the idea with the SHA-256 hash algorithm, which results in a 256-bit MAC. When used properly, this is a highly secure way to integrity-protect data. The .NET Framework supports HMAC-SHA1, which provides a 128-bit MAC via the HMACSHA1 class.

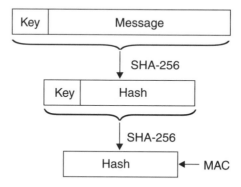

Figure 58.2 HMAC-SHA-256 in action

---

2. The .NET Framework does have an implementation of CBC-MAC based on TripleDES, named MACTripleDES, but please don't use it because of the small block size that both DES and TripleDES use (only 8 bytes, or 64 bits). You don't want a MAC that small!

So, in order to provide "C" and "I" over a network connection between `Alice` and `Bob`, they need to share some secrets. Generally, sharing four secrets is a good idea (Ferguson and Schneier 2003):

1. MAC key for messages sent from `Alice` to `Bob`
2. MAC key for messages sent from `Bob` to `Alice`
3. Encryption key for messages sent from `Alice` to `Bob`
4. Encryption key for messages sent from `Bob` to `Alice`

All four secrets can be derived from a single secret that `Alice` and `Bob` share, which is typically known as the "session key" for their connection. But how do they discover this magical session key? This is where the "A" comes in! A network authentication protocol is really about two things. First, it allows `Alice` and `Bob` to develop trust in each other's identity (`Alice` gets cryptographic proof that her network peer holds `Bob`'s credentials, and vice versa). Second, it allows `Alice` and `Bob` to exchange a session key that can be used to provide the properties of CIA for their ensuing conversation. With these properties in place, we say that `Alice` and `Bob` have established a secure channel.

How does authentication work? That's the tricky part. Except in the unlikely event that `Alice` and `Bob` have met in some private place and exchanged a master key (for example, a passphrase), they'll need help from a third party who can vouch for the other's identity. This third party is known as an authority. Item 59 talks about one type of authority, known as a Kerberos key distribution center, or KDC. Another type is a certificate authority, or CA, that issues digital certificates to parties who need to authenticate with each other.

The most natural form of authenticated key exchange on Windows is Kerberos, and each domain controller running Windows 2000 or greater hosts a Kerberos authority. Support for Kerberos is also provided by most of the built-in Windows networking substrates, including named pipes, RPC, and DCOM. These subsystems use an abstraction layer known as the Security Support Provider Interface (SSPI, Item 65) to authenticate and implement a secure channel. SSPI can also be used directly by third parties building their own networking plumbing.

To summarize, in order to provide the properties of confidentiality, integrity, and authentication for a network connection, we first must perform an authenticated key exchange using a protocol such as Kerberos. Then, for each message we must calculate a MAC over the plaintext, appending it to the message. Finally, we must encrypt the message. The receiver should decrypt the message and verify the attached MAC. The MAC and encryption keys should be derived from the session key that was exchanged during authentication.

The goal of this item isn't to make you think you can run off and implement your own secure channel from scratch. There's not nearly enough detail here for that (for example, I didn't discuss any protections against replay attacks). My goal instead is to give you a basic introduction to the ideas behind secure network communication. I want you to know what it means to integrity-protect a message. Once you have an inkling of how this works, you might feel more comfortable actually using these features when they're available. For an example, look at the COM authentication levels in Item 50. If you're really on fire for this stuff and want to learn more about what it takes to implement a real secure channel, refer to Ferguson and Schneier (2003).

■ 59 ■
What Is Kerberos?

K ERBEROS IS A NETWORK authentication protocol based on conventional cryptography; that is to say, it relies on symmetrical cryptographic algorithms that use the same key for encryption as for decryption (Ferguson and Schneier 2003). Network authentication protocols do two things: help you discover who is on the other end of the wire, and help you and your peer exchange a cryptographic key (also known as a session key) so you can maintain integrity and confidentiality protection for the ensuing conversation. What follows is a simplified description of Kerberos that will help you understand what's going on under the hood in Windows.

Kerberos gets its name from the mythological three-headed dog that guards the entrance to Hell. The three heads can be thought of as representing the three entities involved: the client, the server, and a trusted authority known as the Key Distribution Center, or KDC (in Windows, each domain controller acts as a KDC, with Active Directory hosting the security account database, as mentioned in Item 12). The KDC is the keeper of secrets. Say Alice and Bob are members of some Windows domain. They each share a secret password with the domain controller (KDC) for that domain. Now, technically, the KDC doesn't know the cleartext password but rather a one-way hash, which is used as the basis for a cryptographic "master key." So Alice shares a master key with the KDC, and Bob shares a different master key with the KDC. Alice doesn't know Bob's master key, and Bob doesn't know Alice's, so neither has a direct way of verifying the

the other's identity. The KDC must get involved and introduce `Alice` to `Bob`, and `Alice` and `Bob` must trust what the KDC says (you can see why the security of domain controllers is paramount). Figure 59.1 shows this relationship.

The essence of Kerberos is key distribution. The job of the KDC is to distribute a unique session key to each pair of security principals that want to establish a secure channel. To illustrate this, I'll describe a simplified version of Kerberos first to help you get the basic idea; then I'll show what bits I omitted and provide a more complete story.

Say `Alice` wants to communicate with `Bob`. She sends a message to the KDC stating, "I'm `Alice`, and I'd like to talk to `Bob`. Help me out here, will you?" The KDC obliges by generating a random cryptographic key for `Alice` and `Bob` to use (let's call this K_{ab}) and sends two copies of it back to `Alice`. The first copy is for her to use and is sent to her along with some other information in a data structure encrypted using `Alice`'s master key. The second copy is packaged along with `Alice`'s name in a data structure known as a "ticket." The ticket is encrypted with `Bob`'s master key and is effectively a message to `Bob` saying, "This is your KDC. `Alice` wants to talk to you, and here's K_{ab}, a session key that I've created for you and `Alice` to use. Besides me, only you and `Alice` could possibly know the value of K_{ab}, because I've encrypted it with your respective master keys. If your peer can prove knowledge of this key, then you can safely assume it's `Alice`." Figure 59.2 shows this exchange.

Now `Alice` must send the ticket to `Bob` along with proof that she knows K_{ab}, and she must do it in a way that allows `Bob` to detect replays from attackers listening on the network where `Alice`, `Bob`, and the KDC are conversing. So she sends the ticket to `Bob` along with what's called an **authenticator**, which is simply a data structure containing her name and

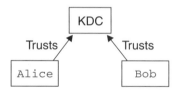

Figure 59.1 The three heads of Kerberos

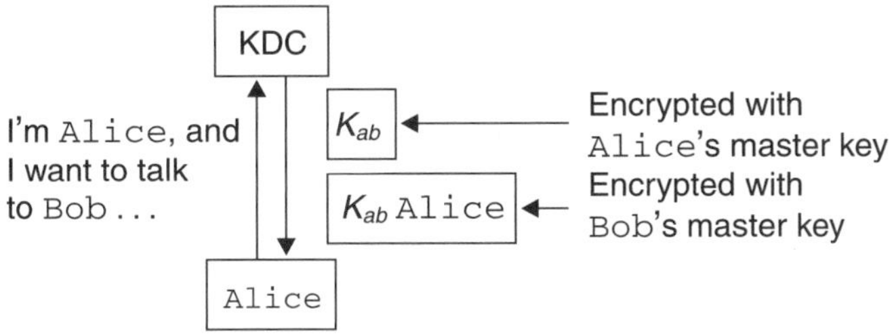

Figure 59.2 **Alice** asks the KDC for a ticket for **Bob**.

the current time, all of which is encrypted with the session key, K_{ab}. Bob takes the ticket, decrypts it, reads the message it holds from the KDC, pulls K_{ab} out of the ticket and decrypts the authenticator using it, and compares the name in the authenticator with the name in the ticket (this provides evidence that the authenticator was indeed encrypted with K_{ab}; otherwise, the name in the authenticator would come out garbled when Bob decrypted it). Finally, Bob checks his replay cache, which is a list of recently seen authenticators, making sure he's never seen this particular authenticator before (this mitigates replay attacks). If Alice's timestamp isn't within five minutes[1] or so of the current UTC time on Bob's wall clock, he simply rejects the request with a hint of what his clock says (time isn't a secret, after all). This allows Bob to prune his replay cache so it doesn't grow without bound, and Alice can retry with a fresh authenticator that Bob will accept. Note that keeping clocks synchronized is important in Kerberos, which is why domain controllers normally provide a time service as well as a Kerberos KDC.

Whoever is on the other end of the wire has claimed to be Alice, and Bob wants to verify that whoever it is really knows K_{ab}, which will prove to him that it's indeed someone who knows Alice's master key. Assuming all goes well, Bob accepts this authenticator as proof that it's Alice on the other end of the wire.

If Alice wants Bob to prove his identity as well (this is the optional mutual authentication feature in Kerberos), she indicates this in her request

---

1. The allowable skew, along with other Kerberos parameters such as ticket lifetime, is configurable via security policy.

to him via a flag. Once Bob is satisfied with Alice's proof, he takes the timestamp she sent, encrypts it with K_{ab}, and sends it back to her. Alice decrypts this and verifies that it's the timestamp she originally sent to Bob. She now knows that whoever is on the other end of the wire knows K_{ab} and infers that it's Bob because only he could have decrypted the ticket to retrieve K_{ab}.[2] Figure 59.3 shows this exchange.

As I explained earlier, this isn't truly Kerberos, but it's close. Real Kerberos includes an extra step for additional security. When Alice first logs in, she actually asks the KDC for what is called a "ticket-granting ticket," or TGT. This is just like the ticket she gets for Bob, except it's designed for use with the KDC and is thus encrypted with a very strong master key known only to the KDC. The TGT contains a session key (let's call it K_{ak}) to be used by Alice in her communications with the KDC throughout the day. So, in Figure 59.2, when Alice requests a ticket for Bob she actually sends along her TGT plus an authenticator with her request. The KDC then sends back Alice's copy of K_{ab} encrypted with K_{ak} (as opposed to Alice's master key, as I described in my earlier, simplified description). What does this buy us? It reduces the exposure of Alice's master key. Theoretically, she doesn't need to even remember her master key once she receives the TGT.[3] Besides, it's a really good idea to avoid

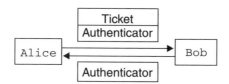

Figure 59.3 Alice authenticates with Bob.

---

2. The KDC also knew K_{ab} at one time (the KDC generated the key in the first place, remember?) and could very well be impersonating Alice or could have leaked K_{ab} to a bad guy, but remember that Alice and Bob must trust the KDC not to play these games. Domain controllers must be carefully guarded against compromise!

3. I say "theoretically" because Windows does cache the client's master key in her logon session for use with an older protocol called NTLM, and to request a new TGT after the one she has can no longer be renewed.

encrypting lots of data with long-term keys (the master key doesn't change until `Alice` changes her password).

To summarize, a Kerberos credential consists of a ticket plus the associated session key (a copy of which resides inside the ticket for the server's use). As a client authenticates with various servers on the network, she collects these credentials in a cache in her logon session (Item 17). The ticket itself is useless to an attacker without the associated key, although there's the possibility of using it to perform a dictionary attack against the server's master key, which is a subject I'll return to later in this item.

From a purely practical standpoint, what do you think will happen if you go into Active Directory and reset the password for a service account? Any tickets issued from that point forward for the service will be encrypted using the new master key. This means you'd better shut down and restart the service process so that it knows its new master key; otherwise, anyone trying to authenticate with that server will fail! What about clients that already authenticated with that server earlier in the day? Their tickets won't be usable after the server restarts with a new master key. When they try to reconnect to the server they will fail to authenticate. Having these clients log out and log back in (or, more simply, clearing the ticket cache using a tool like **kerbtray.exe**, which comes with the Windows 2000 server resource kit) solves the problem. It's probably best to change service account passwords late at night after most folks have gone home!

Here's another practicality about Kerberos. It doesn't work well over the Internet. Imagine being at company A and trying to authenticate with a KDC at company B. The firewall for company A probably isn't going to let you make outgoing requests unless you're doing it over port 80, with HTTP. A Kerberos KDC expects to receive TCP or UDP requests over port 88. So, until we start tunneling Kerberos over port 80 (as we seem to be tunneling everything else these days with Web services), don't expect Kerberos to take over the Internet! Where you'll find it used mostly is on the corporate intranet.

Cross-Domain Authentication and Domain Trusts

What if `Alice` and `Bob` aren't in the same domain? Let's say `Alice` is in `DomA` and `Bob` is in `DomB`. In this case, no one single authority knows both

Alice's and Bob's master keys. This is where trust relationships come in. If DomB trusts DomA, by definition it trusts DomA to issue TGTs on its behalf. So what Alice needs to do in this case is go to her own authority (DomA), present her TGT and a fresh authenticator to prove her identity, and ask for a TGT for DomB. But here's the rub: If DomA issues a TGT for DomB, that ticket must be encrypted using a key that both DomA and DomB share! Otherwise, how would DomB ever be able to decrypt it? This is what a trust relationship in Kerberos establishes: a shared secret between authorities. If you've ever established a trust relationship manually (via the Active Directory Domains and Trusts MMC snap-in), you know that a password is required; this is what that password is used for. (If you set up a manual trust, make sure the password is at least 20 characters long and randomly generated!)

Once Alice gets a TGT for DomB, she can proceed as I described earlier, presenting her TGT plus a fresh authenticator to DomB and asking for a ticket for Bob, then sending Bob this ticket plus a fresh authenticator.

Now, more generally, transitive trusts are possible in Kerberos. If authority A trusts B, and B trusts C, then A trusts C indirectly. But what if a principal in A wanted to authenticate with a server in C? She would have to follow the trust path, getting TGTs for each domain in the path. But because she's caching each ticket in her logon session, she has to transit any given trust path only once per day. That's because once she's got a TGT for a particular authority, she can authenticate directly with that authority as long as her TGT hasn't expired. Once her TGT expires (technically it can be renewed for up to seven days before this happens), she'll need to transit the trust path again from the beginning. Active Directory domains are set up to take advantage of this transitive trust. Each domain you create in a tree has a trust relationship with its parent and all of its children. And the root domain of each tree in a forest has trusts with every other root domain in the forest. This means you can have 100 domains in a forest, and all of them will have Kerberos trusts either directly or indirectly (via transitive trust) with each other. I've shown this in Figure 59.4.

In the figure, Alice in domain C needs to talk to domains C, A, B, and D, in that order, to transit the trust path to the server in domain D. But once she's done that, as long as she doesn't log out (thus losing her logon session and its associated ticket cache), and as long as her tickets haven't expired, she can talk to any servers in domain B (for example) without having to talk

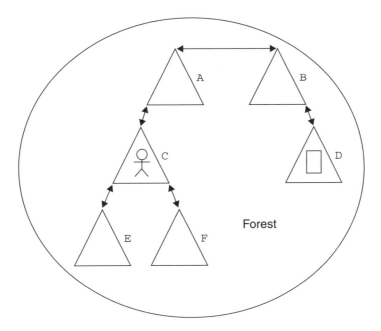

Figure 59.4 Transitive trust in a forest

to domains C or A again. An administrator can short-circuit this trust path by manually adding a trust from D to C as well. This allows Alice to get to resources in domain D a bit quicker and more reliably (otherwise, if domain A or C is out of commission when she first tries to transit the trust path, Alice is out of luck). Note that all of this complexity is hidden from programmers. Even if you were adding Kerberos support to an application manually (as I do in Item 66), you wouldn't need to worry about transiting trust paths. The client-side Kerberos plumbing in Windows takes care of that automatically when you initiate an authentication handshake with a server. But I still think it's important to know what's happening, because you'll develop a better intuition for solving problems that way, and you'll better understand domain administration as well.

What Else Is in a Ticket?

In the previous discussion, I omitted some details in order to focus on how Alice proves her identity to Bob. Let me now fill in some of the more practical details that you might find interesting. The first is that tickets contain group SIDs. This allows a domain controller to communicate domain group membership to servers, avoiding the need for the server to make a network round-trip to discover this information. Considering the way groups work in Windows (Item 20), this can actually mean contacting two domain controllers if the client and servers are in different domains. But it also means that there can be significant latency (typically up to ten hours) in the domain group SIDs a server receives for a client. Say, for example, that the client authenticates with the server first thing in the morning, disconnects, and is removed from a domain group at lunchtime. If the client is still logged in at the end of the day and connects and reauthenticates with that same server, she'll be sending the same ticket to the server, with the same set of groups. The server will believe the client is still in a group when she's actually been removed. The only way to clear up this discrepancy is for the client to retrieve a fresh ticket before going to the server, and that will only happen if the client's ticket cache has been purged or if she's logged out and logged back in. In Item 15, I mentioned the same type of problem that servers have caching security contexts (tokens) for clients. Well, it turns out that even if you throw away the client's token and force her to reauthenticate, when Kerberos is in use it's likely that you'll still have up to ten hours of latency in the resulting group SIDs.

Kerberos tickets also contain times. These times include a window during which the ticket is valid plus a limit on how long the ticket can be "renewed." As I hinted earlier, tickets are valid for ten hours from the time the client first logged in, but they can be renewed before they expire for up to seven days. All of these numbers can be changed via Kerberos security policy, which is part of group policy (Item 74). Renewal allows the KDC to verify that the client's account hasn't been disabled and allows fresh group SIDs to be placed in the new ticket. The time limitations are there to reduce the window during which an attacker can use a stolen ticket.

Kerberos tickets may contain network addresses restricting their use. Thus, if `Alice` is at IP address 67.129.90.150 when she requests a ticket for `Bob`, her ticket may specify that it must be used from 67.129.90.150 and no other address. This makes an attacker's life a bit harder by forcing him to either use the ticket from `Alice`'s machine or spoof `Alice`'s IP address.

User-to-User Authentication

`Bob` (the server in our example) has a master key that may often be exposed to dictionary attacks because the KDC encrypts all tickets for him with his master key. Say `Alice` wants to know `Bob`'s password. She knows that if she asks for a ticket for `Bob`, that ticket will be encrypted with `Bob`'s master key, which is derived from his password. So `Alice` can use a ticket for `Bob` to mount a brute-force or dictionary attack against his password.

With most password-based systems, you need to choose good passwords to foil brute force or dictionary attacks by eavesdroppers. Humans have trouble remembering long passwords, but if you're configuring an account specifically for a daemon (Item 27), remember that a machine can remember much better passwords than a human can! So be sure to use extremely long, randomly generated passwords for servers. For example, if you randomly generate a 20-character password that includes upper- and lower-case letters, numbers, and punctuation, you'll have about 128 bits of entropy, which leads to a very strong master key. Settle for no less! For some sample code that randomly generates passwords like this, you might want to look at my Password Minder tool, which you can download from this book's Web site.

But what if some of our servers aren't daemons? What if we're using Kerberos to do peer-to-peer authentication, and `Bob` is a real human with a less than stellar password? Well, first of all `Bob`'s password better not be too weak, because when he first logs in an attacker eavesdropping on his TGT request can use that information to mount a dictionary attack against his password (the TGT is encrypted using `Bob`'s master key). But throughout the day, as other peers connect to `Bob` they're constantly sending him tickets encrypted with his master key, giving the bad guy even more chances to attack. Plus, didn't I say earlier that Kerberos allows the client to forget her master key once she receives her initial TGT? If `Bob` (a peer-to-peer agent—acting as both a server and a client, or "servent") has forgotten his master key, how can he possibly decrypt incoming tickets?

Kerberos includes a feature known as "user-to-user" authentication to help with these situations. The idea is to avoid encrypting tickets with the master key of a servent. Here's how user-to-user authentication works. Before talking to the KDC, `Alice` first contacts `Bob` and asks for a copy of his initial TGT. Bob sends this to Alice (remember, a ticket alone without the corresponding key is useless—Alice can't use this to pretend she's Bob). Alice then makes her normal request to the KDC, asking for a ticket for Bob. But she includes an additional ticket with her request: Bob's TGT. The KDC decrypts Bob's TGT and retrieves the session key that Bob and the KDC use to communicate. It then uses this session key, which is long and random and thus not vulnerable to dictionary or brute-force attacks (as Bob's master key might be), to encrypt the ticket sent back to Alice. It's a tradeoff between performance and security; an extra round-trip or two in the morning seems like a reasonable price to pay for reduced exposure of Bob's master key. But how does Windows know when to use this feature? How does it know when the server you're contacting is actually a servent with a potentially vulnerable password?

Windows Server 2003 makes this decision based on whether the target server account has been anointed with at least one service principal name (SPN). If you've configured your service to run as Network Service or SYSTEM, then you don't need to do anything special because a machine account always has a set of SPNs defined for it by default. But if you've set up a custom domain account to run your server, you'll want to add an SPN to it; otherwise, you'll be suffering extra round-trips for user-to-user authentication for no good reason. Besides, you'll want your clients to use the SPN to identify the server anyway, as you'll learn in Item 60.

■ 60 ■
What Is a
Service Principal Name (SPN)?

MANY DAEMONS ARE configured to run with domain credentials. For instance, consider a Windows service that runs as `Network Service` on a machine in a domain. This service has the domain credentials of the machine, and clients can use Kerberos to authenticate with it. But if you look at how Kerberos works (Item 59), it seems as though the client needs to know exactly what account the server is running under, because she must ask the KDC for a ticket for that account (the ticket is normally encrypted using a key derived from the service account's password). If the client can't provide this information, how is she ever supposed to authenticate with the server?

Another problem we have is mutual authentication. When a client uses Kerberos to authenticate with, say, `mydaemon` on machine `FOO` via port 4761, the client should receive some assurance that `mydaemon` isn't being spoofed. For example, what if the real machine `FOO` has been disabled and a Trojan machine with the same name has been started on the network? Kerberos can help `mydaemon` assure the client of its authenticity, but how, when the client has no idea what account the daemon is supposed to be using?

Both of these problems are solved by using a service principal name (SPN). If we want the client to obtain tickets and authenticate with a daemon called `mydaemon` running on machine `FOO` and listening on port 4761, we let the client ask for a ticket using a name constructed from that information: `mydaemon/foo:4761`.[1] To make this work, we need to configure Active Directory with a mapping from this name to the account that `mydaemon` is *supposed* to be running under. Now the KDC can use this information to issue the correct ticket. Remember, the directory is the trusted oracle where we store security policy, so we should use it to indicate under which account we want a particular service to run. The name "`mydaemon/foo:4761`" is called an SPN.

With this infrastructure in place, imagine the difficulty an attacker would have trying to spoof a daemon on the network. First he must knock out the real daemon, perhaps by disconnecting it from the network or flooding it with fake connection requests. Then he must start up a new machine on the network with the same name and expose his Trojan service. But since the client is using Kerberos with mutual authentication, she won't talk to the Trojan until he proves that he knows the password for the account under which the real service is configured to run. So the attacker now needs to either discover this password or compromise Active Directory to reconfigure the SPN mapping.

See Item 61 to learn how to use service principal names in practice.

---

1. Note that the text "`mydaemon`" is completely arbitrary: Each service just needs to decide on a unique string that it will use to construct its SPN, and any clients that want to talk to that service will need to form the SPN using that string. This is called the "service class," and for real NT services a reasonable convention is to simply use your service's short name.

■ 61 ■
How to Use Service Principal Names

A NY DAEMON THAT USES Kerberos (Item 59) to authenticate its clients should have a service principal name (SPN) in the directory (Item 60). Configuring an SPN is straightforward; in fact, there's a tool that ships with the server version of Windows called **setspn.exe** that can be used to add these mappings. If you're running Windows 2000, you can find this tool in the Windows 2000 Resource Kit. Or you can write some code yourself to call the Win32 function DsWriteAccountSpn, which is really all that **setspn.exe** does anyway.

The structure of an SPN looks like this: class/host:port/name, where class represents the type of service (for example, "MSSQLSvc," "ldap," or "www") and host is the machine name (either a DNS or NETBIOS name). The port and name fields are optional; port isn't necessary if the daemon is listening on its default port, but it can be useful if several instances of the daemon are running on the same machine, listening on different ports. The name field is used by replicated services such as Active Directory, but most services won't make use of this feature and can omit it.

Here's an example: Say you have a Windows service called weathersvc that runs on a machine called jupiter and listens on the service's default port. On that machine, you've decided to run the service under a domain account named WeatherDaemon. In this case, you add an SPN to the

`WeatherDaemon` account (actually I'm adding two SPNs here; you'll see why shortly).

```
setspn -A weathersvc/jupiter.acme.com MyDomain\WeatherDaemon
setspn -A weathersvc/JUPITER MyDomain\WeatherDaemon
```

Let's say you're also running this same service on a machine called `titus`, but there it runs as `Network Service`. Because it's running with the machine's credentials, you need to add an SPN to the machine account `titus`.

```
setspn -A weathersvc/titus.acme.com MyDomain\titus
setspn -A weathersvc/TITUS MyDomain\titus
```

For each example, I registered two SPNs: one using the DNS name and one using the NETBIOS name of the host. This is convenient because it allows the client to specify either name, but bear in mind that NETBIOS names might not be unique across the directory, and if a duplicate SPN is found in the directory, authentication will fail. If you're worried about this, use only DNS names when registering SPNs, and make sure your clients always use the fully qualified DNS name when making authenticated connections to a server using Kerberos.

SQL Server 2000 uses this mechanism. If you decide to run an instance of it under a domain account, you'll need to add an SPN (the service class in this case is "`MSSQLSvc`"). It's useful to consider how the client-side libraries for SQL Server 2000 pick apart a connection string and form an SPN when they authenticate with a server. It's really quite simple once you understand how SPNs work.

1. Pull the server name out of the connection string.
2. Form the SPN as follows: `string.Format("MSSQLSvc/{0}:1433", hostName)`.
3. Use this SPN when authenticating with the database.

If you build your own Kerberized system, you should incorporate the use of SPNs to ensure that you're getting mutual authentication. This means building client-side code that forms the SPN based on the names of your service class and the host (and perhaps the port) to which the client is connecting. It also means registering an SPN for each instance of your server in Active Directory. I provide an example of this in Item 66.

Remember that this works only if you run your server under a domain account or one of the built-in logon sessions (`Network Service` or `SYSTEM`) on a machine that is part of a domain. SPNs are not used with local accounts because Kerberos isn't used with local accounts!

Also, if you're using named pipes, DCOM, or HTTP, you shouldn't need to add any SPNs because the system maps these services onto a well-known SPN with a service class of "`HOST`." These SPNs are automatically added whenever a machine joins the domain.

■ 62 ■
What Is Delegation?

I N ITEM 31, I described the concept of impersonation, where a server can temporarily take on a client's identity in order to perform some work on the client's behalf. Usually when a server impersonates a client, it's only to access resources that are local to the server. When the server attempts to use the client's credentials to access remote resources, well, that's delegation and by default it's disallowed. If a server (Bob) impersonates a remote client (Alice) and tries to authenticate with another server (Charlie), by default Charlie will see a null session (Item 35) rather than a logon for Alice.

Before Windows embraced Kerberos in Windows 2000, a simple challenge-response authentication protocol called NTLM was in place. Basically this said that to verify Alice's identity, Bob would challenge her by sending a unique number that she would then encrypt with a master key derived from her password. Bob would then send the challenge and Alice's response to a domain controller for verification. Bob didn't know Alice's password, and after this exchange he still didn't know her password. He therefore had no possible way to impersonate Alice on the network because, when Charlie challenged Bob to encrypt a number with Alice's password, Bob couldn't respond. The only way to make this work would be for Alice to tell Bob her password, and that would be very dangerous indeed because passwords are long-term secrets. There would be no practical constraint over Bob's use of Alice's password, either in space or in time. Bob could impersonate Alice to any server for months on end. This is why delegation simply was not supported in Windows NT 4 domains.

But along came Windows 2000 with Kerberos. If you read Item 59 (and I recommend that you do before you continue reading this item), you know that a Kerberos credential isn't the client's password. It's a temporary "ticket" plus a corresponding session key, and that ticket has a lifetime of a single workday. So in Windows 2000 you can flip a switch called "Trust this computer for delegation . . ." in Active Directory, and a server will suddenly be allowed to receive these types of delegated credentials. In fact, Active Directory even advertises this to clients: If Bob is a server account trusted for delegation, any tickets for Bob issued to clients contain a flag: ok-as-delegate.

Let's say you set up an IIS server on an intranet and configure it to use Integrated Windows Authentication (Kerberos). Let's say you also mark that computer account as "trusted for delegation" in Active Directory. When Alice points Internet Explorer to that Web server, during authentication the browser will see the ok-as-delegate flag and will check to see if Alice has a "forwardable" ticket (technically this is a ticket-granting ticket) for her domain authority. This will be the case only if Alice's account hasn't been marked "sensitive and cannot be delegated" in Active Directory. If she has a forwardable ticket, the browser will ask her domain authority for a "forwarded" ticket with a new session key and send that off to the Web server (the session key will be encrypted so an eavesdropper can't use it). The Web server can now use Alice's Kerberos credential (ticket plus session key) to obtain tickets to any other server on the network in her name. A Web programmer doesn't notice any of this magic happening. All he knows is that he can now impersonate his client (Alice) and access remote resources as her! Remember that tickets have a limited lifetime, and this delegated ticket will only be valid for ten hours from when Alice first logged in. So, in essence, Windows 2000 provides delegation that's constrained in time but not in space.

Let's back off of the mechanics for a minute and think about what this means. Before delegation, we had some serious limitations in how we could design multitier systems. Because the middle-tier server couldn't delegate the client's credentials to the back end, the back end had to trust the middle tier to perform any access checks that were necessary (see Figure 62.1).

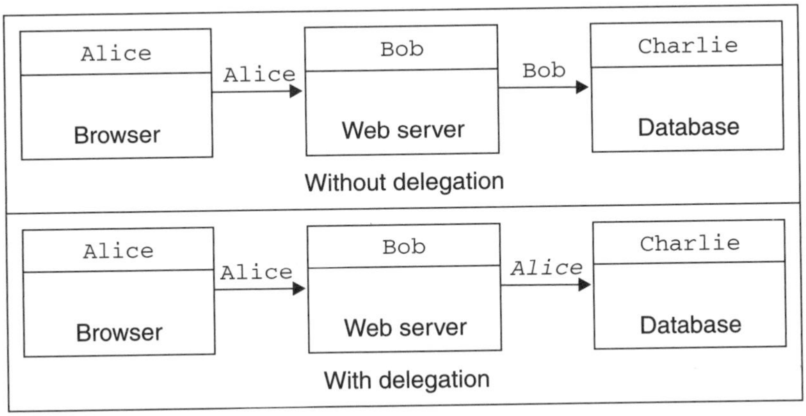

Figure 62.1 A three-tier system without and with delegation

Think about it: No matter who the real client happened to be (Alice or somebody else), the back end always saw the middle tier's identity (Bob). This was one of the main motivations for Microsoft Transaction Server (MTS), which provided a framework for doing these access checks in the middle tier in Windows NT 4, before delegation was supported. That framework was called role-based security, and it still exists today in the successor to MTS, COM+.

With delegation, things look a bit different. Now the middle tier (Bob) can pass through the client's identity directly to the back end. Whereas the middle tier can still perform some role-based access checks, the back end has ultimate authority and can perform very fine-grained access control based on the original client's level of authorization.

There are pros and cons to either scenario. Without delegation, the middle tier can use pooled connections to access the back end. This is faster than warming up a connection for every client. But think about what happens if the middle tier is compromised! Because the middle tier uses its own credentials (Bob) to do work on behalf of all clients, an attacker who compromises it can do anything Bob can do with that back-end server. The attacker can run any stored procedure that Bob can run, can view any tables that Bob can view, and can make any changes that Bob is allowed to make. The back end trusts Bob, so if Bob falls to an attacker, the back end falls immediately as well.

With delegation, the middle tier (Bob) has very little privilege on the back end (possibly none at all), for the clients are the ones granted permissions to the back-end server. If the middle tier is compromised, the attacker has to wait for individual users to connect so he can impersonate them and use their credentials to attack the back end. But each individual user presumably has access only to a very small set of data on the back end. In this scenario, if the middle tier falls to an attacker, the back end is still quite insulated because it doesn't intrinsically trust the middle tier. One problem with this picture is that in Windows 2000 delegation isn't constrained in space. So if the middle tier is attached to servers other than the back end with which it's designed to work, the attacker might use clients' delegated credentials to attack these other servers. This problem is solved in Windows Server 2003, as you'll see. The other problem is that the middle tier can no longer use connection pooling to talk to the back end. You need a new connection for each user you impersonate. (Remember what a database connection is: It's an authenticated connection to the database!)

I happen to think using a mix of the two approaches in Figure 62.1 is your best bet. If you categorize interactions with the back end into low-privileged and high-privileged, you can allow the middle tier to perform all low-privileged interactions using Bob's credentials, making the best use of pooled connections. A high-privileged interaction requires the original client's credentials to be delegated to the back end. If the middle tier is compromised, the attacker has immediate access only to the interactions categorized as low-privileged. Damage is limited in the short term, and your detection countermeasures (Item 2) can kick in and notify the administrator that there's a problem. Not all systems can be built this way, but it's certainly a design worth considering.

Another thing to consider when delegating client credentials is that because the back end now grants permissions directly to clients as opposed to the middle tier, what's to stop the client from connecting directly to the back end instead of going through the middle tier? You probably don't want to allow this, but when talking to a traditional server like SQL Server, there's really no way to constrain this other than using conventional techniques such as firewalls. This is one place where I see Web services coming to the rescue. Because the Web service security specs are so flexible, there's no stopping the middle tier from passing *two sets of credentials* to a Web service back end: his own credentials (Bob) and those of his client (Alice). The back end can do a quick check to make sure Bob's credentials are valid and then use Alice's credentials to perform authorization. This prevents Alice from going directly to the back end, because she doesn't have Bob's credentials! I think it's an interesting idea to consider when building new systems.

Windows Server 2003 makes delegation more palatable by constraining it not only in time but also in space. I show the delegation options in a Windows Server 2003 domain in Figure 62.2. In Windows 2000 there were only two options for allowing an account to delegate client credentials:

- Don't allow this account to delegate client credentials.
- Allow this account to delegate client credentials to any server on the network.

Windows Server 2003 domains add a third option: Allow delegation to specified services only. This mitigates the problem of an attacker who has taken over the middle tier and wants to use delegated client credentials to

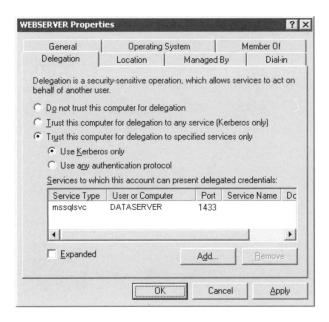

Figure 62.2 Constrained delegation in Windows Server 2003

attack servers that the middle tier wasn't even designed to talk to. With an extension to Kerberos, Windows Server 2003 domain authorities can now constrain delegating servers by restricting whom they can talk to using delegated credentials. In Figure 62.2, the middle-tier server is configured so that it can delegate client credentials, but only to SQL Server running on a machine called DATASERVER. This feature is known as "constrained delegation," and to learn more about how it works under the hood, see Brown (2003).

Delegation is an important security feature in Windows, one that requires virtually no programming (well, you have to impersonate to make it happen, but that's it). It's really a design issue, and one that should be considered early in the life cycle of an N-Tier project. Used carefully, delegation can help slow down an attack. Used carelessly, it can lead to middle-tier servers teeming with juicy client credentials that can be used to attack other network servers. See Item 64 to learn how to use delegation.

■ 63 ■
What Is Protocol Transition?

Protocol transition is a new feature that's been added to Windows Server 2003 domains. Put bluntly, it allows certain designated servers to establish logon sessions with valid Kerberos credentials for an arbitrary domain user without knowing that user's password! As I showed in Item 26, if you're one of these designated servers, you can create a `WindowsIdentity` for a user, with a real token (Item 16) and logon session (Item 17) behind it. Simply use the `WindowsIdentity` constructor that takes a single string argument, the user's account name—technically the user principal name (UPN) for the account, which is typically the user's e-mail address.

There are a couple of scenarios where this can be helpful. The first (and the reason for the name "protocol transition") is when you simply can't use Kerberos to authenticate users on the front end of a distributed application. For example, if users are contacting your server over the Internet (without a VPN connection), they likely won't be able to talk to your domain controller to get the tickets necessary to talk to the server because firewalls prevent them from contacting your domain controller (Item 59). This means you'll need to use some other form of authentication, perhaps a client-side certificate in conjunction with SSL, to authenticate your client. In Windows 2000, whatever authentication protocol you chose, once your middle tier authenticated the client, in order to map the user onto a legitimate Windows user account, the middle tier had to know the password for that account in order to establish a logon session and get a token (typically via the Win32 API `LogonUser` that I discussed in Item 26).

In a perfect world, a user's master key should be known only by that user and her domain authority. But when you need to transition from one authentication protocol (such as SSL) to Kerberos on the back end, the server performing this transition (authenticating the client using SSL in this case and mapping that client onto a Windows account with Kerberos credentials) ends up with a big juicy password database that just screams, "Attack me!" The point of protocol transition is to make it possible for designated servers (think of them as gateways) to be able to perform this service without having to store passwords.

At this point you might be wondering how protocol transition helps. Just because the gateway no longer stores passwords, it can still get a logon for any user it wants (including highly privileged users in the domain). This means an attacker who has compromised the gateway can do the same thing, right? Yes, but protocol transition works hand in hand with the constrained delegation feature in Windows Server 2003 that I discussed in Item 62. In other words, the gateway can't use this feature to obtain tickets for just any servers on the network. Once it logs in the user via protocol transition (without knowing her password, in other words) and impersonates her, when it attempts to use her credentials to talk to other servers on the network, the domain authority only issues tickets for the servers on the gateway's "allow-to-delegate-to" list.

For example, in Figure 63.1, the WEBSERVER gateway will be allowed to log in users without knowing their passwords, but will only be able to use those credentials to talk to SQL Server on a machine called DATASERVER. This sort of constraint wouldn't be possible if WEBSERVER were storing passwords for user accounts. Because we're using protocol transition on WEBSERVER, if that machine is compromised by an attacker, the attacker will find, much to her dismay, that the domain authority simply won't issue tickets for other servers on the network. She won't be able to authenticate with those servers and will be denied access, assuming you've configured your servers to disallow anonymous requests (Item 35)! Sure, the attacker will be able to use a variety of user credentials to get to DATASERVER, but he would have been able to do that (and more) had you stored passwords on WEBSERVER instead. And remember that you should mark highly privi-

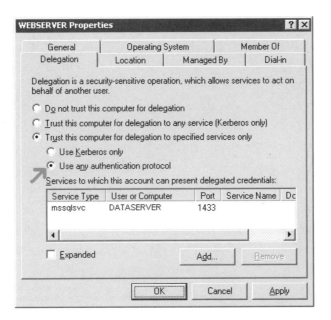

Figure 63.1 Configuring protocol transition for a gateway

leged accounts "sensitive and cannot be delegated" (Item 62), which would restrict the attacker from using those accounts to talk to DATASERVER.

Configuring protocol transition is exactly like configuring constrained delegation, which I cover in Item 64. The only difference is what I've highlighted in Figure 63.1: You must select the option that says "Use any authentication protocol."

Here's another interesting new feature: On any Windows Server 2003 machine that's running in a native Windows Server 2003 domain, you can obtain a token for a domain user without knowing her password. If your server account isn't marked as being trusted to delegate to other servers, you can only use this token to find out what groups the user is in. If your server process is running with the SeTcbPrivilege enabled (SYSTEM is the only security context with this privilege by default, as I discussed in Item 28), you get what's called an impersonation token and you can use it to impersonate and open up local secured objects such as files. Access checks to these resources are made based on the identity in the impersonation token. Without this privilege, you get what's called an identification token, designed only for doing access checks and group lookups. If you try to impersonate using this token, you'll be successful, but if you do anything interesting like try to open a local file, the request will fail.

But even if you get only an identification token, it's still useful because you can use it to see what groups the user is a member of. This has been a really hard problem on Windows 2000, if you can believe it. Recall from Item 20 that group membership lists are decentralized in Windows. Global group memberships are stored in the client's domain, domain local group memberships are stored in the server's domain, and universal group memberships are stored in the Global Catalog. Plus, these domain groups can be nested! Oh, and don't forget local groups, which are stored on individual machines. Trying to discover these group memberships manually is expensive and it's very difficult to get an authoritative answer. The best way to discover the groups for a user is to get a token for her. In the past, however, that required knowing the user's password. With this new feature, you can get a token for a user and get an authoritative list of groups without any hassle. Your server doesn't have to have any special trust to be able to do this (although there's an access check to make sure the server is allowed to read the group memberships for the user).

■ 64 ■
How to Configure Delegation via Security Policy

A DOMAIN ADMINISTRATOR CAN enable a server process to delegate client credentials by designating the account under which that process runs as "trusted for delegation." If the account is a custom user account, say DOMA\Bob, the administrator for DOMA configures the Bob account this way. On the other hand, if the server process is configured to run as either Network Service or SYSTEM, the server is using the machine's credentials and therefore the administrator needs to grant delegation privileges to the computer account for the computer where that server process runs.

On Windows 2000, delegation is a binary choice. Either you allow a principal to delegate client credentials or you don't. To configure a computer account for delegation, bring up the Active Directory Users and Computers console and drill down into a domain's Computers folder. The delegation setting is on the General tab of the property page for the computer account. It's a checkbox with a big warning sign next to it (see Item 62 to learn why delegation can be dangerous). To configure a user account (like DOMA\Bob) just bring up its property sheet and go to the Account tab. Scroll around until you find a checkbox that says "Account is trusted for delegation." While you're there, notice a checkbox that says, "Account is sensitive and cannot be delegated." This is a client-side setting that I discussed in Item 62. Accounts that have this flag set will never be issued "forwardable" tickets. That is to say, the domain authority will never allow their credentials to be delegated, even by servers marked as "trusted for delegation." It's too bad that this setting can't be applied to groups! As it stands, it's a really good idea to mark all highly privileged accounts (such as domain administrator accounts) with this flag to prevent the misuse of powerful credentials on the network.

On Windows Server 2003 things look a lot different. Instead of just a checkbox, there's now a full page of delegation options (I showed this in Item 62). If you bring up a computer account in a Windows Server 2003 domain that's running in Windows Server 2003 native mode (as opposed to Windows 2000 mixed mode), you'll see a tab called "Delegation" that looks like the one I showed in Item 62. There are three radio buttons: The first turns off delegation; the second enables the Windows 2000 form of delegation not constrained in space; and the third enables the extended form of delegation (Brown 2003) implemented by Windows Server 2003 domains. If you choose this third option, you need to add a list of service principal names (SPN) (Item 60) to which this server may delegate client credentials. User accounts don't have the Delegation tab unless they have been assigned at least one SPN, so be sure to add an SPN for your middle-tier server (Item 61) before trying to configure delegation for its user account.

Programmatically, using delegation is easy. Just impersonate your client (Item 32) and then you can authenticate with any of the servers in your "allowed-to-delegate-to" list. Just realize that those servers see the client's security information, not yours.

■ 65 ■
What Is SSPI?

S SPI STANDS FOR the Security Support Provider Interface, which helps a client and server establish and maintain a secure channel, providing confidentiality, integrity, and authentication (Item 58). It abstracts most of the details of performing an authentication handshake and provides methods for integrity-protecting and encrypting data being sent on the wire as well as for decrypting and validating that data on the other side. Providers, such as Kerberos, NTLM, and Negotiate, sit underneath this abstract interface. Figure 65.1 shows the basic architecture.

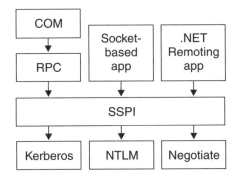

Figure 65.1 The Security Support Provider Interface

Whereas SSPI is used internally by many secure operating system features such as the file system, RPC, and COM, you may need to use it yourself to Kerberize an application that doesn't make use of these higher-level transports. I provide some guidelines on doing this with raw socket-based apps in Item 66, and with .NET Remoting in Item 67.

66

How to Add CIA to a
Socket-Based App Using SSPI

V S.NET 2005 ADDS some very nice support for SSPI, making it almost trivial to establish an authenticated connection over a socket. Kerberizing a socket-based application has never been easier. The essence of this new support lies in a class called NegotiateStream (these details are based on Beta 1 of version 2.0 of the .NET Framework).

Remember, the goal of SSPI is to help add CIA support to a channel (Item 58), so it makes sense to use a stream-based programming model, where the steps are:

1. Perform a handshake to complete an authenticated key exchange
2. Read and write to the stream, which provides integrity protection and encryption

Here's what the class looks like:

```
namespace System.Net.Security {
  public abstract class AuthenticatedStream : Stream
  {
    protected AuthenticatedStream(Stream InnerStream,
                                  bool leaveStreamOpen);
    protected Stream InnerStream            { get; }
    public virtual bool IsAuthenticated        { get; }
    public virtual bool IsMutuallyAuthenticated { get; }
```

```
        public virtual bool IsSigned              { get; }
        public virtual bool IsEncrypted           { get; }
        public virtual bool IsServer              { get; }
    }

    public class NegotiateStream: AuthenticatedStream
    {
      public NegotiateStream(Stream innerStream)
      public NegotiateStream(Stream innerStream,
                             bool leaveStreamOpen);

      // async Authenticate methods omitted for brevity...
      public virtual void ClientAuthenticate()
      public virtual void ClientAuthenticate(
        NetworkCredential      credential,
        string                 targetName);
      public virtual void ClientAuthenticate(
        NetworkCredential      credential,
        string                 targetName,
        ProtectionLevel        requiredProtectionLevel,
        TokenImpersonationLevel allowedImpersonationLevel);

      public virtual void ServerAuthenticate();
      public virtual void ServerAuthenticate(
        NetworkCredential      credential,
        SecurityLevel          requiredProtectionLevel,
        TokenImpersonationLevel requiredImpersonationLevel);

      public virtual TokenImpersonationLevel
        ImpersonationLevel                     { get; }
      public virtual IIdentity RemoteIdentity { get; }
    }
  }
```

There are a few functions on the client and server sides that allow you to implement the handshake asynchronously; I've omitted them for brevity, but their use is pretty obvious once you see the synchronous version.

The `NegotiateStream` class is a lot like a `CryptoStream`, where you simply tie the new stream onto an existing one. As the client pushes bits into her `NegotiateStream`, where they're framed, MAC-protected, and encrypted, the ciphertext is pushed through the underlying stream (which is most likely tied to a socket). The server then pulls data from its `NegotiateStream`, which pulls ciphertext from the underlying stream, decrypts the ciphertext, verifies the MAC, and gives the server the plaintext. The server can also push data back through its stream (assuming the underlying stream supports bidirectional communication), and the client can receive that data in a similar fashion.

The one thing that's different about this stream as opposed to any other is that, if you want CIA protection, the client must first call `ClientAuthenticate` and the server must call `ServerAuthenticate`. These functions map down to SSPI's `InitializeSecurityContext` and `AcceptSecurityContext`, and basically implement an authenticated key exchange using a protocol called SPNEGO, which stands for "secure, protected negotiation." In the negotiation phase, `NegotiateStream` prefers Kerberos (Item 59), but will accept NTLM as a fallback for down-level systems like Windows NT 4, or any time you are using local as opposed to domain accounts on the client and server.

Once the handshake is complete, the server can obtain the client's token (Item 16) via the `RemoteIdentity` property and can impersonate the client via `WindowsIdentity.Impersonate` (Item 32). Given this, the client can protect its identity by specifying an impersonation level during the handshake.

```
namespace System.Security.Principal {
  public enum TokenImpersonationLevel {
    None           = 0,
    Anonymous      = 1,
    Identification = 2,
    Impersonation  = 3,
    Delegation     = 4
  }
}
```

For details on what these different levels mean, please read Item 51. All of my recommendations for using the COM impersonation level apply here as well. For now, suffice it to say that this allows the client to choose programmatically whether or not to allow delegation of its credentials to the server.

The client should also specify a service principal name (SPN) if it wants to use Kerberos. This helps provide mutual authentication as I talked about in Item 60.

There's one very important setting that the client and server must agree on, and that's the level of protection for the channel. For example, if the server were to tell its `NegotiateStream` to encrypt and the client didn't, the client would be sending cleartext data that the server would then try to decrypt, resulting in garbage! Unless you know you'll be running over some secure channel such as IPSEC (Item 68), I implore you to use SecurityLevel.EncryptAndSign, which is the default level if either the client or the server doesn't specify one manually. You might want to allow this to be ratcheted down to SecurityLevel.Sign when debugging in a lab environment: Network packet sniffers used during debugging won't be of much help if you're encrypting everything. In production, however, encrypt those packets!

```
namespace System.Net {
  public enum ProtectionLevel {
    None          = 0, // only provides "A"
    Sign          = 1, // provides "IA"
    EncryptAndSign = 2  // provides "CIA"
  }
}
```

Here is a simple example that shows how to use NegotiateStream in client code:

```
void SpeakSecurelyWithServer(NetworkStream s,
                             string serverHostName) {
  // form a service principal name (SPN)
  string spn = string.Format("SSPISample/{0}",
                             serverHostName);

  // wrap the raw stream in a secure one
  NegotiateStream ns = new NegotiateStream(s);
  ns.ClientAuthenticate(CredentialCache.DefaultNetworkCredentials,
                  spn,
                  ProtectionLevel.EncryptAndSign,
                  TokenImpersonationLevel.Impersonation);

  // verify we achieved mutual authentication
  // (note this will only be true if we're using domain accounts)
  if (!ns.IsMutuallyAuthenticated) {
    Console.WriteLine("Warning: we don't know who the server is!");
  }

  // now we can chat with the server over our secure channel
  using (StreamReader r = new StreamReader(ns))
  using (StreamWriter w = new StreamWriter(ns)) {
    w.WriteLine("GET_PRODUCT_SHIP_DATE");
    w.Flush();
```

```
      string response = r.ReadLine();
      Console.WriteLine(response);
  }
}
```

Note in the model how I formed an SPN based on the target host name. This decouples the client from server configuration, because the client literally requests a Kerberos ticket for `SSPISample/MAC3.acme.com` (let's assume the server is running on a machine called `MAC3`). To make this work, we must tell Active Directory which server account to map this name onto, and we can do this with the **setspn.exe** tool as I showed in Item 61:

```
setspn -A SSPISample/MAC3.acme.com ACME\Bob
```

`setspn.exe` effectively tells the KDC that if it receives a request for a ticket for someone named `SSPISample/MAC3.acme.com`, it should issue a ticket for `ACME\Bob` because that's who the server is configured to run as. This helps assure the client that the server is running under the account it's *supposed* to be running under, but the client doesn't have to know exactly which account that happens to be. If an attacker were spoofing the server, he'd have to know the password for `ACME\Bob` in order to decrypt the ticket, and authentication would fail (none of this will make much sense if you're not familiar with Kerberos, so be sure to read Item 59).

Here's what the server code might look like:

```
void SpeakSecurelyWithClient(NetworkStream s) {
  // wrap the raw stream in a secure one
  NegotiateStream ns = new NegotiateStream(s);
  ns.ServerAuthenticate(
    CredentialCache.DefaultNetworkCredentials,
    ProtectionLevel.EncryptAndSign,
    TokenImpersonationLevel.Identification);

  // record who the client is for this call
  Thread.CurrentPrincipal =
    new WindowsPrincipal(ns.RemoteIdentity);

  using (StreamReader r = new StreamReader(ns))
  using (StreamWriter w = new StreamWriter(ns)) {
    try {
      ProcessRequest(r, w);
    }
```

```
      catch (Exception x) {
        int recordID = RecordDetailedErrorInSecureServerLog(x);
        SendClientAFriendlyButVagueErrorMessage(w, recordID);
      }
    }
  }

  [PrincipalPermission(SecurityAction.Demand, Authenticated=true)]
  void ProcessRequest(StreamReader r, StreamWriter w) {
    string command = r.ReadLine();
    switch (command) {
      case "GET_PRODUCT_SHIP_DATE":
        w.WriteLine("RSN");
        break;
      // ... and so on
    }
  }
```

Note the use of `Thread.CurrentPrincipal` to track the client's identity (Item 33) and the `PrincipalPermissionAttribute` used to gate access to the `ProcessRequest` method so that only authenticated clients are allowed to pass (Item 34).

■ 67 ■
How to Add CIA to
.NET Remoting

V ERSION 1.X of the .NET Framework does not support user authentication, integrity protection, or encryption of the TCP remoting channel. While it is possible to layer this support onto the HTTP channel by
hosting your server objects in IIS, that approach is a bit kludgy, as you'll see.
Version 2.0 of the .NET Framework went into its first beta cycle as I was
wrapping up final edits on this book, and the TCP channel now supports
these important security features, which is great news. This new feature is
based on the NegotiateStream class that I showed in Item 66.

For those who are relying on version 1.x of the .NET Framework, let's
first consider using the HTTP channel and hosting in IIS. To do this, you
create a virtual directory and copy your remoting configuration file into a
web.config file at its root. Figure 67.1 shows an example remoting configuration file, and Figure 67.2 shows the **web.config** file you should end
up with. Note that there are a few differences.

Here's what I changed in moving to the **web.config** file. From top to
bottom, first I removed the application name attribute. This part of the
client's URL will now be controlled by the name of the virtual directory in
IIS. Next, I changed the channel from tcp to http, which is the only supported channel when hosting in IIS. Also note that I removed the port
attribute, because that will be controlled by IIS as well. By default when you

```
<configuration>
 <system.runtime.remoting>
  <application name='MyApp'>
   <channels>
    <channel ref='tcp' port='4242'/>
   </channels>
   <service>
    <wellknown type='Server, server'
               mode='Singleton'
               objectUri='MyEndpoint'/>
   </service>
  </application>
 </system.runtime.remoting>
</configuration>
```

Figure 67.1 A typical remoting configuration file

```
<configuration>
 <system.runtime.remoting>
  <application>
   <channels>
    <channel ref='http'>
     <serverProviders>
      <formatter ref='binary'/>
     </serverProviders>
    </channel>
   </channels>
   <service>
    <wellknown type='Server, server'
               mode='Singleton'
               objectUri='MyEndpoint.rem'/>
   </service>
  </application>
 </system.runtime.remoting>
</configuration>
```

Figure 67.2 Converting to a `web.config` file

use the TCP channel, you're also using the binary formatter, but with HTTP the default is the less efficient SOAP formatter, so I've overridden the default and requested the binary formatter instead. When hosting in IIS, you can use any formatter you like. Finally, note the subtle change in the `objectUri` attribute. I changed `MyEndpoint` to `MyEndpoint.rem`, making it look like a file name. There won't *actually be* any file with this name, but using this format allows the script map in IIS to forward requests for this endpoint to the .NET Framework, where it will then be dispatched to the remoting plumbing (if you look in **machine.config**, you'll find a handler for `.rem` and `.soap` extensions that's supplied by the Remoting team).

Based on the original remoting configuration file, the client would have connected to `tcp://hostname:4242/MyApp/MyEndpoint`. Now that we've moved into IIS, the client connection string changes to `http://hostname:80/vdir/MyEndpoint.rem`, where `hostname` is the name of the Web server and `vdir` is the name of the virtual directory. This really isn't all that hard to do. I've diagrammed the resulting architecture in Figure 67.3. What I want you to note is that any remote calls initiated by the client are sent through IIS and into the server object. These calls can be secured via SSL, Kerberos, and so forth, as I'll talk about shortly. If the server fires events or makes other callbacks to the client, however, IIS knows nothing about the connection from the worker process back to the client. It's a raw connection that has no authentication, integrity, or

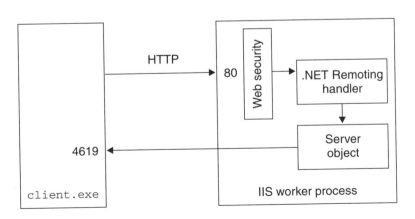

Figure 67.3 Hosting in IIS

encryption on the channel. Hosting in IIS secures only forward calls, not callbacks or events!

If you decide to host in IIS, you'll first want to think about authentication. If the client and server are in a Windows domain, and you want to use the client's domain credentials to authenticate with the server, turn on Windows Integrated Authentication for your virtual directory and disable anonymous access. But note that this won't work out of the box! The .NET Remoting architecture normally prevents clients from disclosing their identities to servers, thus protecting the clients' anonymity. Clearly this is not what you want if your system needs to authenticate clients. To fix this, use a client configuration file as well, as shown in Figure 67.4. You'll probably already have a client configuration file anyway in order to use the HTTP channel with the binary formatter. Note in my client configuration file how I've specified the `useDefaultCredentials` attribute. This isn't well documented, but it tells the remoting plumbing that the client wishes to identify herself to servers using her Windows logon.

Besides the insecure callback problem I described earlier, the other thing that bothers me about this solution is that even if you're using Kerberos to authenticate the client, IIS is simply not designed to use Kerberos to protect the channel. In other words, if all you do is turn on Integrated Windows Authentication and disable anonymous access, you won't get any sort of

```
<configuration>
 <system.runtime.remoting>
  <application>
   <channels>
    <channel ref='http' useDefaultCredentials='true'>
     <clientProviders>
      <formatter ref='binary'/>
     </clientProviders>
    </channel>
   </channels>
  </application>
 </system.runtime.remoting>
</configuration>
```

Figure 67.4 A client-side remoting configuration file

integrity protection or encryption. So there's the potential for connection hijacking, tampering, and eavesdropping attacks. The way to mitigate these attacks is to either require SSL or turn on IPSEC. This seems like overkill to me, which is one reason that I called this solution kludgy at the beginning of this item.

What I really want is Kerberos support directly in the .NET Remoting channel, and fortunately that's exactly what version 2.0 provides. To get started, all you need to do is change your configuration files a bit. Now please note that we are working with a very early implementation, and I would not be surprised if some of these details change before Visual Studio 2005 actually ships. In fact, I plan on making some change requests myself now that I've seen the implementation.

Here's how the TCP channel needs to be configured on the server to require authentication (obviously the port is up to you):

```
<channel ref='tcp' port='4242' authenticationMode='IdentifyCallers'/>
```

And of course if the server requires authentication, the client must comply or she will be denied access. Here's what the client-side reference should look like (refer to Item 51 to help you pick an appropriate `impersonationLevel`):

```
<channel ref='tcp' useDefaultCredentials='true'
impersonationLevel='Impersonate'/>
```

In order for authentication to work with Kerberos, the client needs to specify a service principal name. If the client will be talking only to a single server, she can simply put the SPN in her configuration file. (In this example, I'm assuming she wants to connect to a service of type "Weather-Service." If this makes no sense, revisit Item 60 to learn about SPNs, then follow up with Item 66, which provides a concrete example of the concept.)

```
<channel ref='tcp'
         useDefaultCredentials='true'
         impersonationLevel='Impersonate'
         spn='WeatherService/host.acme.com'/>
```

If the client needs to use different SPNs for different proxies, she should specify the SPN programmatically, which will override any value in the configuration file (or the default value, which is an empty string). For example:

```
IFoo proxy = (IFoo)RemotingServices.Connect(typeof(IFoo),
  "tcp://...");
string spn = string.Format("WeatherService/{0}",
  serverHostName);
ChannelServices.GetChannelSinkProperties(proxy)["spn"] = spn;
```

So far what I've shown you is how to perform authentication, but we still need to add integrity protection and encryption to the channel. Once you have authentication working, it's quite easy to add these two features. Just add another property to both the client- and server-side channel references (I'm going to lobby the .NET Remoting team to change the name of this attribute from `encryption` to `protection`):

```
encryption='EncryptAndSign'
```

Be sure to do this on both the client and server sides.

Now that we have the channel secured, we can talk about how the server discovers (and perhaps impersonates) the client's identity. In the code I'm looking at here in Beta 1, it isn't as clean as it should be. Remember how I specified `authenticationMode='IdentifyCallers'`? Well, you'd expect that the caller's identity would be communicated to the server via `Thread.CurrentPrincipal`, a pattern I described in Item 33. Sadly, in this beta, it's not. In fact, I see no way to retrieve the client's identity through public methods or properties at all right now! It appears as though the only way to discover the client's identity is to go one step further and specify `authenticationMode='ImpersonateCallers'`, which not only sets `Thread.CurrentPrincipal`, but also impersonates the client before calling the method on the object. Hopefully by the time the next beta rolls around, you'll see this fixed so that `Thread.CurrentPrincipal` is set even if you only specify `IdentifyCallers`. I'll be pushing for that change, for certain. You shouldn't have to impersonate the client in order to know who she is!

■ 68 ■
What Is IPSEC?

PSEC IS A NAME that's been given to a suite of security protocols used to secure IP traffic between computers. I'll talk about these individual protocols shortly, but for now let's just talk about the main ideas behind this initiative as a whole. Recall from my discussion of CIA in Item 58 that to secure a channel we want to start with an authenticated key exchange, during which two things happen: The communicating peers develop trust in each other's identity, and they discover a session key that the bad guys won't know. Based on this session key, the peers then provide integrity protection over the channel via MAC protocols (usually HMAC), and the channel is encrypted as well. These countermeasures mitigate lots of different attacks, including spoofing, tampering with packets, connection hijacking, eavesdropping, and replay.

Most IPSEC implementations also provide some form of authorization. For example, in Windows you can do meaningful filtering of incoming IP packets based on the source IP address. This is normally easy for an attacker to skirt around because IP source addresses can be spoofed when not protected. Under IPSEC, however, the source IP address can be authenticated, giving these sorts of filters some real teeth. In fact, IPSEC policies are chosen based on the peer's IP address, so it's possible to have a client that communicates with a secure server over IPSEC but also communicates over an unsecured channel with other machines on the network. IPSEC is not an all-or-nothing proposition.

With IPSEC, the peers are not user principals; rather, they're machines. So when two machines use IPSEC to communicate, they authenticate to one another, ultimately proving that they know some secret that validates their IP addresses. In other words, with `Alice` logged into machine `MAC1` and communicating with `Bob`, logged into `MAC2`, if IPSEC is the only technique securing their communication, `Alice` and `Bob` aren't authenticating each other; `MAC1` and `MAC2` are. If `MAC2` requires all incoming traffic to be secured with IPSEC, the only thing `Bob` knows about any given message from `Alice` is that the IP address on that message wasn't spoofed, that the data wasn't tampered with, and that the plaintext wasn't seen by an eavesdropper on the wire (assuming that both encryption and integrity protections are in place). `Bob` has no proof that it was `Alice` who actually sent the message. He just knows that it originated from `MAC1` (see Figure 68.1). IPSEC is thus very useful for protecting communications between machines, but it doesn't help a server implement any form of user authentication or authorization.

When is IPSEC useful? When you don't have any better alternative. For example, two COM servers talking to one another over DCOM can use COM security to communicate, which under the covers uses SSPI (Item 65), typically using Kerberos authentication. The endpoints of the authentication in this case are the user principals running the processes in question, as shown in Figure 68.2. This is better because the server will get a token (Item 16) for the client and will be able to make authorization decisions based on the client's group memberships. He can also impersonate the client if the need arises (Item 31).

But what if you're not using COM? What if you're using something less mature, like version 1.1 of .NET Remoting, which doesn't provide a secure

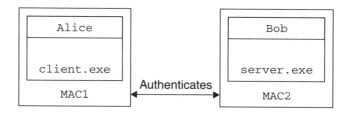

Figure 68.1 Authenticating machines

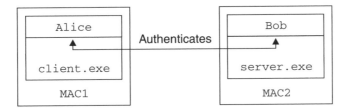

Figure 68.2 Authenticating user principals

channel? This is where IPSEC can come in handy. At least you'll have a secure channel between the machines that are communicating, even if you won't necessarily be able to do user authentication and authorization. While there are ways of adding user authentication to .NET Remoting, such as hosting in IIS, all of the techniques I know of are somewhat kludgy (Item 67). Until version 2.0 of the .NET Framework ships and this support is built in to remoting from the ground up, IPSEC may be the best alternative in your toolbox.

What protocols make up IPSEC? Too many, if you ask Niels Ferguson or Bruce Schneier (Ferguson and Schneier 1999). There are two protocols for channel security: Authentication Header (AH) and Encapsulating Security Payload (ESP). They can be run individually or on top of one another. In addition, they both support two distinct modes of operation: transport and tunnel. AH provides only authentication and integrity protection; it doesn't encrypt the channel. ESP provides full CIA on the channel, but costs a bit more in terms of bandwidth. Ferguson and Schneier (1999) recommend simplifying the protocol suite by eliminating AH and transport mode completely, which would leave ESP in tunnel mode as the only option. I'm going to compromise a bit in Item 69 and suggest that you use ESP in transport mode for securing communications within your organization, as it's the most manageable for LAN communication and still provides full CIA security on the channel.

Key exchange is described by a couple of layered standards: Internet Security Association Key Management Protocol (ISAKMP), and Internet Key Exchange (IKE). These specs talk about how to perform authenticated key exchange to get the channel ready for operation. One last term you should be aware of is the Security Association (SA), which is a little bit like a TCP association, only unidirectional. An SA is identified by a triplet that consists of a peer's IP address, a protocol identifier (AH or ESP), and an index to a set of parameters (such as what encryption and hash algorithms should be used to protect packets). One of the things that the key exchange protocols do is help establish an SA between two machines. In other words, there's lots of negotiation involved here: what protocol to use, which algorithms to use, and so on. Unfortunately none of these IETF standards are easy to read, so if you want to learn more about IPSEC, you might want to pick up a book to guide you, such as *IPSEC: Securing VPNs* (Davis 2001).

On Windows, key exchange can be done one of three ways: Kerberos, X.509 certificates, and a hardcoded master key. Of these three, Kerberos is by far the simplest to use (assuming you're using Active Directory), very secure, and is thus the clear preference. But it will work only if the two machines communicating have a path of trust between them (e.g., they're members of the same forest or their forests are linked with trust relationships). If no trust path exists, you can't use Kerberos; you'll need to use one of the other two options instead, with certificates being the preferable mechanism.

In Item 69, I'll show how to implement IPSEC using a very simple, secure configuration for locking down communication between machines in your organization, where a lot of negotiation isn't really necessary. I'm not going to attempt to tell you how to implement a VPN-secured extranet, where you'll need to deal with multiple platforms, firewalls, NAT, and so on, because that's not only beyond the scope of this book but also beyond the scope of my own expertise.

■ 69 ■
How to Use IPSEC to Protect Your Network

I N WINDOWS, YOU ENABLE IPSEC via security policy. Either you can edit the local security policy of individual machines or you can use domain group policy (Item 74) to configure IPSEC in a consistent way on a whole group of machines, which is a great way to go. Either way you do it, the procedure for configuring IPSEC is the same.

If you look at the security policy for a machine, you'll see a section called IP Security Policies. Figure 69.1 shows what mine looks like on my Windows XP box. It lists several optional policies (strategies, if you will) for applying IPSEC. Notice that they are all disabled by default.

The simplest way to turn on IPSEC support between two computers is to enable the Server policy on the server machine and the Client policy on the client machine. The former says that the server will negotiate IPSEC with the intention of establishing a secure channel, knowing, however, that not all clients will support it. Thus the Server policy allows the client to decide whether a secure connection will be used. The Client policy simply says that, if a server supports IPSEC, the client will agree to use it. You can enable any one of these policies by right-clicking it and selecting Assign, but only one policy may be enabled at any given time, and you can similarly Unassign the active policy to turn off IPSEC support.

A much more secure option is to use the Secure Server policy on the server, which will force all IP communication to be secured with IPSEC or

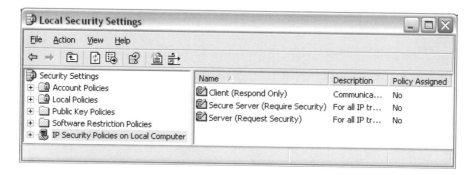

Figure 69.1 Examining IPSEC policy

be rejected. Only client machines with an IPSEC policy enabled will be able to communicate with the server.

But saying, "All IP communication will be secured with IPSEC" is pretty meaningless. Remember that IPSEC is a collection of several protocols (Item 68). To understand what will happen when a particular client connects to a server, you need to drill down into these policies a bit. For example, if you double-click the Secure Server policy, you'll find three different strategies for dealing with peers depending on the type of traffic. Double-click the All IP Traffic option and then click on the Filter Action tab of the resulting dialog. From there, double-click the Require Security filter action (it should be the one whose radio button is checked). You'll see a dialog like the one I've shown in Figure 69.2.

Basically IPSEC allows three options for any given connection to a peer: permit raw (unsecured) communication, block communication completely, or negotiate a secure channel with the peer. Note that the default list of negotiated protocols and algorithms is quite long. This is one place where you can afford to lock things down a bit more. If you're simply locking down machines within your own organization, and you know they'll all be using Microsoft's implementation of IPSEC, by all means restrict the flavors of IPSEC that you're willing to negotiate. Notice that the list contains two encryption and hash algorithms, and if you know much at all about cryptography, you'll know that 3DES is a known secure algorithm in broad use today whereas its older cousin, DES, is easily broken. You'll also know that the SHA1 algorithm is preferable to MD5. So remove any options here that include the two weaker algorithms. That will leave you with one option:

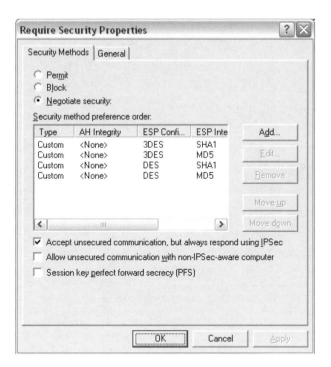

Figure 69.2 Options for negotiating security

the ESP protocol using 3DES encryption with HMAC-SHA1 integrity protection. You can do the same thing for the Client policy on client machines, but there you'll also see the AH protocol being negotiated as a last resort. Remove any entries that use AH because it doesn't support encryption, as I discussed in Item 68.

Another option you should enable is called "Session key perfect forward secrecy (PFS)." This means that, when session keys are swapped out (this happens after a set number of bytes have been exchanged or a fixed amount of time goes by), the new session key won't simply be shipped across the existing secure connection. This would enable an attacker who has recorded all communications between two machines to break one session key and therefore immediately unwind all the rest of the session keys exchanged over time. With PFS, the new session key is exchanged using a protocol called Diffie-Hellman key exchange (Ferguson and Schneier 2003), in which an eavesdropper must break each session key individually. This is a good thing, so be sure to enable it.

In many systems, simply turning on the Secure Server and Client policies and tweaking them as I've suggested will suffice. It's also possible to have the server accept unsecured traffic from certain subnets by adding custom IP filters, but this is more dangerous than simply locking down all traffic to the server.

Try it! Configure a couple of computers in the lab domain environment to use IPSEC and use a network sniffer such as **netmon.exe** on the server to sniff the packets. If you do something simple, such as make an HTTP request, without IPSEC you'll see the request going across in the clear. With IPSEC, however, the request and response will be encrypted.

Another good resource with links to information about IPSEC in Windows can be found in Meier et al. (2003).

PART VI
Miscellaneous

70

How to Store Secrets on a Machine

T HIS HAS GOT TO BE one of the most frequently asked questions I get when I teach security classes: "How should I store my connection strings on the Web server?" It doesn't always take that exact form, but a lot of people out there need to store sensitive data on Web servers and other often-attacked machines. It's a tricky problem with no perfect answers.

Here's the deal. Imagine a Web server that needs a password to connect to some back-end machine running on a platform where Kerberos authentication isn't an option. The server process will need to read that password at some point, and therein lies the problem. Any data that can be read by the server process can be read by an attacker who can compromise the server process. For example, if the attacker can run arbitrary code in the server process, he can read the secret.

So why don't we just encrypt the password so the attacker will see only ciphertext if he goes looking for it? (That's usually the second question.) You've got to remember that encryption algorithms never eliminate secrets. They're designed to take big secrets (like e-mail messages, documents, etc.) and compress them into small secrets, which we call keys. But there's still a secret! It's the key. And if the server program can read the key, the attacker can read it. You haven't gotten rid of the secret by encrypting it; you've only pushed the problem back a bit.

The first thing you should try to do is eliminate the secret if at all possible. By using integrated security with SQL Server, you can avoid having to store passwords in your connection strings, for example. This should be your first avenue of defense!

If you can't eliminate the secret, then protect it using defense in depth (Item 5). You know you'll never have perfect protection (not even close to it), but you want to put up every roadblock possible between your adversary and your secret. So don't do something silly like store the secret in a file that's sitting in a virtual directory on a Web server (`web.config` comes to mind). Web servers have been known to accidentally allow files to be downloaded because of bugs. For example, connection strings in classic ASP pages could be stolen in the past by pointing a Web browser to `page.asp::$DATA` instead of `page.asp`. This fooled IIS into thinking that the request was for a static file because `.asp::$DATA` wouldn't match anything in its script map. But the suffix `::$DATA` has special meaning to the operating system: It indicates the default NTFS stream for the file, which is what you get when you read the contents of the file normally. In other words, asking the file system for `page.aspx::$DATA` is the same as asking it for the contents of `page.aspx`. Thus IIS would serve up the source of the ASP page instead of interpreting it as a script. There have been lots of shenanigans like this over the years, but most folks would agree that you're better off storing sensitive files outside of any virtual directory on a Web server. Even better, keep sensitive files on a different partition than where your virtual directories reside.

You should consider protecting secrets using the Data Protection API (DPAPI). This consists of a couple of Win32 functions that allow you to encrypt (`CryptProtectData`) and decrypt (`CryptUnprotectData`) data using keys controlled by the system. DPAPI also provides integrity protection via a MAC (Item 58), so if the data is tampered with by someone who doesn't know the key, the `unprotect` function will fail.

Using DPAPI, you can encrypt data with a user's login credentials (which means you need to decrypt the data in the same security context in which it was encrypted), or you can encrypt the data using the machine's credentials. If you encrypt with the user's credentials, when the user is not logged in to the machine, her key is not present on the machine at all, which is fantastic! But when you store secrets that need to be accessed by a server that runs 24/7 and the server is logged in all the time, you may as well use the machine's credentials. That makes administration easier. For example, if your server runs as `Network Service`, you don't want the administrator to have to encrypt secrets while running as `Network Service`. So my examples here use the machine's credentials.

Note that DPAPI only works if you decrypt the data on the same machine on which it was encrypted, so be careful how you use it in a load-balanced environment. For example, if one machine encrypts the data and stores it in a database, don't expect another machine to be able to read and decrypt it. And remember, an attacker who can run code on the machine can call these functions as easily as you can! All we're doing here is ensuring that, if the attacker reads a file with secret data in it, he gets ciphertext instead of plaintext. Either he needs to get root access to the machine and compromise the machine's DPAPI key, or he needs to be able to run code on the machine to call the decryption function.[1] We're not making it impossible, but we're putting a protection countermeasure in his way to slow down the attack (Item 2).

DPAPI is wrapped by the .NET Framework version 2.0, but for those of you using 1.x, I've written a class in Managed C++ called `Secret` to help, and I've shown the two static methods it exposes in Figure 70.1.

Here's an example of its usage from a C# program:

```
using System;
using KBC.WindowsSecurityUtilities;

class TestSecret {
  static void Main(string[] args) {
    if (args.Length != 1) {
      Console.WriteLine("usage: testsecret secret");
      return;
    }
    string plaintext = args[0];
    string ciphertext =
      Secret.EncryptWithMachineKey(plaintext, "TestSecret");
    Console.WriteLine("Encrypted string: {0}", ciphertext);
    plaintext =
      Secret.DecryptWithMachineKey(ciphertext, "TestSecret");
    Console.WriteLine("Decrypted string: {0}", plaintext);
  }
}
```

---

1. Less obvious would be the attacker obtaining a "ghosted" image of the operating system, which would have the same machine key!

```
String* Secret::EncryptWithMachineKey(
    String* plaintext,
    String* additionalEntropy) {

    if (0 == plaintext) {
        throw new ArgumentException(S"plaintext required");
    }
    if (0 == additionalEntropy ||
        0 == additionalEntropy->Length) {
        throw new ArgumentException(
            S"additionalEntropy required");
    }
    const wchar_t __pin* pszPlaintext =
        PtrToStringChars(plaintext);
    DATA_BLOB dataIn = {
        plaintext->Length * sizeof(wchar_t),
        (BYTE*)pszPlaintext };

    const wchar_t __pin* pszAdditionalEntropy =
        PtrToStringChars(additionalEntropy);
    DATA_BLOB entropy = {
        additionalEntropy->Length * sizeof(wchar_t),
        (BYTE*)pszAdditionalEntropy };

    DATA_BLOB dataOut;
    if (!CryptProtectData(&dataIn, L"secret_data", &entropy,
                          0, 0,
                          CRYPTPROTECT_LOCAL_MACHINE |
                          CRYPTPROTECT_UI_FORBIDDEN,
                          &dataOut)) {
        throwWin32Exception(L"CryptProtectData");
    }

    Byte ciphertext[] = new Byte[dataOut.cbData];
    Byte __pin* p = &ciphertext[0];
    CopyMemory(p, dataOut.pbData, dataOut.cbData);
    LocalFree(dataOut.pbData);

    return Convert::ToBase64String(ciphertext);
}

String* Secret::DecryptWithMachineKey(
    String* base64EncodedCiphertext,
    String* additionalEntropy) {

    if (0 == base64EncodedCiphertext) {
        throw new ArgumentException(
            S"base64EncodedCiphertext required");
    }
```

continues

```
    if (0 == additionalEntropy ||
        0 == additionalEntropy->Length) {
        throw new ArgumentException(
            S"additionalEntropy required");
    }
    Byte ciphertext[] = Convert::FromBase64String(
        base64EncodedCiphertext);
    Byte __pin* pCiphertext = &ciphertext[0];
    DATA_BLOB dataIn = {
        ciphertext->Length,
        (BYTE*)pCiphertext };

    const wchar_t __pin* pszAdditionalEntropy =
        PtrToStringChars(additionalEntropy);
    DATA_BLOB entropy = {
        additionalEntropy->Length * sizeof(wchar_t),
        (BYTE*)pszAdditionalEntropy };

    DATA_BLOB dataOut;
    if (!CryptUnprotectData(&dataIn, 0, &entropy, 0, 0,
        CRYPTPROTECT_UI_FORBIDDEN, &dataOut)) {
        throwWin32Exception(L"CryptUnprotectData");
    }

    String* plaintext = new String(
        (wchar_t*)dataOut.pbData,
        0, dataOut.cbData / sizeof(wchar_t));
    LocalFree(dataOut.pbData);

    return plaintext;
}
```

Figure 70.1 Wrapping DPAPI in Managed C++

One thing that Secret doesn't address is erasability. This is something that managed environments like the .NET Framework and Java aren't very good about handling. How do you erase a string once you're done with the secret data that it holds? Wait for the garbage collector to collect it? Even then there's no guarantee it will be overwritten anytime soon. You could store the secret in a byte array and then overwrite the array when you're done, but what if a garbage collection occurs and the array is compacted (i.e., copied to another location in memory)? And this says nothing about paging: I don't know of a way to lock managed heap memory so it's not paged out to a swapfile. Finally, a byte array is useless if the function that needs the data expects a string, and this is where we usually get nailed. Have you ever seen a constructor for `SqlConnection` that accepts a connection string in the form of a byte array? I certainly haven't. The only ones who can help us here are the .NET Framework team, I'm afraid. This is an area that needs improved support by the runtime.[2]

Another thing that `Secret` doesn't address is where the ciphertext should be stored once it's encrypted. Your best bet is to put the ciphertext in a file or registry key that won't be easily accessible to an attacker, and put a strong DACL (Item 43) on it. By strong, I mean one that allows administrators to read and write the secret and that allows the account your server runs under to read it.

Secrets in ASP.NET Configuration Files

ASP.NET uses DPAPI for the few secrets that are part of its configuration. From an administrative command prompt, you run a tool called **aspnet_setreg** to encrypt a secret and tuck it away in the registry. Here's an example:

```
aspnet_setreg -k:SOFTWARE\MyApp\MySecret -p:"Attack at dawn"
```

The tool prints out lengthy instructions on what to do next, but suffice it to say that there is now a registry key (HKLM/SOFTWARE/MyApp/MySecret/ASPNET_SETREG) that holds a value named `password`, which contains the ciphertext for `Attack at dawn`. You can now replace a secret in your ASP.NET configuration file with the following string: HKLM/SOFTWARE/MyApp/MySecret/ASPNET_SETREG, password, and ASP.NET will know what to do: It will read the ciphertext from that key and then use DPAPI to decrypt it using the machine key. Of course, this only works for keys that ASP.NET knows about. I've listed those keys below.

```
<identity userName='...' password='...' />
<processModel userName='...' password='...' />
<sessionState stateConnectionString='...' sqlConnectionString='...' />
```

---

2. Version 2.0 of the .NET Framework provides a class called `SecureString`, which uses a combination of DPAPI in-memory encryption and aggressive reclamation via `IDisposable` to keep its contents secure. But it's still not clear how this solves the problem when `SqlConnection` expects an instance of `System.String`! Perhaps we'll see this fixed in a later beta.

This isn't a bad mechanism to emulate if you need to manage your own secrets. I've heard rumors that a feature like this is slated to be generalized for use on any section of an XML configuration file in a future version of ASP.NET. As for today, check out knowledge base article 329290 for more details on obtaining and using **aspnet_setreg.exe**.

The DataProtection Class

Version 2.0 of the .NET Framework introduces a class called Data-Protection that wraps DPAPI. It's simple to use; in fact, it looks almost exactly like the wrapper class I provided in the previous section. I've shown an example in Figure 70.2.

The output from this application follows. You might be surprised by the size of the ciphertext, but please realize that encrypting data doesn't cause it to get bigger. The ciphertext is so long because DPAPI is doing more than

```
using System;
using System.Text;
using System.Security.Cryptography;

class Program {
  const string applicationEntropy = "Some application secret";
  static void Main() {
    string secret = "Attack at dawn";
    Console.WriteLine("Encrypting: {0}", secret);
    string base64Ciphertext = Encrypt(secret);
    Console.WriteLine("Decrypting: {0}", base64Ciphertext);
    Console.WriteLine("Result: {0}", Decrypt(base64Ciphertext));
  }
  static string Encrypt(string plaintext) {
    byte[] encodedPlaintext = Encoding.UTF8.GetBytes(plaintext);
    byte[] encodedEntropy = Encoding.UTF8.GetBytes(
      applicationEntropy);

    byte[] ciphertext = ProtectedData.Protect(encodedPlaintext,
      encodedEntropy, DataProtectionScope.LocalMachine);

    return Convert.ToBase64String(ciphertext);
  }
```

continues

Figure 70.2 Using the **ProtectedData** class

```
static string Decrypt(string base64Ciphertext) {
  byte[] ciphertext = Convert.FromBase64String(base64Ciphertext);
  byte[] encodedEntropy = Encoding.UTF8.GetBytes(
    applicationEntropy);

  byte[] encodedPlaintext = ProtectedData.Unprotect(ciphertext,
    encodedEntropy, DataProtectionScope.LocalMachine);

  return Encoding.UTF8.GetString(encodedPlaintext);
  }
}
```

Figure 70.2 Using the `ProtectedData` class *(continued)*

just encrypting: It's also integrity-protecting the data (Item 58). So the ciphertext includes a message authentication code (MAC) along with some other metadata that DPAPI needs, such as an encrypted copy of the unique derived key used to actually encrypt the data. The ciphertext is also base64 encoded, which increases the size as well.

```
Encrypting: Attack at dawn
Decrypting: AQAAANCMnd8BFdERjHoAwE/Cl+sBAAAAbcJjHJOz8kOjJ+hqZRZHS
gQAAAACAAAAAAADZgAAqAAAABAAAABXEBvjoNiqmbvOsn5M56dpAAAAAASAAACgAA
AAEAAAAM2yg+TTDbC1DFcjO9kKE1QQAAAGa+tMkvYVFo3W6eaDfuDqRQAAAAdo4n
0OtQqpUOdhx7A6gIWBqSBgw==
Result: Attack at dawn
```

■ 71 ■
How to Prompt for a Password

Prompting the user for credentials is a tricky business. First of all, it's best never to do this if you can avoid it because it trains the user to type his password whenever asked. How do you know that next time it won't be a Trojan horse asking? The operating system itself takes this pretty seriously. On a server, you have to press **control+alt+delete** before the operating system will ask for credentials. Have you ever wondered why this is? This key sequence can't be trapped by user-mode code; it can only be trapped by privileged code (kernel-mode code), which is part of the operating system. This is what's called a "secure attention sequence": you're literally getting the attention of the real operating system and asking it to come forward and prompt you for credentials. If the operating system takes it this seriously, you should too! If there's any way to rely on the user's implicit logon credentials, by all means do so. Kerberos (Item 59) is the normal way to leverage these credentials when communicating with remote machines. I showed how to Kerberize applications using SSPI in Items 66 and 67 and most of the built-in infrastructure on the Windows platform supports Kerberos already.

If you have no choice but to ask the user for a password, it's best to follow some basic guidelines. Don't echo the password so that someone looking over the user's shoulder can see it. This means setting `TextMode=Password` in ASP.NET text boxes that collect passwords, and setting the `PasswordChar` property in Windows forms text boxes that do the same.

Also, never, ever copy the old password into a password-style text box for display to the user. There is a tool called Revelation (and many others like it), which temporarily turns off the password style on edit boxes just to show the user whatever secret is lurking behind those asterisks! Instead, initialize the edit box with a long string of spaces if you use anything at all.

Windows XP introduced some new functions for collecting credentials, but you can't use them unless you know your clients have upgraded from Windows 2000, which is somewhat problematic as of this writing. So I'll show you a routine that I've been using for a long time to collect passwords from .NET console applications, followed by a GUI version that uses a Win32 function introduced in Windows XP. The console routine is shown in Figure 71.1 and is a Managed C++ routine. The trick is to turn off input echo before reading the password. The entire example is available on this book's Web site.

```cpp
String* PasswordPrompt::GetPasswordFromCmdLine() {
    // turn off console echo
    HANDLE hConsole = GetStdHandle(STD_INPUT_HANDLE);
    DWORD oldMode;
    if (!GetConsoleMode(hConsole, &oldMode)) {
        throwWin32Exception(S"GetConsoleMode");
    }
    DWORD newMode = oldMode & ~ENABLE_ECHO_INPUT;
    if (!SetConsoleMode(hConsole, newMode)) {
        throwWin32Exception(S"SetConsoleMode");
    }

    Console::Write(S"Enter password: ");
    String* pwd = Console::ReadLine();
    Console::WriteLine();

    // restore console echo
    if (!SetConsoleMode(hConsole, oldMode)) {
        throwWin32Exception(S"SetConsoleMode");
    }
    return pwd;
}
```

Figure 71.1 Prompting for a password from a console application

Figure 71.2 shows another Managed C++ routine that uses the `CredUIPromptForCredentials` function introduced in Windows XP. The inputs to this function include an optional parent window (which is disabled while the modal password prompt is displayed) as well as optional texts for a message and the dialog caption. The `targetServer` argument

```cpp
String* PasswordPrompt::PromptUserForPassword(
    System::Windows::Forms::Control* parentWindow,
    String* messageText,
    String* captionText,
    String* targetServer,
    CredUIOptions options,
    String** userName) {

    if (!targetServer) {
        throw new ArgumentException(
            S"targetResourceName required");
    }

    const wchar_t __pin* _targetServer =
        PtrToStringChars(targetServer);
    const wchar_t __pin* _messageText =
        PtrToStringChars(messageText);
    const wchar_t __pin* _captionText =
        PtrToStringChars(captionText);    // if the caller passed us a
user name,
    // use that as the default in the prompt
    wchar_t user[256];
    const int maxUserChars = sizeof user / sizeof *user - 1;
    user[0] = L'\0';
    if (*userName) {
        const int cch = (*userName)->Length;
        if (cch > maxUserChars) {
            throw new ArgumentException(
                S"User name too long");
        }
        const wchar_t __pin* _userName =
            PtrToStringChars(*userName);
        CopyMemory(user, _userName, cch * sizeof *user);
        user[cch] = L'\0';
    }
```

continues

Figure 71.2 Prompting for a password from a GUI application

```
HWND parent = 0;
if (parentWindow) {
    parent = (HWND)parentWindow->Handle.ToPointer();
}

CREDUI_INFO info = {
    sizeof info,
    parent,
    _messageText,
    _captionText,
    NULL
};
wchar_t pwd[256];

DWORD status = CredUIPromptForCredentials(
    &info, _targetServer, 0, 0,
    user, sizeof user / sizeof *user,
    pwd,  sizeof pwd  / sizeof *pwd,
    0, options);

switch (status) {
    case NO_ERROR:
        *userName = new String(user);
        break;
    case ERROR_CANCELLED:
        return 0;
    default:
        throwWin32Exception(
            S"CredUIPromptForCredentials", status);
}
return new String(pwd);
}
```

Figure 71.2 Prompting for a password from a GUI application   *(continued)*

is used to help form a generic message, "Connect to [targetServer]", and is used as the default authority if the user doesn't provide a fully qualified user account name. For example, if you set `targetServer=XYZZY`, and the user types in `Alice` as the user name, the resulting account name— `XYZZY\Alice`. `userName`—is an in/out argument. If you pass in a non-null user name, the user needs to type in only the password. On return, this argument holds the user name typed by the user (possibly modified by the `targetServer` argument as I described). Finally, there is a whole suite of options, but one I recommend is `CredUIOptions.DoNotPersist`, which gets rid of the silly option that encourages users to persist their passwords on the machine using DPAPI (Item 70). I call it silly because virtually all of the organizations I've worked with have security policies that tell their employees not to use this feature. Even, umm, Microsoft.

Here's a code snippet in C# that prompts for a password via the GUI. Figure 71.3 shows the resulting dialog. I plan to publish another version of this class that uses the new SecureString class in version 2.0 of the .NET Framework. Subscribe to the RSS feed from this book's Web site for announcements.

```csharp
string name = null;
string pwd = PasswordPrompt.PromptUserForPassword(
    null,
    "MessageText",
    "CaptionText",
    "XYZZY",
    CredUIOptions.DoNotPersist,
    ref name);

if (null != pwd) {
    Console.WriteLine("user: {0}", name);
    Console.WriteLine("pass: {0}", pwd);
}
else {
    Console.WriteLine("User cancelled the prompt.");
}
```

Figure 71.3 The credential UI

▎72▪

How to Programmatically Lock the Console

H AVE YOU EVER configured your screensaver to require a password or, on Windows XP, to "show the Welcome screen"? I've seen some special-purpose programs that need to implement similar behavior: locking the interactive console under certain conditions. It's easy to do, so I've included it here. The function you need to call is in Win32, and it's called LockWorkstation. Here's a C# program that locks the console when run:

```
using System.Runtime.InteropServices;

class LockItUp {
  static void Main() {
    LockWorkStation();
  }
  [DllImport("user32.dll")]
  static extern void LockWorkStation();
}
```

After this program runs, the default desktop will be hidden and the Winlogon desktop will be displayed. All programs will continue to run as normal, and the interactive user will still be logged on. However, she'll have to re-enter her password to get back to her desktop.

■ 73 ■

How to Programmatically Log Off or Reboot the Machine

L OGGING OFF LOGICALLY means ending your logon session (Item 17), which means closing any processes that have tokens (Item 16) that point to your logon session. Win32 provides a function to do this called ExitWindowsEx. It looks at the logon session of the code that called it and then closes all processes running within that session. If the interactive user is being logged off, the Winlogon desktop will become active afterward. The C# code for this is shown in Figure 73.1.

```
using System.Runtime.InteropServices;

class LogOff {
  static void Main() {
    ExitWindowsEx(0, 0);
  }
  [DllImport("user32.dll")]
  static extern bool ExitWindowsEx(uint flags, uint reason);
}
```

Figure 73.1 Forcing a logoff programmatically

You can also force a reboot using `ExitWindowsEx`, but you must have (and enable) a privilege called `SeShutdownPrivilege` in order to do that (Item 22). The C# code for rebooting the machine is shown in Figure 73.2. Note that it uses a helper class that I developed in Item 22 to enable the privilege.

```csharp
using System;
using System.Runtime.InteropServices;
using KBC.WindowsSecurityUtilities;

class RebootMachine {
  static void Main() {
    // enable the Shutdown privilege
    try {
      using (Token.EnablePrivilege("SeShutdownPrivilege",
             true)) {
        // reboot - pick a reason code that
        // makes sense for what you're doing
        ExitWindowsEx(EWX_REBOOT,
          SHTDN_REASON_MAJOR_APPLICATION   |
          SHTDN_REASON_MINOR_INSTALLATION |
          SHTDN_REASON_FLAG_PLANNED);
      }
    }
    catch (Exception) {
      Console.WriteLine("You need a privilege"  +
                        " to run this program:" +
                        " Shut down the system");
      return;
    }
  }
  [DllImport("user32.dll")]
  static extern bool ExitWindowsEx(uint flags, uint reason);

  // from Win32 header file: reason.h
  const uint SHTDN_REASON_MAJOR_APPLICATION  = 0x00040000;
  const uint SHTDN_REASON_MINOR_INSTALLATION = 0x00000002;
  const uint SHTDN_REASON_FLAG_PLANNED       = 0x80000000;

  // from Win32 header file: winuser.h
  const uint EWX_REBOOT = 0x00000002;
}
```

Figure 73.2 Forcing a reboot programmatically

∎ 74 ∎
What is Group Policy?

ADMINISTRATORS OF LARGE Windows installations don't configure each workstation and server in the enterprise individually. Rather, they use a mechanism known as group policy to specify security policy and other settings that should be used throughout the domain. As a designer or developer you should know at least a little bit about this mechanism, because it's often used to lock down security throughout an enterprise. It's also used to distribute software applications and patches, as I discuss in Item 75.

You can do some exploring of group policy even if you're at home working on a Windows XP box and not a member of a domain. From an administrative command prompt, just run **gpedit.msc** to look at a few of the settings on your computer that can be affected by group policy. First of all, note that at the very highest level, group policy is split into two categories: Computer Configuration and User Configuration. Each time a computer in a domain boots up, it downloads the Computer Configuration section of any group policies in Active Directory that pertain to that computer. Similarly, each time a user logs in to a machine interactively, an automatic download of the User Configuration section of any pertinent group policy occurs. In a domain environment, security settings on your workstation may change when you boot up or log in because a domain administrator made changes in policy somewhere upstream.

If you drill down in both the Computer and User Configurations, into Windows Settings, and then into Security Settings, you'll see that the vast majority of security policy is controlled in the Computer Configuration section (see Figure 74.1). Here's where privileges are granted, auditing is enabled, and IPSEC is configured, for example. If you look at a group policy object (GPO) in a domain setting, you'll see even more security settings. For example, you can specify ACLs on files, directories, registry keys, and even services.

If you have administrative access to a domain, you can see where group policy is configured. Just run the Active Directory Users and Computers console and drill down into a domain. The most common place where group policy is used is on individual domains. If you right-click a domain and ask for its properties, then click the Group Policy tab, you'll see a list of links to GPOs in Active Directory that apply to that domain. By default

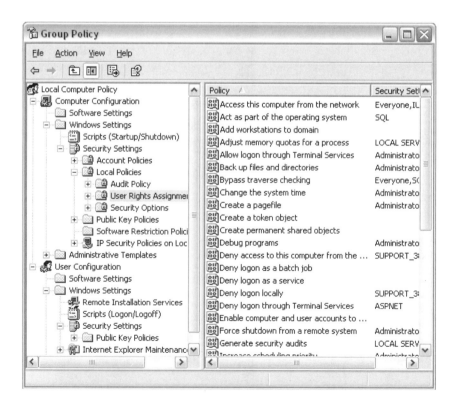

Figure 74.1 Exploring group policy

there's only one, the Default Domain Policy, and for a lot of systems that one policy will suffice. Often more than one GPO applies to any given user or machine. Suffice it to say that in most nontrivial Windows deployments, security settings are usually synchronized throughout a domain using group policy.

I've added a new GPO in Figure 74.2. What's interesting about these policies is that they look really complex to begin with, but they don't say anything at all until you drill into them and start setting policy. For example, note how in Figure 74.2, in the section of my policy that deals with privileges (Item 21), none of the privileges are defined except for the `SeBackupPrivilege`, which I said should be granted to a domain group called `ACME\Backup`. By leaving those other settings as Not Defined, I'm indicating that my policy will have no effect at all on those settings. If no group policy in Active Directory defines a particular setting, the local administrator is free to choose the value of that setting herself. After rebooting a computer in the domain, I took a snapshot of what its local security

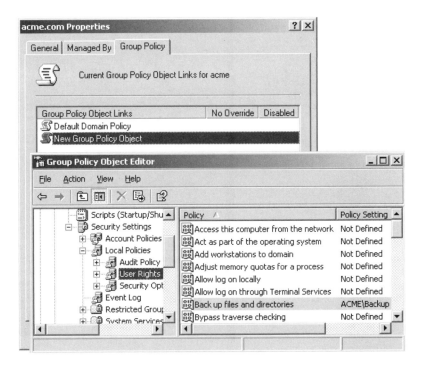

Figure 74.2 Adding a new group policy object

policy looked like (Figure 74.3). It's a little subtle, but note how the icon for `SeBackupPrivilege` is different in the local policy. This is telling you that it's been set by group policy and can no longer be configured locally. In fact, if you double-click the privilege in the local security policy, you'll see that you're prevented from changing it.[1]

There are a number of places that group policy can come from. My demonstration was of a group policy object attached to a domain, but technically these objects can also be associated with an organizational unit (OU) or a site in Active Directory. The policies higher in the tree generally take precedence over those lower in the tree, but there are switches that you can throw (such as No Override or Block Policy Inheritance) that help manage conflicts. You can read more about these details in the Windows 2000 Server Resource Kit.[2]

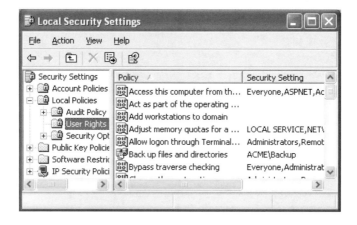

Figure 74.3 Local security policy after a group policy download

---

1. The GUI prevents you from changing it, but an administrator of a machine owns that machine and can ultimately change these settings locally. One way would be programmatically: You could even use the code I provide in Item 23 to do this (not that I'm suggesting you do). Just keep in mind that if you want these domain-wide settings and restrictions to have any teeth, you better not allow individual users to administer their own machines in the domain!

2. This is part of the MSDN Library (you do subscribe, don't you?). The section on group policy is in the *Distributed Systems Guide*, in a part called Desktop Configuration Management.

Most security settings in group policy are specified in the Computer Configuration section, which is applied each time the computer boots. But what if you want to get these computer settings refreshed without having to reboot your machine? There are a couple of ways this can happen. The first is to force a manual refresh by running **gpupdate** from a command line (if you're on a Windows 2000 box, the command is a bit different but achieves the same thing: **secedit /refreshpolicy machine_policy**). The second way is to force a periodic refresh of policy, which you can specify by drilling down into the Computer Configuration of a group policy object. Drill into Administrative Templates/System/Group Policy. Here you'll find settings that control auto-refresh. Oh, and if you happen to force an update of policy while you're looking at, say, the local security policy editor, the GUI won't immediately refresh and show the new policy in force. To force the GUI to display the new settings, right-click on the Security Settings node and choose Reload.

For further reading, check out Item 75 to learn how to use group policy to deploy software.

■ 75 ■
How to Deploy Software Securely via Group Policy

A s I write this, the vast majority of developers are running as administrators on their own machines as they develop code (Item 8). If a developer needs a new software application, she just pops in the installation disk and installs it herself. This leads some developers to think that this is how software is installed everywhere. I just want to point out that this isn't the case in many enterprises.

In a secure domain environment, to prevent chaos and accidental (or even purposeful) security breaches, most users don't have administrative rights on the machines they use. The domain administrator is in charge. So how does software get installed throughout an enterprise if the users themselves don't install it? Does the domain administrator roll around on his chair to each workstation installing the software manually using the power of his administrative login? I hope not! As of Windows 2000, a feature known as "IntelliMirror" makes deploying software throughout a domain (or an entire enterprise) considerably easier. This feature is designed to work with the Microsoft Installer, so to get the most out of it you really need to deploy software by using `MSI` files.

IntelliMirror works through group policy (Item 74). There's a folder in each group policy object called `Software Settings`. Well, actually, there are two of these: one under the Computer Configuration section and one under the User Configuration section. If you drill into either of these folders for a group policy object in Active Directory, you'll find a node called *Software Installation*. If you have an **MSI** file you'd like to deploy, you have three options. You can "publish" the file, in which case it becomes available to users from the control panel via Add/Remove Programs. Or you can "assign" the file, which is a little more functional. If you assign the file to a user, a link to the application shows up on that user's Start menu the next time she logs in. The first time she clicks the link, the Windows installer installs the application. The Windows installer runs as SYSTEM, so you have plenty of privilege (arguably too much in many cases!) to install whatever files are necessary. Finally, you can assign the file to a computer, and the next time the computer boots, your **MSI** file will be run by the installer, once again as SYSTEM. I've shown an example of this in Figure 75.1. This is how many companies deploy patches, service packs, and also .NET Framework code access security policy.

Why am I telling you this? Well, for two reasons. First, if you have some piece of software that you need to install throughout a domain or enterprise, you should make sure you build an **MSI** installation so you can take advantage of this feature. Just knowing that this feature exists is useful! Second, you need to realize that if your software is deployed this way, it will be installed under one security context (and a highly privileged one at that) and run under a different (restricted) security context: the user of the workstation where your software is installed. So, as I discussed toward the

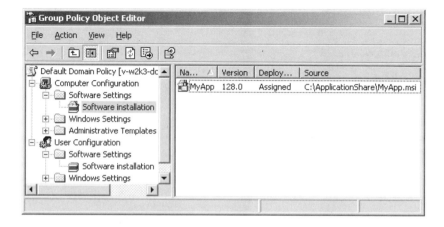

Figure 75.1 Deploying software via group policy

end of Item 9, be sure you design your application with these two security contexts in mind. Your installer program shouldn't be messing with any settings in the user profile (Item 19), for example, because it won't be running in the security context of any legitimate user who will be using the application. It will most likely be running as SYSTEM. Keep these deployments in mind when writing installers.

Bibliography

Box, D. 1998. *Essential COM.* Reading, MA: Addison-Wesley.

Brown, K. 2004. Security headaches? Take ASP.NET 2.0! *MSDN Magazine,* June.

Brown, K. 2003. Security briefs: Exploring S4U Kerberos extensions in Windows Server 2003. *MSDN Magazine,* April.

Brown, K. 2000a. Handle logons in Windows NT and Windows 2000 with your own logon session broker. *MSJ Magazine,* February.

Brown, K. 2000b. *Programming Windows Security.* Reading, MA: Addison-Wesley.

Brumme, C. 2003. Initializing code. C. Brumme's Weblog: blogs.gotdotnet.com/cbrumme/.

Davis, C. R. 2001. *IPSEC: Securing VPNs.* Berkeley, CA: McGraw-Hill.

Ferguson, N., and Schneier, B. 2003. *Practical Cryptography.* New York: John Wiley and Sons.

Ferguson, N., and Schneier, B. 1999. *A Cryptographic Evaluation of IPsec.* Mountain View, CA: Counterpane Internet Security.

Howard, M., and LeBlanc, D. 2002. *Writing Secure Code.* Redmond, WA: Microsoft Press.

McClure, S., et al. 2001. *Hacking Exposed: Network Security Secrets and Solutions,* 3rd ed. Berkeley, CA: Osborne/McGraw-Hill.

McPherson, D. *Role-Based Access Control for Multi-Tier Applications Using Authorization Manager.* Microsoft Corporation: http://www.microsoft.com/technet/prodtechnol/windowsserver2003/technologies/ management/athmanwp.mspx.

Meier, J. D., et al. 2003. *Improving Web Application Security: Threats and Countermeasures.* Redmond, WA: Microsoft Corporation.

Mitnick, K. 2002. *The Art of Deception.* Indianapolis, IN: John Wiley and Sons.

Rammer, I. 2002. *Advanced .NET Remoting.* Berkeley, CA: APress.

Saltzer, J. H. 1975. The protection of information in computer systems. *Proceedings of the IEEE* 63:9, 1278–1308.

Schneier, B. 2003. *Beyond Fear: Thinking Sensibly about Security in an Uncertain World.* New York: Copernicus Books.

Schneier, B. 2000. *Secrets and Lies.* New York: John Wiley and Sons.

Smith, R. 2002. The biometrics dilemma. *Black Hat Briefings.* http://www.blackhat.com/html/bh-media-archives/ bh-archives-2002.html

Sontag, S., and Drew, C. 1998. *Blind Man's Bluff: The Untold Story of American Submarine Espionage.* New York: PublicAffairs.

Stevens, W. R. 1990. *UNIX Network Programming.* Englewood Cliffs, NJ: Prentice-Hall.

Swiderski, F., and Snyder, W. 2004. *Threat Modeling.* Redmond, WA: Microsoft Press.

Tunstall, C., and Cole, G. 2003. *Developing WMI Solutions.* Reading, MA: Addison-Wesley.

Viega, J., and McGraw, G. 2002. *Building Secure Software.* Reading, MA: Addison-Wesley.

Index